The Complete Idiot's

WordPerfect for Windows Short...

Editing and Formatting Shortcut Keys

Press	To
Ctrl+Z	Undo your last action
Ctrl+Shift+R	Redo an undone action
Ctrl+Shift+Z	Undelete
Ctrl+C	Copy the selected block
Ctrl+X	Cut the selected block
Ctrl+V	Paste the cut or copied block
F2	Find and Replace
F9	Select a font
Ctrl+B	Bold characters
Ctrl+I	Italicize characters
Ctrl+U	Underline characters
Ctrl+W	Use WordPerfect's characters
Alt+F8	Select a style
Ctrl+Enter	Insert a hard page break

Navigation Shortcut Keys

Press	To Move to the
Ctrl+→	Next word
Ctrl+←	Previous word
End	End of the line
Home	Beginning of the line
Ctrl+↓	Next paragraph
Ctrl+↑	
Page Do...	
Page Up	
Alt+Page Down	Beginning of next page
Alt+Page Up	Beginning of previous page
Ctrl+End	End of the document
Ctrl+Home	Top of the document
Ctrl+G	Any page (Go To command)

General WordPerfect Shortcut Keys

Press	To
Ctrl+O	Open a document
Ctrl+N	Start a new document
Ctrl+T	Use a template
Ctrl+S	Save a document
Ctrl+P	Print a document
Ctrl+F4	Close a document
F12	Create a table
F1	Start Help
Ctrl+F1	Start Spell Check
Alt+F1	Start Thesaurus
Alt+Shift+F1	Start Grammatik
Ctrl+Shift+F1	Start QuickCorrect
Alt+F4	Exit WordPerfect for Windows

The Power Bar: Formatting Made Easy

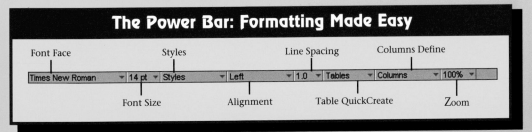

The Ruler Bar: Fast Tabs, Margins, and More

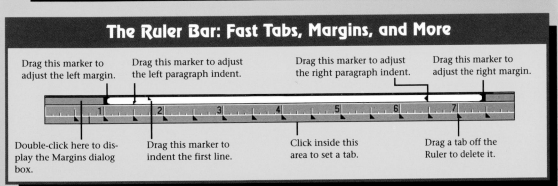

tear here

A Toolbars Highlight Film

WordPerfect 6.1 Toolbar Highlights

New Blank Document	Open
Save	Print
Cut	Copy
Paste	Undo
Redo	Bold
Italics	Underline
QuickFormat	New Document
Paragraph Format	Insert Bullet
Make It Fit	Image
TextArt	Page/Zoom Full
Spell Check	Grammatik

Font Toolbar Highlights

Font	Double Underline
Outline	Small Caps
Redline	Strikeout
Superscript	Strikeout

Format Toolbar Highlights

Tab Set	Indent
Double Indent	Hanging Indent
Page Margins	Justify Left
Justify Center	Justify Right
Justify Full	Justify All

Graphics Toolbar Highlights

Text Box	Edit Box
Draw	Chart
Horizontal Line	Vertical Line

Tables Toolbar Highlights

Table Expert	Table Format
Number Type	Row/Column Indicators
Size Column to Fit	Formula Bar

The

COMPLETE

IDIOT'S

GUIDE TO

WordPerfect®
for Windows,™

Second Edition

by Paul McFedries

**alpha
books**

A Division of Macmillan Publishing
A Prentice Hall Macmillan Company
201 W. 103rd Street, Indianapolis, IN 46290

International Standard Book Number:1-56761-543-0
Library of Congress Catalog Card Number: 94-79169

96 95 94   8 7 6 5 4 3 2

Interpretation of the printing code: the rightmost number of the first series of numbers is the year of the book's printing; the rightmost number of the second series of numbers is the number of the book's printing. For example, a printing code of 94-2 shows that the second printing of the book occurred in 1994.

Screen reproductions in this book were created by means of the program Collage Complete from Inner Media, Inc., Hollis, NH.

Printed in the United States of America

Publisher
Marie Butler-Knight

Acquisitions Editor
Barry Pruett

Managing Editor
Elizabeth Keaffaber

Product Development Manager
Faithe Wempen

Development Editor
Heather Stith

Production Editor
Mark Enochs

Copy Editor
Audra Gable

Cover Designer
Scott Cook

Designer
Barbara Kordesh

Illustrations
Judd Winick

Indexer
Bront Davis

Production Team
*Gary Adair, Dan Caparo, Brad Chinn, Kim Cofer, Lisa Daugherty,
David Dean, Cynthia Drouin, Dave Eason, Jennifer Eberhardt, David Garratt,
Erika Millen, Beth Rago, Bobbi Satterfield, Karen Walsh, Robert Wolf*

*Special thanks to C. Herbert Feltner for ensuring
the technical accuracy of this book.*

Contents at a Glance

v

Contents

Introduction

If you've ever tried to have a conversation with a so-called computer "expert," you know they have this uncanny ability to make the rest of us feel like complete idiots within five seconds. They prattle on in their techno-jargon, throwing in the odd "of course" and "obviously" to make it clear that any fool with half a brain ought to know this stuff. Well, I say we thumb our collective noses at the world's computer geeks! Not only are we *not* idiots, but we're smart enough to know a thing or two ourselves:

> ➤ We're smart enough to know that "cool" isn't defined by how many back issues of *Popular Mechanics* we keep in the bathroom. We simply don't need a lot of technical details (and we don't wear pocket protectors, either).

> ➤ We're smart enough to know that it doesn't make sense to learn absolutely *everything* about WordPerfect for Windows. We just need to know enough to get our work done, thank you.

> ➤ We're smart enough to know that life's too short to read five kazillion pages of arcane (and mostly useless) information. We have lives to lead, after all.

A Book for Smart WordPerfect Idiots

If you're no fool, but the computer gurus of the world make you feel like one, welcome to *The Complete Idiot's Guide to WordPerfect for Windows*. This is a book for those of us who aren't (and don't even want to be) computer wizards. This is also a book for those of us who have a job to do—a job that includes working with WordPerfect for Windows—and we just want to get it done as quickly and painlessly as possible. This is *not* one of those absurdly serious, put-a-crease-in-your-brow-and-we'll-begin kinds of books. On the contrary, we'll even try to have—gasp!—a little fun as we go along.

You'll also be happy to know that this book doesn't assume you have any previous experience with WordPerfect for Windows. This means we'll begin each topic at the beginning and build your knowledge from there. But you won't find any long-winded discussions of boring technical details. With *The Complete Idiot's Guide to WordPerfect for Windows*, you get just the facts you *need* to know, not everything there *is* to know. All the information is presented in short, easy-to-digest chunks that you can easily skim through to find just the information you want.

How This Book Is Set Up

I'm assuming you have a life away from your computer screen, so *The Complete Idiot's Guide to WordPerfect for Windows* is set up so you don't have to read it cover to cover. If you want to know how to print, for example, just turn to the printing chapter. To make things easier to find, I've organized the book into five more or less sensible sections:

Part I—Day-to-Day Skills

WordPerfect for Windows follows the old 80-20 rule: you'll spend 80 percent of your time working with 20 percent of the program's features. The nine chapters in this section cover most of that 20 percent. You'll learn basic stuff such as starting WordPerfect for Windows (Chapter 3), using the keyboard and mouse (Chapter 4), saving your work (Chapter 7), and printing a document (Chapter 9).

Part II—Getting It Right: Editing Stuff

The benefits of a word processor over a typewriter are legion, but one of the biggest pluses is being able to edit a document right on the screen. These three chapters show you how to delete—and undelete—text (Chapter 10), how to move chunks of text around (Chapter 11), and how to find stuff in your documents (Chapter 12).

Part III—Looking Good: Formatting Stuff

Because looking good is often as important as *being* good, WordPerfect for Windows gives you a fistful of ways to format your documents. The six chapters in Part III introduce you to these various options. You'll learn how to format individual characters (Chapter 13), lines and paragraphs (Chapter 14), and pages (Chapter 15). I'll also show you how to create envelopes and labels (Chapter 16) and how to streamline your work with styles (Chapter 18).

Part IV—Fiddling with Your Files

The documents you create in WordPerfect for Windows—whether they're letters, memos, or mystery novels—are stored inside your computer as *files*. This section shows you how to work with multiple files at once (Chapter 19), how to manage files in WordPerfect for Windows instead of fumbling around with Windows' File Manager (Chapter 20), and how to find files quickly with QuickLists and QuickFinder (Chapter 21).

Part V—Wielding WordPerfect for Windows' Tools

The book ends with nine chapters that take you through some of WordPerfect for Windows' collection of tools and utilities. Chapters 22 and 23 check out the spell checker, thesaurus, and grammar-checker that are built right into WordPerfect for Windows. You'll also get to play with graphics (Chapter 24), WordPerfect Draw (Chapter 25), and tables (Chapter 26), and I'll also show you how to customize WordPerfect for Windows (Chapter 28). Chapter 29 helps you get the most out of WordPerfect for Windows by taking you through 10 practical ideas you can use at home or at the office. The final chapter takes you through the necessary drudgery of installing WordPerfect for Windows (just in case you can't talk your local computer whiz into doing it for you).

The Complete Idiot's Guide to WordPerfect for Windows also includes a glossary that'll help you make sense of all those bizarre computer terms as well as a handy tear-out reference card that gives you easy access to important (or just plain handy) WordPerfect for Windows stuff.

What's New in the Second Edition

Sending a book out to market is a little like watching one of your kids leave home and head out into the world. Will she be all right? Will other people accept her? Will she be successful in her chosen field? Will she be displayed prominently at the front of the store? (Well, okay, we probably don't want our kids displayed prominently in the front of stores.) I'm happy to report that *The Complete Idiot's Guide to WordPerfect for Windows'* first venture into the cold, cruel world has been a resounding success. I've received a lot of comments from people saying they liked the book and really enjoyed the approach. Thanks!

The only complaints I heard were from people who wanted more! Well, you got it. This second edition beefs up the coverage of the same WordPerfect for Windows features you use every day. The second edition also includes the following:

➤ Complete coverage of all the useful new features that those busy WordPerfect programmers added to version 6.1. This includes QuickCorrect, QuickFormat, and lots more.

➤ A greater emphasis on those WordPerfect for Windows features that can make your writing life easier. For example, I've moved the coverage of the insanely convenient Toolbar and Power Bar to an earlier chapter (Chapter 5). This way, as you read the rest of the book, I can point out which buttons you can use to work with the other WordPerfect for Windows features.

➤ Increased coverage of WordPerfect for Windows' formatting features. This includes coverage of creating envelopes and labels, as well as how to use styles to make formatting a breeze.

➤ The "Wielding WordPerfect for Windows' Tools" section includes new chapters on using graphics and tables. These are features that can give even the most mundane document a truly professional touch (and, best of all, they're remarkably easy to use).

➤ There is, as I've already mentioned, a separate "WordPerfect for Windows Ideas" chapter that gives you all kinds of ways to put WordPerfect for Windows to work at home and at the office.

Features of This Book

The Complete Idiot's Guide to WordPerfect for Windows is designed so you can get the information you need fast and then get on with your life. If you ever need to type something (it comes up occasionally with word processors), it will appear like this:

type this

WordPerfect for Windows, it seems, has thousands of features, and most of them are accessible by pressing certain *key combinations* on your computer's keyboard. I explain more about this in Chapter 4, "Keyboard and Mouse Basics," but you should know that I'll be writing these key combinations by separating the two keys with a plus sign (+).

For example, I may say something like "Press **Ctrl+S** to save a document." The "Ctrl+S" part means you hold down the **Ctrl** key, tap the **S** key, and then release **Ctrl**. (Don't worry: you are in no way required to memorize these keyboard contortions to become a competent WordPerfect for Windows user.)

Also, look for the following icons that will help you learn just what you need to know:

These boxes contain notes and technical info about WordPerfect for Windows that are (hopefully!) interesting and useful.

This icon defines geeky computer terms in plain English.

There are always dangerous ways to do things on a computer; this icon will tell you how to avoid them.

If you rearrange the letters in "complete idiot," you end up with "de cool tip time," and that's just what this icon means. It presents you with handy tips that show you easier ways to get things done in WordPerfect for Windows.

Acknowledgments (The Kudos and Huzzahs Dept.)

Ah, so many people to thank, so little time. From the first edition, let's start with Acquisitions Editor Steve Poland: thanks for thinking of me. Development Editor Faithe Wempen: it was great being a team again; thanks for another job well done. Managing Editor Liz Keaffaber: thanks for keeping me in line (take a vacation!). Production Editor Annalise DiPaolo: always a pleasure (good luck in the future). Copy Editor Barry Childs-Helton and Tech Editor Kelly Oliver: thanks for making me look good.

The second edition was graced by the presence of Development Editor Heather Stith, Copy Editor Audra Gable, and Production Editor Mark Enochs. Thanks to all for another great job!

Part I
Day-to-Day Skills

Let's face it, WordPerfect for Windows is one intimidating program: all those installation disks and the overstuffed manuals bursting at the seams. The good news is that most of that stuff doesn't apply to the likes of you and me. All we really need are a few basic features that'll let us get our work done with a minimum of fuss and bother. In a sense, that's what this whole book is about, but the chapters here in Part I set the stage for everything else. You'll be learning basic stuff such as how to start WordPerfect, how to use your keyboard and mouse, and how to use things like the pull-down menus and dialog boxes to make your life easier. Believe me, if you can get through this stuff (if you can dress yourself, you can handle any of this), the rest will be a day at the beach.

SKIP HAD SOME TROUBLE WITH THE NEW SOFTWARE

Chapter 1

The Least You Need to Know

I know, I know. You can't wait to get started. What is it? A looming deadline? Unfettered curiosity? A type-A personality? Well, not to worry. This chapter gets you up to speed quickly by presenting a just-the-facts description of the 10 most important WordPerfect for Windows tasks. Of course, I discuss each of these items in more detail elsewhere in the book; so just in case you'd like to know more, I'll also point out the relevant chapters. If you're one of those people who likes to read ahead to the good bits, this chapter's for you.

1. Entering Text

Once you have loaded WordPerfect for Windows, you can start typing right away. There are no complicated commands to run, and no messy formulas to remember. You don't even have to press Enter at the end of every line the way you do with a typewriter (where the same key is called "Return"). WordPerfect for Windows wraps your text onto the next line, free of charge. The only time you need to press Enter is when you want to start a new paragraph. If you make a mistake, just press the Backspace key to wipe it out.

Chapter 3, "Diving In: Your First WordPerfect for Windows Session," gives you a few more tips about entering text. For the lowdown on editing your documents, skim through Part II, "Getting It Right: Editing Stuff."

2. Using Pull-Down Menus

Pull-down menus are hidden menus that list the various commands available for each WordPerfect for Windows task. The *menu bar* (the horizontal strip just below the top of the screen) lists the various menu names (File, Edit, View and so on). To pull down a menu with a mouse, move the mouse pointer into the menu bar and click on the menu name. ("Click" means to press and release the left mouse button.) If you want to use the keyboard, first find the underlined letter in the menu name. Then hold down the **Alt** key and press that letter.

Once your menu is displayed, you select a command. With the mouse, simply click on the command. With your keyboard, you use the up and down arrow keys to highlight the command you want and then press **Enter**.

To learn more about pull-down menus, see Chapter 5, "Easy Street: Using the Menus, Toolbars, and Power Bar."

3. Opening a Document

When you start WordPerfect for Windows, you get a blank screen that's ready for your input. If you'd prefer to work with an existing document, you need to open it. To do so, pull down the File menu and select the Open command (or simply press **Ctrl+O**) to display the Open File dialog box. Type the full name of the file you want to open into the Filename box. If the file is in a different drive or directory, be sure to include the drive letter and/or the directory name. When you're ready, select the **OK** button or press **Enter**.

For more information on the Open command, see Chapter 7, "Day-to-Day Drudgery I: Saving, Opening, and Closing." To learn more about dialog boxes, see Chapter 6, "Talking to WordPerfect for Windows' Dialog Boxes."

4. Saving a File

One of the most gut-wrenching experiences in computerdom occurs when you work on a document for hours, and then lose everything because of a system crash or power failure. You can minimize this damage by saving your work regularly; just pull down WordPerfect for Windows' File menu and select the Save command, or press **Ctrl+S**. If you're saving a new file, the Save As dialog box will appear. Use the

Filename box to give the file a name. When you're finished, select **OK** to close the dialog box.

See Chapter 7, "Day-To-Day Drudgery I: Saving, Opening, and Closing," for more details about saving your work.

5. Marking a Block of Text

Much of what you do in WordPerfect for Windows—whether it's cutting, copying, formatting, or printing—involves highlighting a block of text beforehand. Here's how you do it:

➤ With the keyboard, position the cursor to the left of the first character in the block, hold down the **Shift** key, and then use the arrow keys (or Page Up and Page Down if you have a lot of ground to cover) to highlight the block.

➤ With the mouse, point at the first character in the block, and then drag the mouse to move the pointer over the block.

You'll find lots more block info in Chapter 11, "Block Partying: Working with Blocks of Text." To learn how to drag a mouse, see Chapter 4, "Keyboard and Mouse Basics."

6. Formatting Characters

To make your documents stand out from the crowd, use WordPerfect for Windows' *character formatting* commands. With these commands you can do simple formats like **bold** and *italics*, but you can also get into fancy stuff like different fonts, outlining, and shadowing. Just pull down the Format menu (the Layout menu in version 6.0) and select the Font command (or press **F9**), and then choose the options you want from the Font dialog box that appears.

You can find the full scoop on all this in Chapter 13, "Making Your Characters Look Good."

7. Undoing a Mistake

The WordPerfect for Windows programmers thoughtfully included an Undo command you can use to reverse your most recent action. This is great if you've just made a formatting gaffe, or if you "cut" something when you should have "copied" it. To use the Undo feature, just pull down the Edit menu and select the Undo command (or you can simply press **Ctrl+Z**).

But wait, there's more. WordPerfect for Windows also has an Undelete feature that can get you out of trouble if (heaven forbid) you've just deleted your entire day's work. To use it, first select Undelete from the Edit menu (in version 6, you can press **Ctrl+Shift+Z**). Your most recent deletion appears highlighted in the text, and WordPerfect for Windows displays the Undelete dialog box. Select the Restore button to restore the highlighted text. Select Previous or Next to take a look at the other stored deletions (WordPerfect for Windows stores the last three deletions). When you have the text you want, select Restore.

You'll learn more about Undo in Chapter 11, "Block Partying: Working with Blocks of Text," and you'll learn more about Undelete in Chapter 10, "Deleting Text (and Undeleting It, Too)."

8. Printing a File

Once you've finished working with a document, you'll want to print a copy to show your friends and colleagues. To do this, pull down the File menu and select the Print command (or press **F5**). The Print dialog box appears. It enables you to specify how much of the document to print, the number of copies, and various other settings. When you're ready to print, select the Print button.

For more printing info, take a look at Chapter 9, "Getting It Down on Paper: Printing Documents."

9. Checking Your Spelling

People are so picky these days that they'll often write off a document (and the person who wrote it) just because of a simple spelling mistake. To avoid this ignominious fate, take advantage of Spell Check—WordPerfect for Windows' built-in spell checker.

To run Spell Check, select the Spell Check command from the Tools menu. WordPerfect for Windows laboriously checks every word in your document and displays any word it doesn't recognize, along with a suggested replacement. Select Replace to replace the word.

Spell Check is a powerful program with all kinds of fun options. To get all the facts, turn to Chapter 22, "Using the Spell Checker and Thesaurus."

10. Quitting WordPerfect for Windows

When you've finished with WordPerfect for Windows, you can quit the program by pulling down the File menu and selecting the Exit command (or by pressing **Alt+F4**). If you've made changes to any open documents, WordPerfect for Windows will ask whether you want to save them. Select **Yes** to save changes; select **No** to exit without saving.

See Chapter 3, "Diving In: Your First WordPerfect for Windows Session," for some additional stuff on quitting WordPerfect for Windows.

Chapter 2

Word Processing: A Primer

In This Chapter

➤ What is word processing?

➤ Is word processing a good thing?

➤ How does WordPerfect for Windows fit in?

➤ What's new with version 6.1?

➤ Occasional outbursts as the author gets a thing or two off his chest

Word processing. Personally, I've never liked the term. It sounds so cold and so, well, computer-like. I mean, processing words? What the heck does that mean? The bank processes checks, the IRS processes tax returns. Who processes words? We write them, play with them, misuse them, misspell them, forget them—but process them? No.

But the computer geeks of the world decided long ago that's what it should be called, so it looks like we're stuck with it. Despite these misgivings, this chapter takes a look at this whole word processing thing. What is it? What can you do with it? Why should you care?

So Just What Is This Word Processing Thing?

Well, in the most basic, watch-their-eyes-glaze-over terms, *word processing* is using a computer to write, edit, format, and print documents. Yeah, I know, it doesn't sound very glamorous, but it's not really supposed to be. I mean, think about it. Most of the writing we do is grunt work anyway: memos, letters, essays, diatribes and tirades of one sort or another. All we really need is to get the words down, dot the i's and cross the t's, make it presentable, and then get some hard copy that we can ship out. Everything else—whether it's putting together a newsletter or writing a doctoral thesis—is just an extension of this basic stuff.

Your Computer Is Not a Typewriter

All word processors have some kind of work area that you use for writing. Generally speaking, you just start pecking away on the computer's keyboard and the characters appear like magic on the screen.

Works just like a typewriter, right? Wrong. Oh sure, the keyboard looks somewhat familiar: the letters and numbers are arranged more or less the same, the Spacebar is where it should be, and your old friends the Shift and Tab keys are there. Things may look the same, but baby, this ain't no Selectric.

The biggest difference, of course, is that the word processor has the muscle of a full-fledged computer behind it. Computers may be a lot dumber than we are (and don't let anyone tell you otherwise), but even the cheapest PC clone is way smarter than the most high-falutin' typewriter. For example, on a typewriter, a bell sounds to warn you when you near the end of a line. That's not bad, but the dumb beast still expects you to finish the line yourself and then press the Return key (or—gasp—crank the carriage return bar) to start a new line. A word processor, on the other hand, handles this chore for you. If you near the end of a line, you can blissfully continue typing, and the program will start a new line automatically. It'll even carry over any word you happen to be in the middle of.

Editing: Getting It Right

Word processors really begin to earn their stripes when it comes time to make changes in a document. With a typewriter, you can fix small

10

mistakes, but you still have to fumble around with correction ribbons or (yuck) that ugly White-Out stuff. If you accidentally leave out a sentence or paragraph, forget about it. You've got to type the whole thing over.

Word processors, however, exist to fix mistakes. Type the wrong character? Just press a button to delete it. Forget a paragraph? Just insert it where it needs to go. Want to move a section of text from the beginning of the document to the end? No problem: just "cut" it out and "paste" it in the appropriate place. Want to replace every instance of *affect* with *effect*? (I can never remember which is which, either.) Most word processors (including WordPerfect for Windows) have a "search and replace" command that'll do just that.

And this is just the tip of the iceberg. A full-featured program like WordPerfect for Windows has all kinds of strange and wonderful ways to get the job done right (including, thank goodness, a spell checker!).

Formatting: Looking Good on Paper

Writing and editing are important of course, but the area where word processors really shine is *formatting*. It's not enough, in these image-conscious times, merely to hand someone a piece of paper with a bunch of words on it. Documents today need impact to get their message across. The formatting options in most word processors can help.

You can use **bold** to make things stand out, or *italics* for emphasis. You can center text or set tabs with just a few keystrokes. In some of the better programs, you can also organize your words into columns, or wrap them around a picture. In the really high-end word processors (WordPerfect for Windows is one), you can even add cool features such as footnotes and tables of contents without breaking a sweat. If you can picture it in your head, you can probably do it with today's word processors.

Printing: Getting Hard Copy

Once you've finished changing a document, you'll need to print it out for others to see. It sounds like there wouldn't be much to this; just run some sort of "Print" command and the thing prints. But you have the choice of printing only certain parts of a document (a single page or even a single paragraph, for example) or printing multiple copies; or, if you have more than one printer, you choose which one you want to use. Some programs even let you see a page-by-page preview of what the document will look like.

Is Word Processing a Good Thing?

This may sound like a silly question to ask after extolling the numerous virtues of word processing programs. And it may be moot in any case, because word processing is by far the most popular category of computer software. Some people do have concerns, however, about what word processing is doing to our minds—so we may as well tackle those concerns before we go any further.

Problem 1: Word Processors Encourage Sloppy Writing

This is the most common problem put forth by so-called "writing experts." You usually hear three kinds of complaints:

➤ If a section of text doesn't work for some reason, people using word processors don't rewrite the whole thing from scratch. Instead, in trying to get their point across, they tend to insert more words and sentences. The usual result is bloated, overexplained thoughts that ramble incoherently.

➤ Most word-processor screens show only about half a page at a time, so people tend to see the trees (words, sentences, and paragraphs) instead of the forest (the entire document). As a result, word processing documents tend to lack organization, and they scatter separate pieces of the overall argument willy-nilly.

➤ The advent of the electronic thesaurus has made it easier to utilize cumbrous, orchidaceous words that serve only to obfuscate intendment and subjugate perspicuity.

My answer to these charges is that word processors don't write sloppily, *people* do. Forthwith, here are some suggestions you can use to avoid sloppiness in your own prose:

➤ Wherever possible, read your text out loud. If it doesn't flow off your tongue, it won't flow through someone's brain.

➤ If a sentence or paragraph doesn't feel right, try rewriting it from scratch instead of patching it up. If you can't bring yourself to delete it, at least move it off the screen where you can't see it (so you won't be influenced by it).

➤ A good word processor (such as WordPerfect for Windows) has outlining features that can help you organize large documents. This is a bit of an advanced topic, but it's worthwhile to learn before starting on that new novel.

➤ The best writing is clear and straightforward, without a lot of pretentious words that confuse more than they impress.

Problem 2: Word Processors Waste Time

You could see this one coming. Today's top-of-the-line word processors have so many bells and whistles that you can end up spending all your time fussing about with obscure fonts and complicated desktop publishing features. People often compound the problem by printing the document every time they make the slightest change. This just wastes paper and consumes valuable natural resources.

Again, these are behavioral problems, not word processor problems. On the one hand, it really is best to leave your work simple and uncluttered with fancy elements. This will keep your documents readable and your meaning clear. On the other hand, the best way to get familiar with any kind of software is to experiment with different features, and try out whatever looks interesting. You won't wreck anything, and most programs will warn you if you're about to do something disastrous. And besides, you've got to have *some* fun.

Programs that come fully loaded with complicated options are called **fritterware** because you often end up frittering away your time playing around with the fun stuff instead of getting work done.

Problem 3: Word Processors Create Illiterates

The same people who complained that calculators would turn our kids into math dropouts are now crying that computer spell checkers and grammar checkers will turn us all into illiterate slobs who wouldn't know a participle if it was dangled in front of us.

This one's easy to answer, folks: Nuts to them, I say! If we can get our machines to handle the rote work of spelling and grammar, I'm all for it. After all, meaning is what's most important. Why not take the time that we would normally spend with our noses in dusty dictionaries, and use it to craft our concepts and polish our prose?

How Does WordPerfect for Windows Fit into All This?

If word processing was boxing (and on those days when our computers make us feel like putting our fist through our screens, I suppose it *is* something like the sweet science), a puny program like Notepad (the text editor that comes with Windows) would be in the flyweight division and Write (the more full-featured word processor that you also get free with Windows) would be a middleweight. This means that a muscular program like WordPerfect for Windows would have to be a heavyweight, because there are few chores this software can't handle.

As you'll soon see, WordPerfect for Windows has something for everyone. If all you need is basic editing features for things like letters and memos, WordPerfect for Windows will handle these chores with a few simple commands. If you need to put together large, complex documents, WordPerfect for Windows has features such as outlining, indexing, and footnotes that'll handle the biggest job without complaint. If your interests lean more toward desktop publishing (creating newsletters, brochures, and the like), WordPerfect for Windows can do page layout, columns of text, and graphics with the best of them. In other words, WordPerfect for Windows works the way you do, not the other way around.

What You See Is What You Get

One of the biggest advantages of WordPerfect for Windows (especially if you've ever used a DOS word processor) is that it operates in what is known as *graphics mode*. This means that when you format your documents (making characters bold or italic, or using different fonts, for example), you can see the changes right on-screen, instead of having to wait for a printout.

With WordPerfect for Windows, what you see on your screen is what you get when you print. This not only saves time when formatting and laying out your documents, but it also saves trees because you don't have to print out every little change to see if it looks right.

What's New in Version 6.1?

WordPerfect for Windows version 6.1 is more than just a mere upgrade from version 6.0a. Oh sure, it squashes a few bugs (that's programmer lingo for software errors; they're also called, sarcastically, *undocumented features*) and is a bit faster, but it also includes a few new or retooled features that should make your writing life a bit easier. Here's a rundown of the major changes you'll find in version 6.1:

The feature that enables you to see on your computer screen what you end up getting from your printer is called **WYSIWYG** (What-You-See-Is-What-You-Get). It's pronounced wizzy wig. (I swear I'm not making this up.)

➤ A feature—it's called QuickCorrect—that can fix some spelling mistakes as soon as you type them.

➤ Revamped Power Bar and Toolbar that put even more common features only a mouse-click or two away.

➤ Multiple levels of undo. This means you can reverse not just your last gaffe, but your last 10 or 20, or whatever. And, just in case you change your mind, you can also redo something you've just undone.

➤ Beefed up versions of the spell checker, thesaurus, and grammar checker.

➤ New and improved incarnations of the TextArt and WordPerfect Draw programs that have all kinds of added bells and whistles.

This book covers all of these new version 6.1 features and more. But don't feel left out if you're still using either version 6.0 or 6.0a; I'll point out the differences between versions as we go along.

The Least You Need to Know

This chapter took you on a quick tour of the shiny, happy world of word processing. Here's a recap of some of the sights we saw along the way:

➤ Word processing is a dumb name for using a computer to write, edit, format, and print documents.

➤ Your keyboard may look like a typewriter, but thanks to the computer in the box behind it, it's a lot smarter and a lot easier to use than a typewriter. Most editing and formatting commands are just a few keystrokes or mouse clicks away.

➤ Word processing is a good thing if you approach it the right way. Keep things simple, use the program's features to make your life easier, and don't be afraid to experiment.

➤ WordPerfect for Windows is a popular word processor because it works the way you do. Version 6.1 has all kinds of cool new features that'll keep you entertained for hours.

Chapter 3

Diving In: Your First WordPerfect for Windows Session

In This Chapter

➤ Starting WordPerfect for Windows

➤ Taking a tour around the screen

➤ Entering text

➤ Exiting WordPerfect for Windows

➤ A heartwarming story about skiing

The first time I ever went skiing, my friends (who, of course, were all experts and had little patience for a rank beginner) took me for a couple of token runs down the bunny hill and then whisked me to the top of some huge mountain. (With friends like these...)

In our travels down the mountain, we'd often come upon the steep, mogul-filled hills that my friends loved. These suckers scared the heck out of me, so I'd just follow everyone else, and I always made it down somehow. But I'd usually see groups of skiers standing at the top of these hills, fidgeting nervously, afraid to go down, but not able to turn back. In honor of these nervous-nellies, I developed my skiing motto: "Better a leg broken by boldness than a spirit broken by fear."

I tell you this story now, as we stand at the edge of WordPerfect for Windows Hill, to inspire you to, as the ads say, "Just do it." Follow my lead, and we'll get through without a hitch.

Preflight Checklist

Before starting WordPerfect for Windows, you should make sure you've got everything you need. Here's a quick checklist:

Is Your Computer On?

This is, of course, important. Make sure not only that your computer is up and running, but that you've powered up anything else you'll need (such as your monitor or printer).

Is WordPerfect for Windows Installed?

If you haven't yet installed the program, you have two choices:

➤ Find the nearest computer guru and ask him or her to install the program for you. This is the easiest method (for you, anyway), and you'll find most gurus can be easily cajoled with flattery ("Say, that's a *nice* pocket protector!").

➤ If you can't find a guru or you'd like to give it a go yourself, you'll find WordPerfect's installation program to be friendlier than most. Forge ahead to Chapter 30, "Installing WordPerfect for Windows," to run through the appropriate steps.

Are You in Windows?

Before you can fire up WordPerfect for Windows, you need to start Windows. (This assumes, of course, that Windows is installed on your computer. If it's not, you'll need to march out to your local computer store and shell out the bucks to buy a copy, because WordPerfect for Windows is useless without it.)

If you see a box on your screen that says **Program Manager** at the top, you're in Windows. Otherwise, from the DOS prompt (which looks like C>, or C:\>, or some variation on this theme), type **WIN** and press **Enter**.

If you don't see anything that looks like Windows or the DOS prompt, you're likely in some other program. Here are some possibilities:

The MS-DOS Shell program. If you see the words **MS-DOS Shell** at the top of your screen, hold down your keyboard's **Alt** key and press **F4** to return to DOS.

Some kind of menu system. Your computer might be set up with a menu system that gives you a list of programs to run. If you're lucky, you may see a Windows option. If so, great! Just select the option to start Windows. Otherwise, look for an option called "Exit to DOS," "Quit," or something similar. You can also try pressing the **Esc** key.

Is the Ambiance Just Right?

Make sure your surroundings are comfortable and your favorite computer accessories are nearby (a good, strong cup of coffee, relaxing background music, and a copy of *Feel the Fear and Do It Anyway*).

The Three-Step Program for Starting WordPerfect for Windows

With Windows loaded, you should now see a box on your screen that says **Program Manager** at the top. If you don't, find the nearest guru and tell her that some dork in a book wants you to be in Program Manager. Better yet, why not learn how to do it yourself by picking up a copy of *The Complete Idiot's Guide to Windows* by the same dork? (Ah, yes, that *was* a shameless plug, wasn't it?)

The boxes you see (such as Program Manager and WPWin 6.1) are called **windows**. The little pictures you see infesting Program Manager's boxes are called **icons**.

Without further ado, here are the steps you need to follow to get WordPerfect for Windows up and running:

1. Hold down the **Alt** key on your keyboard and tap **W**. You'll see a menu of options.

19

2. Look for the option named either **WPWin 6.1** or **WPWin 6.0** (depending on which version you have) and press the number you see beside it. This displays a box with the same name, as shown in the following figure.

3. Look inside the WPWin 6.1 (or WPWin 6.0) box for a little picture labeled "WPWin 6.1" (or "WPWin 6.0"). You start WordPerfect for Windows by "selecting" this picture in one of these ways:

   ➤ With a mouse, move the pointer so it rests on the picture, and then press the left button twice quickly.

   ➤ With the keyboard, press the arrow keys until the WPWin 6.1 label is highlighted. Then press **Enter**.

This is the icon you use to start WordPerfect for Windows.

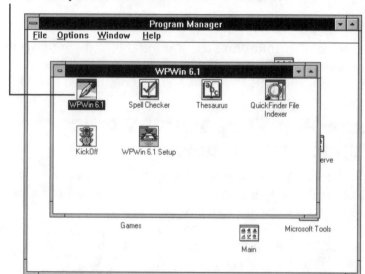

You start WordPerfect for Windows by selecting the WPWin 6.1 picture.

Checking Out the WordPerfect for Windows Screen

WordPerfect for Windows will take a few seconds to crank itself up to speed. When it finally does, you'll see the following screen.

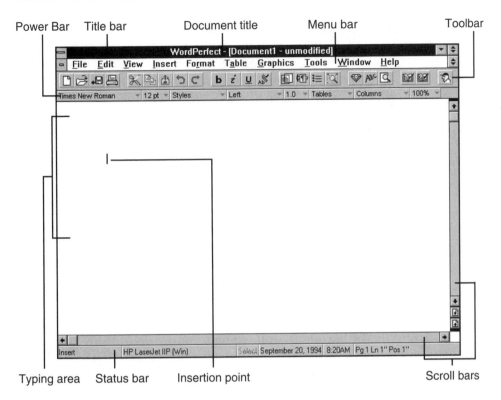

The WordPerfect for Windows screen in all its glory.

The WordPerfect for Windows screen is somewhat stark, but it's certainly not empty. Here's a quick rundown of what's there:

➤ **The typing area**   This large, blank expanse covers most of the screen. This is where it all happens; everything you type will appear in this area. Think of it as the digital equivalent of a blank sheet of paper.

➤ **The insertion point**   This small, blinking line has a single purpose in life: it tells you where the next character you type will appear. Go ahead and press a letter on your keyboard. See how it shows up on-screen right where the insertion point was? The insertion point itself leaps ahead to tell you where your next character will appear. (Press **Backspace** to get rid of the character you typed.)

➤ **The title bar** This area (besides reminding you that you're using WordPerfect) tells you the name of the current document. This is important because in WordPerfect for Windows you can have a bunch of documents open at the same time (yes, there *are* times when this is useful). This area also gives you helpful hints about what WordPerfect for Windows' commands and buttons mean. (I'll show you what I mean in Chapter 5, "Easy Street: Using the Menus, Toolbars, and Power Bar.")

➤ **The menu bar** This is the second line from the top of the screen (File, Edit, View, and so on). Although you'd never know to look at it, this innocuous-looking line is actually your gateway to every single WordPerfect for Windows feature. WordPerfect accomplishes this prodigious feat through the miracle of pull-down menus. You'll learn all about these magical beasts in Chapter 5, "Easy Street: Using the Menus, Toolbars, and Power Bar."

➤ **The Toolbar** Lying just beneath the menu bar, this feature (which was new in version 6) undoubtedly makes your life easier. Each of the little squares you see represents a commonly used WordPerfect for Windows task (such as saving a file). All you have to do is click the mouse button to perform a task with any one of these buttons. I'll give you the details on using the Toolbar in Chapter 5.

➤ **The Power Bar** Below the toolbar, you'll find the Power Bar. This is a collection of lists for things like fonts and styles. Again, Chapter 5 is the place to learn how to wield the Power Bar.

➤ **Scroll bars** These things make it easy to navigate your longer documents with a mouse. See Chapter 8 "Day-to-Day Drudgery II: Navigating Documents," for the full lowdown.

➤ **The status bar** Bars, bars, and more bars! This one gives you various tidbits of information, including (in version 6.1) the current date and time. The stuff on the right side looks pretty incomprehensible, doesn't it? This data is actually quite useful, although you probably won't appreciate it until you've used the program a bit. Here's a summary of what's there:

Info   **What It Means**

Pg 1   This is the page number you're on (Pg 1, Pg 2, and so on).

Ln 1"   This tells you what line the insertion point is on. The position is measured in inches (that's what the double-prime symbol (") means) from the top of the page. It starts at 1" because you have a one-inch margin at the top of the page.

Pos 1"   This tells you the horizontal position of the insertion point. The position is measured in inches from the left edge of the page. Again, it starts at 1" because there's a one-inch margin on the left side of the page.

If you're starting version 6.1, you'll see a dialog box asking you whether you want to use the QuickStart coach. If you can ignore the silly name, you can use "coaches" to learn more about various aspects of WordPerfect for Windows. In this case, the coach can give you a brief introduction to WordPerfect for Windows 6.1. If you'd like to give it a whirl, click on Yes. If you'd prefer to bypass this nonsense, click on the No button. (Not sure what "clicking" means? Bound ahead to Chapter 4, "Keyboard and Mouse Basics," to get the scoop.)

Now What?

Okay, you've got this big-bucks word processor loaded, the insertion point is blinking away insistently, and the large, blank typing area seems to cry out to be filled with happy little characters. What else do you need to know before you get started? Well, in a word, nothing! That's right, just start pecking away on your keyboard, and your brilliance will be displayed for all to see. This is the beauty of WordPerfect for Windows (if beauty is the right term): the program gets out of your way so you can get down to the business of writing. Here are a few things to watch for when typing:

Margins are the (usually) empty areas that surround your text on the page. WordPerfect for Windows' standard margins are one inch high on the top and bottom, and one inch wide on the sides. See Chapter 15, "Making Your Pages Look Good," to learn how to change margin sizes.

➤ If you're used to typing with a typewriter, you may be tempted to press the Enter key when you approach the end of a line. Fortunately, you don't have to bother because WordPerfect for Windows handles that chore for you. When you've filled up a line, WordPerfect for Windows moves the text onto the next line automatically. Even if you're smack in the middle of a word, the program will automatically truck the entire word onto the next line, no questions asked. (This feature is called *word wrap*.) The only time you need to press Enter is when you want to start a new paragraph.

➤ If you make a mistake, just press the **Backspace** key to wipe it out. (If you don't see any key with the word Backspace on it, look for a left-pointing arrow (←) on the right end of the row with all the numbers.)

➤ As you type, some of the stuff in the status bar will change. As you move across the screen, the column position (Pos) will increase; when you move to a new line, the row position (Ln) will increase.

➤ If you're entering a lot of text, you may be startled to see a line suddenly appear across the screen. No, there's nothing wrong with your screen. It just means that you've moved to a second page, and to show you where one page ends and the next begins, WordPerfect for Windows displays a line (it's called a *page break*). As proof that you're on a new page, check out the status bar: WordPerfect for Windows bumps the page number (Pg) up to 2, and resets the line position to 1" (since you're now at the top of a new page).

Getting Help

If you run into a problem with WordPerfect for Windows, or if you simply find yourself in a strange part of town, you probably want to get help fast before panic sets in. Thoughtfully, the WordPerfect programmers have provided you with a handy online Help system. You start this system in one of two ways:

➤ Press **F1** to get help that is *context-sensitive*. This means the help screen that appears is related to whatever task you're in the middle of.

➤ Select a command from the Help menu. (You can display the Help menu by holding down **Alt** and pressing **H**.)

I won't go into the details of the Help system here. However, if you think you'll be using it regularly, Chapter 5, "Easy Street: Using the Menus, Toolbars, and Power Bar," and Chapter 6, "Talking to WordPerfect for Windows' Dialog Boxes," will tell you everything you need to know to navigate the Help system's windows. (By the way, to close a Help window, hold down **Alt** and press **F4**.)

Exiting WordPerfect for Windows

I know, I know, you're just starting to have fun, and here I am telling you how to exit the program. Well, you've gotta do it sometime, so you may as well know the drill:

1. Begin by pressing **Alt+F** (hold down the **Alt** key, press **F**, and then release both). You'll suddenly see a big list of stuff appear on your screen. This is your first look at one of the pull-down menus that I mentioned earlier.

2. Ignore everything you see except the line near the bottom of the list that says Exit. There are several ways to select this command, but for now, the easiest is simply to press **X**. If you've made changes to any open documents, WordPerfect for Windows asks whether you want to save them.

You can skip steps 1 and 2 by simply holding down the **Alt** key, pressing **F4**, and then releasing **Alt**.

3. You have three choices at this point:

➤ If you don't want to save your changes, press **N** (for No).

➤ If you do want to save your changes, press **Y** (for Yes). If you see a box titled Save As, type a name that is eight letters or fewer (for now, don't use any punctuation marks or spaces in the name; see Chapter 7 for details on what is and isn't legal in creating a file name). Then press **Enter**.

➤ If you change your mind and decide you don't want to exit after all, press the **Esc** key.

4. If you've made changes to more than one document, you may have to repeat steps 2 and 3 a few times.

The Least You Need to Know

In this chapter, you made the big leap and learned how to start WordPerfect for Windows. The rest of the chapter wasn't terribly strenuous (I hope), but here's a quick summary anyway:

➤ Before starting WordPerfect for Windows, make sure Windows is loaded.

➤ In Program Manager, select the **WPWin 6.1** (or **WPWin 6.0**) window and then select the **WPWin 6.1** (or **WPWin 6.0**) icon.

➤ To enter text, just start typing. Remember that you don't have to press Enter at the end of each line.

➤ To exit WordPerfect for Windows, hold down **Alt**, press **F**, and then press **X** (or just press **Alt+F4**). If the program asks if you want to save your changes, select Yes or No, or press **Esc** to cancel.

Chapter 4

Keyboard and Mouse Basics

In This Chapter

➤ A tour around the keyboard

➤ WordPerfect for Windows keyboarding basics

➤ The mouse made easy

➤ Musings on the ins and outs of garbage

"Garbage in, garbage out." That's an old expression computer geeks like to use to explain why things go haywire in software programs. Feed computers junk, and you get junk back because the dumb beasts just aren't smart enough to know the difference. In other words, input is everything.

When using WordPerfect for Windows, you have two ways of *inputting* stuff (that is, of putting stuff into your computer): you can use the keyboard or the mouse. You don't have to become a keyboard connoisseur or a mouse maven to use WordPerfect for Windows, but to avoid the "garbage in" thing, it helps to digest a few basics. This chapter tells you all you need to know.

The Keyboard: A Guided Tour

Keyboards come in all shapes and sizes; like the proverbial snowflakes, it seems no two are alike. However, they all share a few common features, and most are laid out more or less the way you see in this figure.

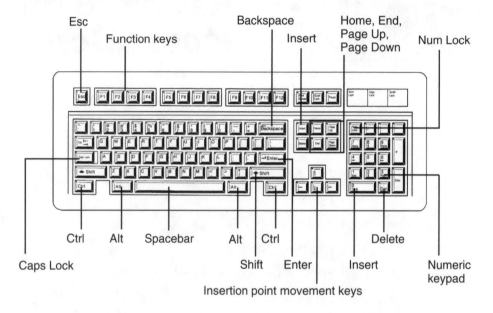

A typical PC keyboard. Just to be a pain, your computer manufacturer may have put the keys in slightly different positions.

Letters, Numbers, and Other Strangers

The bulk of the keyboard is taken up by the basic letters, numbers, punctuation marks, and other special characters that you'll be using most often (and some, like ~ and ^, that you may never use). This area of the keyboard is called the *alphanumeric keypad*.

Shift and Caps Lock

Just like a typewriter, you use the Shift key to get capital letters. For keys with two symbols (except the ones on the numeric keypad; I'll talk about those later), hold down **Shift** to get the upper symbol. If you want to type nothing but capital letters for a stretch, it's better to press the **Caps Lock** key (similar to a typewriter's Shift Lock key). However, this only works for letters; to get the other symbols (such as **$** and **+**), you still need to use **Shift**. When you want to switch back to normal letters, press **Caps Lock** again.

> Typing teachers always suggest limbering up your fingers before getting down to heavy typing. One of the best ways to do this is to type out *pangrams*—sentences that use all 26 letters of the alphabet. The standard pangram that everybody (sort of) knows is *The quick brown fox jumps over the lazy dog.* This is fine, but it's a bit dull. Try some of these on for size:
>
> Pack my box with five dozen liquor jugs.
> The five boxing wizards jump quickly.
> Judges vomit; few quiz pharynx block.
> Sexy zebras just prowl and vie for quick, hot matings.

Ctrl, Alt, and Those Bizarre WordPerfect Key Combinations

If you press **Ctrl** (it's pronounced "control") or **Alt**, nothing much happens—but that's okay because nothing much is supposed to happen. You don't use these keys by themselves, but as part of *key combinations*. (The Shift key often gets into the act as well.)

Let's try an example so you can see what I mean. Hold down the **Ctrl** key with one hand, use the other to tap the **W** on your keyboard, and then release **Ctrl**. Like magic, a box entitled **WordPerfect Characters** appears on your screen. The point of this exercise isn't to do anything with this box (which you can get rid of by pressing the **Esc** key; or turn to Chapter 13, "Making Your Characters Look Good," to figure out what it does), but to show you that you can get WordPerfect's attention simply by entering certain combinations of keys. Using the **Ctrl** and **W** combo is like saying, "Hey, I wanna see the WordPerfect Characters box on the screen!"

WordPerfect for Windows has all kinds of these strange-but-useful key combinations, so we need some kind of shorthand for verbose instructions like "Hold down the **Ctrl** key, tap **W**, and then release **Ctrl**." From now on, instead of this mouthful, I'll just say "Press **Ctrl+W**" (or whatever).

The Esc Key

If you find yourself in some strange WordPerfect for Windows neighborhood, and you're not sure what to do next, you can usually get back to Kansas not by clicking your ruby slippers, but by pressing the **Esc** key until things look more familiar.

The Insertion Point Movement Keys

One of the principal differences between a word processor and a typewriter is that the word processor enables you to leap around to any place in the document to fix blunders or just to check things out. You do this with the *insertion point movement* keys, which you'll find either on a separate keypad or mixed in among the numeric keypad keys.

You'll be learning all kinds of fun navigation stuff in Chapter 8, "Day-to-Day Drudgery II: Navigating Documents," but for now, here's a quick summary of some basic insertion point movement techniques.

 If you press a key on the numeric keypad and instead of getting a number, the insertion points moves, you have Num Lock turned off. Just tap the **Num Lock** key to enable the numbers. Most keyboards have a Num Lock indicator light that tells you when Num Lock is on.

Press	To move the insertion point
←	Left one character
→	Right one character
↑	Up one line
↓	Down one line
Page Up	To the top of the screen
Page Down	To the bottom of the screen

The Numeric Keypad

On each type of keyboard, the numeric keypad serves two functions. When the Num Lock key is on, you can use the numeric keypad to enter numbers. Turn Num Lock off to enable the keypad's insertion point movement keys, and you can use them to navigate a document. Some keyboards (called *extended keyboards*) have a separate keypad for the insertion point movement keys so you can keep Num Lock on all the time.

The Function Keys

The *function keys* are located either to the left of the alphanumeric keypad, or across the top of the keyboard. There are usually 12 function keys (although some older keyboards have only 10), and they're labeled F1, F2, and so on. In WordPerfect for Windows, you use these keys either by themselves or as part of key combinations to perform commands. For example, you can press the **Alt+F4** key combination to quickly exit WordPerfect for Windows.

A Note About Notebook Keyboards

If you're ever forced to type for an extended period on a notebook or laptop keyboard, you have my deepest sympathies. Not only are these suckers cramped, but they have all the feel of a piece of cement. To make things even worse, there's usually no separate numeric keypad, so the insertion point movement keys are scattered about willy-nilly. On some notebooks, the insertion point keys are hidden among the letters, and you have to hold down a special key (usually labeled "Fn") to get at them. (Groan!)

So what's my point? Well, just that you need to be a little more careful when using a notebook keyboard. Fingers that would normally fly (relatively speaking) on a regular keyboard will be bumping into each other in the cramped confines of the notebook layout. One solution that many notebooks offer is the capability of hooking up a separate numeric keypad—or even a full-fledged keyboard. You should check into this; it's definitely worth it.

WordPerfect for Windows Keyboarding for Non-Typists

Contrary to popular belief, getting the most out of WordPerfect for Windows doesn't mean you have to become some kind of touch-typing, thousand-words-per-minute keyboard demon. Heck, I've been using computer keyboards for years, and I wouldn't know what touch-typing was if it bit me in the face. In this section, we'll just go through a few things that should make your life at the keyboard easier.

The Enter Key Redux

When you use a typewriter, a little bell goes off as you near the end of each line. This sound warns you to finish off the current word (or to add only a couple of small ones) and then press Return to start a new line. WordPerfect for Windows frees you from this old-fashioned drudgery; it starts new lines for you automatically. If you're smack in the middle of a word, this feature will even transport the whole word to the next line. So even though you ex-typewriter types may be sorely tempted to do so, *don't* press Enter as you near the end of a line. Just keep typing—WordPerfect will handle all the hard stuff. (You'll probably find you miss the little bell, though. Oh, well.)

You can press **Enter** when you need to start a new paragraph. WordPerfect for Windows creates a new, blank line and moves the insertion point to the beginning of it. You can also use Enter to insert blank lines in your text. Just position the insertion point at the beginning of a line and press **Enter**. The new line appears above the current line.

Quick Fixes: Using Backspace and Delete

You'll be learning all kinds of fancy techniques for editing your documents in Part II. For now, though, you can use the Backspace and Delete keys to get rid of small typos. Just use the arrow keys to position the insertion point appropriately, and then use the Backspace and Delete keys as described here.

Backspace   Use this key to delete the character immediately to the left of the insertion point. (If your keyboard doesn't sport a key that says "Backspace" on it, look for a left-pointing arrow: ←. It should be to the right of all the numbers on the top row.)

Delete   Use this key to delete the character immediately to the right of the insertion point.

Switching to Typeover Mode

If you position the insertion point in the middle of some text, WordPerfect inserts anything you type between the existing characters. (Why, yes, that *is* why they call it the *insertion* point.) If you're redoing a few words, you could delete them first and then retype, but usually it's easier just to type over them. To do this, you need to put

WordPerfect for Windows in *Typeover mode* by pressing the **Insert** key. (I know, I know, that doesn't make sense, but bear with me.) The word **Typeover** appears in the status bar, and when you type again, the new characters replace the existing ones. To resume normal operations, just press **Insert** again.

Key Combination Contortions

WordPerfect for Windows has a key combination for just about anything you'd ever want to do with the program, and I'll be letting you in on many of them as we go through this book.

Most people find it faster to use one hand for these key combinations, but I'll warn you now to expect some real contortions if you do. This is especially true for key combos that use either Ctrl or Alt and the function keys. Some of these nasty devils can be quite a stretch for all but the biggest hands (although things are made easier by some thoughtful computer companies that put Ctrl and Alt keys on both sides of the Spacebar). My advice? Don't strain yourself unnecessarily. Use two hands if you have to.

The problem with Typeover mode is that one of these days (inevitably) you'll forget to turn it off, and you'll end up wiping out all kinds of important prose. When this happens, press **Ctrl+Z** to undo the typeover, and then press **Insert** to return to the friendly confines of Insert mode.

Mouse Machinations

Learning how to use a mouse is by no means an essential WordPerfect for Windows survival skill. However, you'll find that it makes many everyday tasks just plain faster and easier. The good news is that using a mouse takes no extraordinary physical skills. If you can use a fork without poking yourself in the eye, you should have no trouble wielding a mouse.

The Basic Mouse Technique

A mouse is a marvelous little mechanical miracle that can seem incomprehensible to the uninitiated. The basic idea, though, is simple: you move the mouse on its pad or on your desk, and a small pointer (see

the figure below) moves correspondingly on your screen. By positioning the pointer on strategic screen areas, you can select text, operate
the pull-down menus, and choose all kinds of WordPerfect for Windows options. Not bad for a rodent!

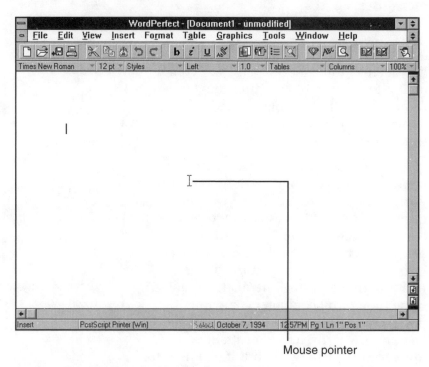

Mouse pointer

The WordPerfect for Windows mouse pointer.

If you don't see the mouse pointer on your screen, but you know you have a mouse installed, just wiggle the mouse a bit, and the pointer should appear. WordPerfect for Windows always hides the pointer when you're typing.

Using a mouse is straightforward, but it does take some getting used to. Here's the basic technique:

1. Turn the mouse so that its cable extends away from you.

2. Place your hand over the mouse in such a way that:

   ➤ The part of the mouse nearest you nestles snugly in the palm of your hand.

34

➤ Your index and middle fingers rest lightly on the two mouse buttons. (If your mouse has three buttons, rest your fingers on the two outside buttons; leave the middle one alone for now.)

➤ Your thumb and ring finger hold the mouse gently on either side.

3. Move the mouse around on its pad or on your desk. Notice how the mouse pointer on the screen moves in the same direction as the mouse itself.

The proper way to hold a mouse.

WordPerfect's Mouse Pointers

One of the most confusing things about using a mouse is that the pointer often changes shape without warning. This is perfectly normal behavior, but it can be disconcerting for mouse rookies. To prepare you for the inevitable, here's a field guide to some of the mouse pointers you'll encounter in your WordPerfect for Windows travels:

This pointer	Appears when
I	You move the mouse inside the typing area.
↖	You move the mouse into any of the regions surrounding the typing area (the title bar, menu bar, and so on).

You're moving any of WordPerfect for Windows' graphic objects.

 You're changing the size of a graphic object.

 You're moving the WordPerfect for Windows Toolbar.

 WordPerfect for Windows is busy with something. This dreaded pointer means you won't be able to do anything else until the program has finished its business.

The Hard Part: Controlling the Darn Thing!

Although moving the mouse pointer is simple enough, controlling the pesky little thing is another matter. Most new mouse users complain that the pointer seems to move erratically, or that they move to one part of the screen and then run out of room to maneuver. To help out, here are a few tips that will get you well on your way to becoming a mouse expert:

A person who spends lots of time in front of his screen is called a **mouse potato** (which is, of course, the computer equivalent of a couch potato).

➤ Don't grab the mouse as though you were going to throw it across the room (although you may, on occasion, be sorely tempted to do so). A light touch is all you need.

➤ The distance the mouse pointer travels on the screen depends on how quickly you move the mouse. If you move the mouse very slowly for about an inch, the pointer moves about the same distance (a little more, actually). However, if you move the mouse very fast for about an inch, the pointer leaps across the screen.

➤ If you find yourself at the edge of the mouse pad but the pointer isn't where you want it to be, simply pick up the mouse and move it to the middle of the pad. This doesn't affect the position of the pointer, but it does allow you to continue on your way.

Mouse Actions

Here's a list of the actions you can perform with a mouse:

Point   Move the mouse pointer so it rests on a specific screen location.

Click   Press and release the left mouse button. (You always use the left button unless you're specifically told otherwise.)

Right-click   This is similar to plain clicking, except that you press and release the right mouse button.

Double-click   Not surprisingly, this means you quickly press and release the left mouse button twice in succession.

Drag   This has nothing to do with dressing funny. It simply means you press and hold down the left mouse button, and then move the mouse.

The Least You Need to Know

This chapter gave you the lowdown on using the keyboard and mouse in WordPerfect for Windows. Here are a few highlights:

➤ You'll spend most of your typing time pecking out letters, numbers, and punctuation in the alphanumeric keypad.

➤ You use the **Ctrl** and **Alt** keys (and sometimes **Shift**) in combination with other keys to access WordPerfect's commands.

➤ The insertion point movement keys help you move around in a document. They appear in a separate keypad, or mixed in with the numeric keypad (in which case, you have to turn Num Lock off to get at them).

➤ Use the numeric keypad to enter numbers into your documents quickly. Make sure you turn **Num Lock** on before using these keys.

➤ The function keys are the 12 (or sometimes only 10) keys labeled F1, F2, and so on. In WordPerfect for Windows, you use these either by themselves or in combination with other keys to run certain commands.

➤ A mouse can make WordPerfect for Windows easier to use, but it does take some getting used to.

Chapter 5

Easy Street: Using the Menus, Toolbars, and Power Bar

In This Chapter

➤ What are pull-down menus?

➤ How to use pull-down menus with a mouse and keyboard

➤ Checking out the oh-so-handy Toolbars

➤ Easy formatting with the Power Bar thing

➤ Complete coverage of some handy tools that let you work with WordPerfect for Windows the easy way

You (or your company) didn't shell out the big bucks for WordPerfect for Windows so you could type all day. To get the most out of your investment, you need to use the program's other features. "Okay, so how do I access those features?" Well, if you read the last chapter, you know that one way is by using key combinations. But key combinations, while often quicker, have two major drawbacks:

➤ You either have to memorize them (shudder) or you have to interpret WordPerfect's arcane keyboard template (a task akin to deciphering the Dead Sea Scrolls).

➤ They can be physically brutal unless you have basketball-player-sized hands.

Fortunately, WordPerfect for Windows gives you no less than three easier alternatives: *pull-down menus*, *Toolbars*, and the *Power Bar*. The pull-down menus group commands in logical chunks, are a snap to use (especially with a mouse), and provide access to every WordPerfect for Windows feature. The Toolbar and Power Bar are even handier because they make it possible for mouse users to access common WordPerfect for Windows tasks with a click or two of a button. Sound good? Then read on, and I'll show you how they work.

What the Heck Are Pull-Down Menus?

Take a good look at the desk you're sitting at. (If you're not sitting at a desk, picturing one in your head will do.) You've probably got an area where you do your work, surrounded by various tools (pens, pencils, and so on) and things that keep you informed (such as a clock and calendar). You probably also see a few drawers, from which you get your work and in which you store your desk tools.

The WordPerfect for Windows screen is a lot like a desk. You have the typing area to work in, of course, and you have the status bar to keep you informed. The pull-down menus, then, work just like desk drawers. When you need to get more work (open a document) or access a WordPerfect for Windows command, you simply open the appropriate menu and select the menu option that runs the command.

Why You Pull Down Instead of Up or Out

Why are they called "pull-down" menus? Well, because they're hidden inside the menu bar near the top of the screen. Selecting any of the ten menu bar options (File, Edit, View, and so on) displays a menu of choices, as you can see in the File menu.

File	
New...	Ctrl+T
Open...	Ctrl+O
Close	Ctrl+F4
Save	Ctrl+S
Save As...	F3
Master Document	▶
Compare Document	▶
Document Summary...	
Document Info...	
Print...	Ctrl+P
Exit	Alt+F4

WordPerfect for Windows' File pull-down menu.

The effect, you'll note, is as though you pulled the menu down from the menu bar. See, sometimes this stuff actually makes sense!

How to Use Pull-Down Menus with a Mouse

If you have a mouse, using pull-down menus is a breeze. All you do is move the mouse pointer into the menu bar area (the pointer will change to an arrow), and then click on the name of the menu you want to pull down. For example, clicking on File in the menu bar pulls down the File menu.

Once you have a menu displayed, you need to select one of the commands. This is simple enough: just click on the command you want to run. Depending on what you select, one of three things will happen:

> The choices you see listed in a pull-down menu are called **commands**. You use these commands to tell WordPerfect for Windows what you want it to do next.

➤ WordPerfect for Windows will run the command.

➤ Another menu will appear. In this case, just click on the command you want to run from the new menu.

➤ Something called a *dialog box* will appear to get further info from you. See Chapter 6, "Talking to WordPerfect for Windows' Dialog Boxes," for details on using dialog boxes.

What do you do if you pull down a menu and discover you don't want to select a command? No problem. To return to the document, simply click anywhere inside the document. To pull down a different menu, click on the menu name.

How to Use Pull-Down Menus with the Keyboard

The secret to accessing pull-down menus from the keyboard is to look for the underlined letter in each menu bar option. For example, look at the "F" in File and the "E" in Edit. These underlined letters are the menu options' *hot keys*. (In geekier circles, they're also known as *accelerator keys*.) How do they work? Simple: you just hold down the **Alt** key, press the hot key letter (or number) on your keyboard, and then release **Alt**. For example, to pull down the File menu, use the **Alt+F** key combination.

To select one of the menu commands, use the up and down arrow keys to highlight the command you want (a *highlight bar* moves up and down to mark the current command), and then press **Enter**. As I explained in the mouse section, one of three things will happen depending on which one you select:

➤ The command will run.

➤ Another menu will appear. In this case, use the arrow keys to select the command you want from the new menu, and then press **Enter**.

➤ A dialog box will appear, asking you for more information.

If you pull down a menu and discover you don't want to select a command, you can return to the document by pressing Alt. Or, to pull down a different menu, press **Alt** plus the letter of the new menu.

More Fun Pull-Down Menu Stuff

If you've been pulling down some menus, you may have noticed a few strange things. For example, did you notice that some commands have a triangle on the right-hand side of the menu? Or that some are followed by three ominous-looking dots? Or that others also list a key (or key combination)? These are just a few of the normal features found in pull-down menus, and you can take advantage of them to make your life easier. The rest of this section summarizes these features. I'll be using the Format menu (shown in the following figure) as an example, so you might want to pull it down now to follow along. (If you're using version 6.0, pull down the Layout menu, instead.)

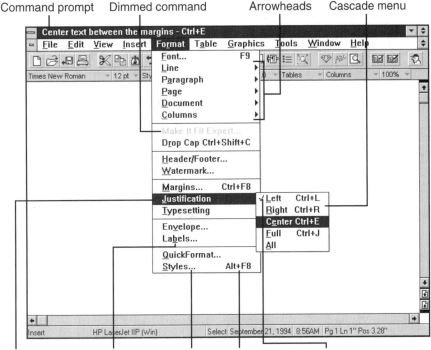

WordPerfect for Windows' umpteen pull-down menu features.

The Highlight Bar

As you move through a menu with your keyboard, a black bar appears across the menu. This is called the *highlight bar*, and it indicates the current command. As I've said, one way you can execute a command is by pressing **Enter** when the command is highlighted.

Command Prompts: Helpful Hints

WordPerfect for Windows has so many commands that it's just about impossible (and probably not very useful) to remember what each one does. Fortunately, you don't have to, because whenever you highlight a command, WordPerfect displays a prompt in the title bar that gives you a brief description of the command. If this description seems reasonable, go ahead and select the command. If it doesn't, you're free to move on.

As a reminder, you highlight a command in a pull-down menu by using the up and down arrow keys to scroll through the list. Is there any way to highlight a command with the mouse? Sure! You just need to use a slightly different technique for pulling down a menu: move the pointer over the menu name, press the left mouse button and *hold it down*. Keep the button held down and move the mouse pointer through the menu commands. (This is called *dragging* the mouse.) As the pointer hits each command, the prompt appears in the title bar. To select a command, just release the mouse button while the command you want is highlighted. To remove the menu without selecting a command, move the pointer off the menu and then release the button.

Underlined Characters: More Hot Keys

Every command in a pull-down menu has one underlined character. This is the command's hot key; it means that once you've displayed a menu, you can select any command simply by pressing its underlined letter on your keyboard. (For this reason, command hot keys are also known as *selection letters*.) For example, in the Format menu, you could select, say, the Font command simply by pressing **F**. (If you're itching to try this out, go ahead and press **F**. You'll eventually see a box named Font on your screen. I'll discuss font stuff in Chapter 13, "Making Your Characters Look Good," so for now just press **Esc** to return to your document.)

I can hear you now: "Okay, so let's get this straight. Each menu has a hot key, and to pull down a menu, I have to hold down Alt and press the hot key letter. Each menu command also has a hot key, but to select the command, I press the letter *without* holding down the Alt key. Is it just me, or is this confusing?" It *is* confusing at first, but it's just one of those dumb Windows things we have to live with. My advice? Use your mouse for all this menu monkeying around.

Shortcut Keys: The Fast Way to Work

Some menu commands also show a key or key combination on the right-hand side of the menu. These are called *shortcut keys*: they allow you to bypass the menus altogether and activate a command quickly from your keyboard. For example, you can select the Format menu's **Margins** command simply by pressing **Ctrl+F8**. (If you try this, press **Esc** to remove the Margins dialog box that appears. To learn about working with page margins, see Chapter 15, "Making Your Pages Look Good.")

Once you've worked with WordPerfect for Windows for awhile, you may find it faster to use shortcut keys for the commands you use most often.

I know it's confusing, but the shortcut keys only work when you don't have a menu displayed. If you press a key combination with a menu pulled down, WordPerfect for Windows will ignore it and wait for you to do something sensible.

Arrowheads (Menus, Menus, and More Menus)

With some commands, you'll see an arrowhead (▶) on the right side of the menu. This tells you that yet another menu (called a *cascade menu*) will appear when you select this command. For example, select the Justification command from the Format menu to see a menu of commands for justifying text. (Press **Esc** to remove the new menu. I'll talk about each of these commands in Chapter 14, "Making Your Lines and Paragraphs Look Good.")

The Ellipsis (The Three-Dot Thing)

An *ellipsis* (...) after a command name indicates that a dialog box will appear when you select the option. WordPerfect for Windows uses dialog boxes to ask you for more information or to confirm a command you requested. For example, if you select the Format menu's Font command, a dialog box appears to find out what kind of font you want to use. (Press **Esc** to remove this dialog box.) See Chapter 6, "Talking to WordPerfect for Windows' Dialog Boxes," for more dialog box details.

Check Marks: The Active Command

Some commands operate like light switches: they toggle certain features of the program on and off. When the feature is on, a small check mark appears to the left of the command to let you know. Selecting the command (or sometimes a different command) turns off the feature and removes the check mark. If you select the command again, the feature is turned back on, and the check mark reappears.

Let's work through an example so you can see what I mean:

1. Pull down the View menu and take a look at the Status Bar command; it should have a check mark beside it. This means WordPerfect for Windows' status bar is active (or turned on).

2. Now select the Status Bar command. This deactivates the command, which means that WordPerfect for Windows no longer displays the status bar on-screen.

3. To bring back the status bar, first pull down the View menu. Notice that the Status Bar command no longer has a check mark beside it. Select the Status Bar command, and WordPerfect for Windows redisplays the status bar.

What You Can't Do: The Dimmed Options

You'll sometimes see menu options that appear in a lighter color than the others. These are called *dimmed options*, and the dimming indicates that you can't select them (for now, anyway). A dimmed option is usually WordPerfect's way of telling you that you must do something else with the program before the option will become active.

Quick Command Fun with QuickMenus

WordPerfect for Windows version 6 introduced a new feature that gave mouse users a real bonus: QuickMenus. These menus display a short list of commands related to a specific feature. All you do is place the mouse pointer over the feature and then right-click. When the menu appears, just click (the left button this time) on the command you want.

For example, if you right-click in the typing area (but not in any of the margins), you'll see the QuickMenu shown in the following figure. Notice how the options are all related to working with the text in a document. (To get rid of the QuickMenu, click anywhere in the typing area.)

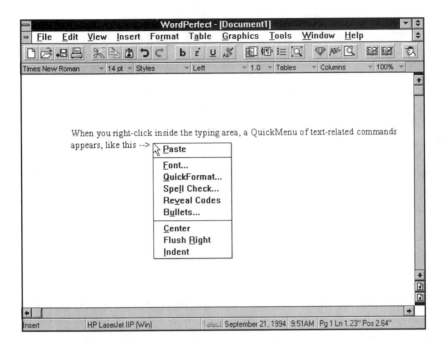

One of WordPerfect for Windows' handy QuickMenus.

QuickMenus are available for text, the left margin, headers and footers, Toolbars, the Power Bar, the status bar, scroll bars, tables, and graphics, among other things.

The Toolbar: Easy Command Access

In the bad old days of computers (way back in the '80s!), the only way to run a command in most programs was to press a key or key combination. Users complained, though, because not only was it hard to remember the proper keystrokes, but the hand contortions were crippling people for life.

In response to these complaints, the world's programming geniuses came up with pull-down menus and dialog boxes. These were a big improvement, but then people whined about having to wade through dozens of menus and windows to get to the command they needed. (You just can't please some people.)

Don't have a Toolbar on your screen? No sweat: just pull down the View menu and activate the Toolbar command. (If you're using version 6.0, activate the **Button Bar** command, instead.)

So now we have *bars*. Whether they're called "power" bars or "tool" bars or "sushi" bars, they're all designed to give you push-button access to common commands and features. No unsightly key combinations to remember; no menu and dialog box forests to get lost in.

WordPerfect for Windows has gotten into the act in a big way by offering you both a Toolbar (or, if you're still using version 6.0, a Button Bar) and a Power Bar.

Test Driving the Toolbar

Each of the Toolbar buttons you see represents a common WordPerfect for Windows task. All you have to do is click on a button, and WordPerfect runs the task, no questions asked. For example, clicking on the Print button displays the Print dialog box. Okay, so which one is the Print button? Ah, there's the rub. Most of those tiny pictures are pretty obscure, so icon-interpretation is fast becoming one of the '90s' most coveted skills. Fortunately, the WordPerfect for Windows pro-grammers decided to have mercy on us all and included not one, but *two* methods for identifying Toolbar buttons. Just point the mouse at the button you're furrowing your brow over, and then look for the following two things:

➤ The title bar displays a brief description of what the button does.

➤ The button's title appears below the mouse pointer (this is called a QuickTip).

As a public service throughout this book, I'll let you know when-ever a WordPerfect for Windows feature is accessible from a Toolbar button, like this:

 Click on this Toolbar button to display the Print dialog box.

Displaying a Different Toolbar

WordPerfect for Windows actually comes with no less than fifteen(!) different Toolbars (you can only display one at a time, however). Why so many? Well, the other Toolbars are designed for specific tasks. For example, if you'll be doing a lot of character formatting, you'll probably want to display the Font Toolbar because it's chock full of buttons that perform various character formatting chores. (Check out Chapter 13 "Making Your Characters Look Good," to sink your teeth into this character formatting stuff.) In some cases, WordPerfect for Windows is smart enough to display the appropriate Toolbar automatically. For example, if you're working inside a table (which I'll show you how to do in Chapter 26, "Techniques for Terrific Tables"), the program courteously displays the Table Toolbar.

To display a different Toolbar, right-click on the current Toolbar, and then click on the Toolbar you want (Design Tools, Font, and so on) from the QuickMenu that appears.

The Power Bar: Easy Formatting Access

Just when you thought things couldn't get any easier, WordPerfect for Windows also includes yet another screen element: the Power Bar. The Power Bar is a collection of lists that give you easy mouse access to some of WordPerfect for Windows' formatting features.

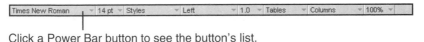

Click a Power Bar button to see the button's list.

WordPerfect for Windows' Power Bar.

Most of the Power Bar buttons contain a list of formatting choices. For example, the first button contains a list of all the fonts on your system. You display the list just by clicking the button. (If you decide not to select anything from the list, you can hide it either by clicking the button again, or by clicking inside the typing area.) As with the Toolbars, I'll show you how to use each Power Bar list in the appropriate section of this book.

Is your Power Bar missing in action? You can get it back by pulling down the View menu and activating the Power Bar command.

The Least You Need to Know

This chapter explained WordPerfect for Windows' pull-down menus, and showed you how to use them with both a mouse and keyboard. You also learned about the Toolbars and the Power Bar. Here's a summary of what you now know:

➤ Pull-down menus are a lot like desk drawers because they store tools (commands) that you use with WordPerfect for Windows.

➤ To pull down a menu with the mouse, simply click on the menu name in the menu bar.

➤ To pull down a menu with the keyboard, look for the menu's hot key and then, while holding down **Alt**, press the key on your keyboard.

➤ Once you pull down a menu, you can select a command by using your keyboard's up and down arrow keys to highlight the command and then pressing **Enter**. If you have a mouse, just click on the command you want.

➤ QuickMenus present you with a short list of commands related to a specific screen area. Right-click on the area to display its QuickMenu. Click on a QuickMenu command to select it.

➤ The Toolbars and Power Bar put common WordPerfect for Windows tasks and formatting chores only a mouse click away. To display a different Toolbar, right-click the Toolbar and select the one you want from the QuickMenu.

Chapter 6

Talking to WordPerfect for Windows' Dialog Boxes

In This Chapter

➤ What is a dialog box?

➤ Getting around in dialog boxes

➤ Learning about dialog box buttons, boxes, and lists

➤ Odd dialog box details for curious computer consumers

As you work with WordPerfect for Windows, little boxes will appear incessantly on your screen to prompt you for more information (and generally just confuse the heck out of things). These are called *dialog boxes*, and they're WordPerfect's way of saying "Talk to me!" This chapter looks at these chatty little beasts, and offers some helpful tips for surviving their relentless onslaught.

Where Do They Come From?

Dialog boxes may sometimes seem to appear out of nowhere, but they generally show up after you select certain options from WordPerfect for Windows' pull-down menus, press certain key combinations, or click on certain buttons in the Toolbar. Whether or not a dialog box appears depends on whether the program needs more information from you. For example, if you select the File menu's Print command, WordPerfect for Windows displays the Print dialog box to ask you which printer to use, how many copies you want to print, and so on.

You can always tell a menu command will generate a dialog box if there are three dots (...) after the command name. These three dots (they're known as an *ellipsis*) tell you that some kind of dialog box will appear if you select the option. This gives you time to prepare yourself mentally for the ordeal to come.

Dialog Box Basics

Here are a few points about dialog boxes to keep in mind as you work through this chapter:

➤ Dialog boxes always have a title at the top of the box. This lets you know if you selected the right command.

➤ Dialog boxes like to monopolize your attention. When one is on-screen, you can't do other things (such as enter text in the typing area or select a pull-down menu). You have to deal with the dialog box first, and then you can do other things.

➤ The various objects you see inside a dialog box are called *controls* because you use them to control the way the dialog box works.

➤ Every control has a name that identifies it.

Navigating Controls

Before you learn how these controls operate, you need to be able to move among them. (This section applies only to keyboard users. Mouse users select a control merely by clicking on it.)

The first thing you need to be able to figure out is which control is currently selected. (This can be easy or hard depending on how many controls the dialog box has.) You need to look for one of two things:

➤ If the control displays text inside a box, the control is active either when the text is highlighted or when you see an insertion point cursor blinking on and off inside the box.

➤ All other controls display a dotted outline around their name when they're selected.

Think of these guidelines as "You are here" signs on a map and keep them in mind as you move through WordPerfect for Windows' dialog boxes.

Once you know where you are, you can move around by pressing **Tab**, which moves, more or less, top to bottom and left to right through the controls, or **Shift+Tab**, which moves bottom to top and right to left. To get used to working with dialog boxes, make sure you can find the currently selected control before pressing Tab (or Shift+Tab) to move on.

Navigating Dialog Box Groups

Most WordPerfect for Windows dialog boxes organize related controls into groups and surround them with a box. For example, the Zoom dialog box shown later in this chapter has a Zoom group, and the Font dialog box (also shown later in this chapter) has an Appearance group. When you're inside one of these groups, you can usually select another control in the group simply by pressing the underlined letter in the control. For example, in the Zoom group, you could select the Full Page control by pressing **F**.

If you're outside a group, you can still select a control inside the group quickly. Just hold down **Alt** and press the underlined letter in the control's name.

Working with Command Buttons

The most basic dialog box control is the *command button*. The dialog box shown in the following figure has four command buttons: OK, Cancel, Use as Default, and Help. (To display this dialog box, select the Edit menu's Repeat command.) When you select a command button, you're telling WordPerfect for Windows to execute the command written on the face of the button.

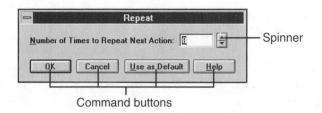

Command buttons

Command buttons execute the command written on their face.

To select a command button with a mouse, just click on the button. To select a command button from the keyboard, press **Tab** until the command button you want is selected (the button name is surrounded by a dotted outline), and then press **Enter**.

WordPerfect for Windows uses command buttons for all kinds of things, but three are particularly common: OK, Cancel, and Help. Here's what they do:

Select the OK button when you've finished with the dialog box and you want to put all your selections into effect. This is the "Make it so" button.

Select the Cancel button to cancel the dialog box. It's useful for those times when you panic and realize that you're looking at the wrong dialog box or when you've made a mess of your selections. This is the "Belay that last order" button.

Select the Help button when you haven't the faintest idea what you're doing and you'd like WordPerfect for Windows to give you a hint. This is the "Please explain" button.

If you take a close look at the Repeat dialog box shown above, you'll see that the OK command button has a darker outline than the other buttons. What gives? Well, this darker outline identifies the OK button as the *default* button for the dialog box. This means that, no matter which other control is currently selected, you can select that button just by pressing **Enter**. Here's another bit of fascinating dialog box lore: you can select the Cancel button by pressing the **Esc** key.

Working with Text Boxes

A *text box* is a screen area in which you type text information such as a description or a file name. When you first select a text box, you'll see a blinking insertion point inside the box (if it's empty) and highlighted text (if it's not). The Document Summary dialog box shown in the following figure contains several text boxes. (Select Document Summary from the File menu to display this dialog box.)

Text boxes

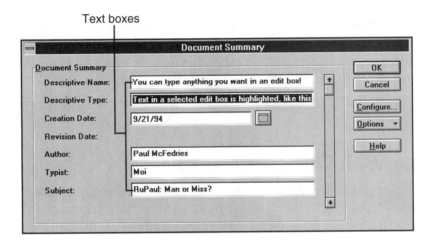

You type text information into text boxes.

To use a text box with a mouse, click inside the box at the point where you want the new text to appear, and then start typing. (If the box is empty, you can just click anywhere inside the box.) To use a text box from your keyboard, press **Tab** either until you see the insertion point in the box or until you see the text in the box highlighted. If the box is empty, you can just start typing. If the box already contains text, however, you need to be a little careful. Why? Because if the text is highlighted, WordPerfect for Windows will delete the existing text and replace it with your typing! If this is what you want, fine. Otherwise, press either the left arrow or right arrow key to remove the highlight, and then enter your text. If you make any mistakes when typing, you can use the Backspace and Delete keys to expunge the offending letters.

If you accidentally blow away some highlighted text box text, you can get it back by pressing **Alt+Backspace**.

Working with Spinners

Spinners are controls that let you scroll up or down through a series of numbers. For example, in the Repeat dialog box shown earlier, the Number of Times to Repeat Next Action control is a spinner.

Spinners have two parts:

➤ On the left you'll see a text box into which you can type the number you want (boring).

➤ On the right you'll see two buttons with upward and downward pointing arrows. Click on the upward pointing arrow to increase the number shown in the text box. Click on the downward pointing arrow to decrease the number. For some real fun, press and hold down the mouse button on one of the arrows and watch the numbers really fly!

Working with Option Buttons

Option buttons are WordPerfect for Windows' equivalent of the old multiple-choice questions you had to struggle with in school. You're given two or more choices, and you're only allowed to pick one. In the dialog box shown in the following figure, there are nine option buttons. (To eyeball this dialog box, pull down the View menu and select the Zoom command.) As you can see, an option button consists of a small circle with a label beside it that tells you what the option is.

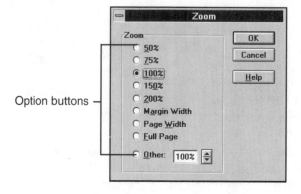

You can only select one option button at a time.

How do you activate an option button? If you have a mouse, simply click on the option you want (you can either click on the button itself or on its name). Notice that a black dot appears inside the circle of the button that you activate. From the keyboard, press **Tab** until one of the option buttons is selected (it's name is surrounded by a dotted outline), and then use the up and down arrow keys to pick out the one you want.

Working with List Boxes

A *list box* is a small window that displays a list of items, such as file names or directories. A highlight bar shows the currently selected item in the list. The Open File dialog box shown in the following figure has two list boxes. If you'd like to display this dialog box on your screen, pull down the **Graphics** menu and select the **Im**age command (or the Figure command, if you're using version 6.0).

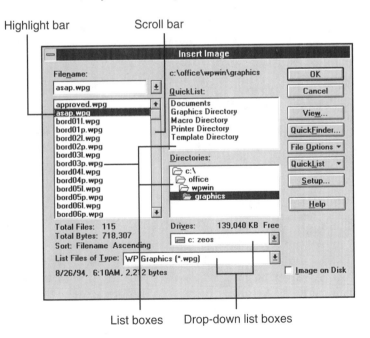

This dialog box has several examples of list controls.

To use a mouse to select an item from a list box, simply click on the item if it's visible. If it's not visible, use the scroll bars to display the

Here's a spiffy tip that can save you oodles of time. Once you're inside a list box, press the first letter of the item you want. WordPerfect for Windows leaps down the list and highlights the first item in the list that starts with the letter you pressed. If you keep typing, WordPerfect tries to find any item that matches the letters you've entered.

item, and then click on it. (If you're a little leery of those scroll bar things, see the section titled "A Brief Scroll Bar Primer," later in this chapter.)

To select a list box item using your keyboard, press **Tab** until an item in the list is selected (you'll see a dotted line around the item). Then use the up and down arrow keys (or Page Up and Page Down if the list is a long one) to highlight the item you want.

The two list boxes shown in the Insert Image dialog box above are slightly different. The Directories control is a pure list box. The Filename control, however, is technically called a *combination list box*, because it combines a text box with a list box. This means that, in addition to selecting an item from the list, you could type in what you want in the text box above it.

Working with Drop-Down Lists

A *drop-down list* is like a combination of a list box and a pull-down menu. The box shows the currently selected item, and the downward-pointing arrow gives you access to a list that drops down (hence the name) from which you can select a different item. Drop-down list boxes usually contain lists of related items such as font names or document files. The Insert Image dialog box has two drop-down list boxes: List Files of Type and Drives.

To use a mouse to select an item from a drop-down list, first click on the downward-pointing arrow on the right side of the control. This opens the list to display its options. Now click on the item you want. If you don't see the item, use the scroll bar to view more of the list. (If you're not sure how a scroll bar works, see the next section.)

To use your keyboard to select an item from a drop-down list, follow these steps:

1. Press **Tab** until the item inside the drop-down list's text box is selected.

2. Press the down arrow key to open the list.

3. Use the up and down arrow keys to highlight the item you want.

4. Press **Enter**.

A Brief Scroll Bar Primer

You'll be learning more about scroll bars in Chapter 8, "Day-to-Day Drudgery II: Navigating Documents," but I'll give you a brief introduction here so you'll be able to use the drop-down lists.

Some lists contain too many items to fit inside the box. In this case, a scroll bar appears on the right-hand side of the box to make it easier to navigate the list. The box inside the scroll bar (called, appropriately enough, the *scroll box*) tells you where you are in the list. For example, if the scroll box is halfway between the top and the bottom of the scroll bar, you're approximately halfway down the list.

To navigate a list with the scroll bar, use the following mouse techniques:

➤ To scroll through the list one item at a time, click on the arrow at the top of the scroll bar (to move up) or the arrow at the bottom of the scroll bar (to move down).

➤ To jump quickly through the list, click inside the scroll bar between the scroll box and the top (to move up) or between the scroll box and the bottom (to move down).

➤ To move to a specific part of the list, drag the scroll box up or down.

Working with Check Boxes

The real world is constantly presenting us with a series of either/or choices. You're either watching Oprah or you're not; you're either eating Heavenly Hash or you're not. That kind of thing. WordPerfect for Windows handles these sorts of yes-or-no, on-or-off decisions with a control called a *check box*. The check box presents you with an option that you can either activate (check) or not.

In the Font dialog box shown in the following figure (select Font from either the Format menu if you're using version 6.1, or the Layout menu if you're using 6.0), the Appearance group contains no less than ten check boxes. As you can see, a check box consists of a small square and a label that tells you what the check box controls. You know a check box is activated when you see an "X" inside the square; it's deactivated when the square is empty.

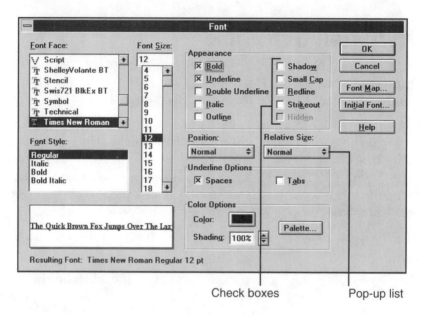

Check boxes   Pop-up list

The Font dialog box contains all kinds of check boxes.

To activate a check box with a mouse, click on the box or on its name. To deactivate the box, just click on the box again.

To activate a check box from the keyboard, press **Tab** until the check box you want is highlighted and then press the **Spacebar**. To deactivate the check box, press the **Spacebar** again.

Working with Pop-Up Lists

Pop-up lists are a cross between a command button and a list. Instead of showing a command name, the button face always shows the current selection from the list. In the Font dialog box shown above, there are two pop-up lists: Position and Relative Size.

To work with a pop-up list using a mouse, place the pointer over the appropriate pop-up list, and press and hold down the left mouse button. When the list appears, keep the mouse button pressed and move the pointer up or down until the selection you want is highlighted. Then release the button.

From the keyboard, follow these steps:

1. Press **Tab** until you select the button name.

2. To scroll through the choices without popping up the list, press the up or down arrow keys. To pop up the list, press either **Alt+up arrow** or **Alt+down arrow** (you'll see that the current selection has a check mark beside it). Then use the up and down arrow keys to highlight the item you want.

3. If you popped up the list, press **Enter** to select your choice.

The Least You Need to Know

This chapter showed you the ins and outs of using dialog boxes to communicate with WordPerfect for Windows. We covered a lot of ground, and you learned all kinds of new things. If it's not all clear in your head right now, don't worry about it because, believe me, you'll be getting plenty of practice. In the meantime, here's some important stuff to remember:

➤ WordPerfect for Windows uses dialog boxes to ask you for more information or to confirm that the command you've selected is what you really want to do.

➤ Mouse users work with controls merely by clicking on them. Keyboard jockeys use the **Tab** key (or **Shift+Tab**) to move through the dialog box controls.

➤ Many controls have underlined letters. When you're in a group, you can select these controls by pressing the letter on your keyboard. Outside the group, you can select a control by holding down **Alt** and pressing the control's underlined letter.

➤ Most dialog boxes use the OK, Cancel, and Help buttons. Select **OK** to exit the dialog box and put your choices into effect. Select **Cancel** to bail out of a dialog box without doing anything. Select **Help** to find out just what the heck is going on.

61

Chapter 7

Day-to-Day Drudgery I: Saving, Opening, and Closing

In This Chapter

➤ Saving a document

➤ Saving a document under a different name

➤ Opening and retrieving a document

➤ Closing a document

➤ Dreary—but nonetheless vital—skills that you'll be using day-in and day-out

WordPerfect for Windows is jam-packed with powerful features that let you do everything but wax the cat. But even with all that power at your fingertips, you still have to deal with the drudgery of opening and saving documents (the subject of this chapter) and navigating your way through large files (which I'll save for Chapter 8).

Save Your Work, Save Your Life

Most people learn about saving documents the hard way. For me, it was a power failure that wiped out an entire day's writing. Believe me, that kind of thing can make you old before your time.

Why is saving necessary? Well, when you open a document, WordPerfect for Windows copies it from its safe haven on your hard disk to the volatile confines of your computer's memory. When you shut off your computer (or if a power failure forces it off), everything in memory is wiped out. If you haven't saved your document to your hard disk, you'll lose all the changes you made.

Saving a New Document

When you first start WordPerfect, the program displays a blank typing area that you can use to begin a fresh document. If you've used this blank file, you can save your work by pulling down the File menu and selecting the **Save** command or by pressing **Ctrl+S**. WordPerfect needs to know the name you want to use for the new file, so you'll see the Save As dialog box shown in the following figure.

 Instead of selecting the **Save** command, you can also click on this button in any Toolbar.

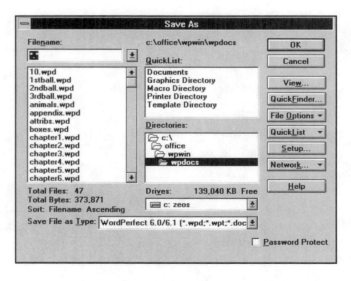

When you save a new document, WordPerfect for Windows displays the Save As dialog box so you can name the file.

Enter the name you want to use in the Filename text box. File names usually contain a period flanked by a *primary name* on the left and an *extension* on the right. Unfortunately, computers are *really* picky about what names you give your files. Use an illegal character or the wrong format, and your machine will get all huffy and display some kind of testy error message.

To avoid this unpleasantness, you need to know what sort of hoops you're expected to jump through. When naming your documents, make sure you observe the sacred File Name Commandments handed down by the great DOS Nerd Gods:

1. Thou shalt not use more than eight characters for the file's primary name.

2. Thou shalt not use more than three characters for the file's extension.

3. Thou shalt separate the primary name and the extension with a period.

4. Thou shalt not use a space or any of the other forbidden characters: + = \ | [ ] ; : , . < > ? /

5. Thou shalt not take the name of an existing file.

Even though extensions are optional, most people use them because they're handy for identifying what type of file you're dealing with. If you don't give an extension, WordPerfect for Windows automatically adds a .WPD extension, so you don't need to worry about it.

When you're done, select the **OK** button. If all is well, WordPerfect saves the file and returns you to the document. However, if you enter an illegal name, WordPerfect for Windows responds in one of the following ways:

➤ If your primary name is too long, WordPerfect lops it off at eight characters; if your extension is too long, WordPerfect spits out the extraneous letters and just uses the first three characters.

➤ If you enter an illegal character in the name, WordPerfect displays an error message. Select **OK** to return to the Save As dialog box. Expunge the offending character, and then try again.

➤ If you give the document a file name that already exists, WordPerfect warns you, asking if you want to replace the existing file. If you choose to replace the file, it's gone for good—and no amount of hocus-pocus will get it back. If you're absolutely, positively sure you won't ever need the other file, select **Yes**; otherwise select **No** to return to the Save As dialog box, and then enter a different file name.

Saving an Existing Document

Even if you've saved a new document, you're still not out of the woods. If you make changes to the file, you need to save them as well. Happily, WordPerfect for Windows makes saving your work as easy as shooting fish in a barrel. In fact, I can tell you the whole thing in a single sentence: To save the document you're working on, either pull down the File menu and select the Save command, or just press **Ctrl+S**. That's it!

 Again, you can also save an existing document by clicking on this button in any Toolbar.

How Often Should You Save?

Saving your work is vital, but few people do it often enough. How often is "often enough"? Here's a quiz you can take to see if you know.

You should save your work when:

a. You have a delay while you think of what to say next (a common occurrence for many of us).

b. You've just entered a long passage.

c. You've just formatted a large section of text.

d. You've just rearranged a bunch of stuff.

e. You've just retrieved another document into the current one.

f. There's a thunderstorm raging outside your office.

g. All of the above.

The answer, of course, is **g**. All of the above. Saving is so easy that you really should do it as often as you can. Use **a.** through **f.** as guidelines for deciding when it's time to save. (You may be wondering why the heck you need to save your work during thunderstorms. Superstition? No, the problem is that lightning strikes can cause power surges in electrical outlets. Don't worry, you're in no danger of being jolted through your keyboard; but these surges do have a nasty habit of wreaking untold havoc on your sensitive data.)

Saving is so important that the WordPerfect for Windows programmers built in an "automatic save" feature. This feature saves a backup copy of your document every ten minutes. If a power failure or some other calamity shuts down the program prematurely, WordPerfect for Windows will let you know the backup exists the next time you start the program. You can then load the backup and continue working. To change the frequency of these automatic saves, see Chapter 28, "Customizing WordPerfect for Windows."

Protecting a Document with a Password

If your document contains important information, you can protect it from snoops by assigning it a password. If anyone tries to open the file, he'll have to enter the correct password or he's out of luck. To assign a password when you're saving a new document, follow these steps:

1. In the Save As dialog box, activate the **P**assword Protect check box.

2. Select **OK** when you're ready to save the file. WordPerfect for Windows displays the Password Protection dialog box (shown in the following figure).

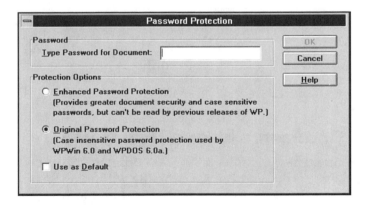

Use the Password Protection dialog box to assign a password to sensitive documents.

3. In the Type Password for Document text box, enter the password you want to use. For added safety, WordPerfect for Windows displays the password in asterisks (just in case those darn snoops are looking over your shoulder).

4. If you're using version 6.1, the Protection Options group enables you to choose from two kinds of password protection:

Enhanced Password Protection   This is the new and improved password protection scheme developed for version 6.1. It uses some kind of fancy-schmancy technique that provides even greater security for your documents. Also, this scheme is *case-sensitive*, which means that you can only open the document if you enter the same combination of upper-case and lowercase letters that you used when you set up the password. For example, if you enter **GuessMe** as your password, WordPerfect for Windows won't open the document if you enter **guessme**, **GUESSME**, or **GuEsSmE** as the password.

Original Password Protection   This is the password protection scheme used in version 6.0. Select this option if you think someone still using 6.0 (or 6.0a) might need the document.

 If you forget your password, you're out of luck because there's no way to retrieve it. To prevent this, try to keep your passwords relatively short (5 or 6 letters) and meaningful. However, using obvious things like your name or birth date won't fool anyone.

5. Select **OK**. WordPerfect for Windows asks you to confirm your password.

6. Type your password again and select **OK**.

Saving a Document Under a New Name

The File menu also includes a Save As command. This command is a lot like Save, except you can save the file with a new name or to a new location. This is useful for creating a new file that is very similar (but not identical) to an existing file. Instead of creating the new file from scratch, just open the existing file, make the changes, and then use the Save As command (or just press **F3**) to save your changes to the new file. The old file remains as it was.

This is also useful for adding a password to an existing file or removing a previously assigned password. Just open the file and select Save As from the File menu. In the Save As dialog box, activate or deactivate the **Password Protect** check box (whichever is appropriate), and then select **OK** (don't change the name of the file). When WordPerfect for Windows asks if you want to replace the file, select **Yes**. If you're adding password protection, you'll have to enter a password as described in the previous section.

Opening a Document

Each time you start WordPerfect for Windows, you see a blank typing area waiting patiently for you to type something. Most of the time, though, you'll want to work with an existing document you've saved sometime in the past. To do this, you need to tell WordPerfect for Windows to grab the appropriate file from wherever it's stored on disk, and *open* it in your computer's memory.

To open a document, pull down the File menu and select the **Open** command, or press **Ctrl+O**. You'll see the Open File dialog box shown in the following figure.

 Click on this tool in any Toolbar to display the Open File dialog box.

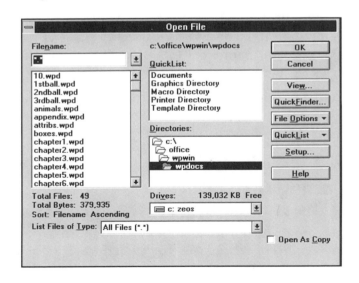

Selecting the Open command from the File menu displays the Open File dialog box.

The purpose of the Open File dialog box is to give you a reasonably coherent view of the files on your hard disk. The idea is that you browse through the files and then select the one you want to open. You'll be seeing this dialog box (or a variation of it) more often than you want to know, so let's take a closer look at just how you go about selecting a file.

Opening a File: The Apartment Hunting Analogy

To make this process of searching for a file a little more comprehensible, let's set up a simple analogy: the apartment search. When you're looking for an apartment, you first decide what city you want to live in. Once you know that, you can narrow your search to a specific area of the city. Finally, you narrow your search even further by deciding what type of apartment you want (studio, 1-bedroom, and so on). When all this is done, you end up with a short list of possible apartments, and you select the one you want from this list. Okay, let's put this analogy to work.

Step 1: Selecting the Correct Drive (The City)

You can store files on your hard disk or on floppy disks, so the first step is to make sure that you're dealing with the right drive. In our apartment hunting analogy, this is like selecting a city in which to live. The Drives drop-down list box displays the current drive, and you can use it to select a different drive, if necessary. (For all the gory details on drop-down list boxes, see Chapter 6, "Talking to WordPerfect for Windows' Dialog Boxes.")

If you're going to select a floppy drive from the Drives list, make sure there's a disk in the drive. Otherwise, your computer makes a rude noise (on my system it sounds like somebody burping!) and posts a nasty message on-screen telling you, basically, to get your act together.

Step 2: Selecting the Correct Directory (The Neighborhood)

Just as cities are divided into neighborhoods, disks are divided into storage areas called *directories*. Use the Directories list box to select the correct directory for your file. If you're using version 6.1, WordPerfect for Windows sets up a default directory called C:\OFFICE\WPWIN\ WPDOCS for storing your WordPerfect documents (in version 6.0, it's called C:\WPWIN60\WPDOCS). If you use this directory when saving your files, you probably won't need to select a different directory. (If you forget how to select items from a list box, head back to Chapter 6 for a quick refresher course.)

Step 3: Displaying the Proper File Type (The Type of Apartment)

There are many kinds of apartments and there are many kinds of files. And although a directory may contain dozens or even hundreds of files, there are only a few that you really need to look at. Use the List Files of Type drop-down list box to narrow the number of files WordPerfect displays. WordPerfect for Windows 6 uses the .WPD extension to identify its files, and those are probably the ones displayed in the Open File dialog box. If the Filename list is cluttered with other types of files, or if you've been saving your files with a different extension, you'll need to select the appropriate type from this drop-down list box.

Step 4: Selecting a File (The Apartment)

Now you're ready to make your selection. You've narrowed your search, and the Filename list box displays the finalists. Double-click on the file you want to open, or highlight it and select **OK**.

If you're not sure that a file is the one you want, highlight it and select the View button. WordPerfect for Windows displays the document in a Viewer window. To view other documents, just click on them in the Open File dialog box while the Viewer window is still open. When you see the one you want, select **OK**. If you want to close the Viewer window before selecting a document, press **Alt+F4**.

Opening Recent Files

If you want to reopen a document you worked with recently, you may not have to go through all this rigmarole. WordPerfect for Windows gives you two methods that may prove easier:

➤ Pull down the File menu and look at the bottom. The names you see below the Exit command are the last four files you used. If one of them is the document you want, you're in luck! Just select it from the menu, and WordPerfect for Windows opens it for you automatically.

➤ If you're using version 6.1, the Filename control in the Open File dialog box has a drop-down list at the top. If you click on the downward-pointing arrow, you'll see a list of the last 10 files you've opened (the most recent file is at the top of the list). You can choose a file from this list and then select **OK** to open it.

Retrieving a File

When you retrieve a document, WordPerfect for Windows makes a copy of the file and adds it to the current file at the insertion point position. This is a handy way of reusing material in another document.

Text that you use repeatedly is called **boilerplate**. It's the word processing equivalent of the old maxim, "Don't reinvent the wheel."

When you want to retrieve a file, here are the steps you need to follow:

1. Position the insertion point where you want the new text to appear.

2. Pull down the Insert menu and select the File command. WordPerfect for Windows displays the Insert File dialog box (which looks and works just like the Open File dialog box).

3. Highlight the name of the document you want to insert.

4. Select the Insert button. WordPerfect for Windows grabs the text from the document you chose, and then adds it to the current document.

A Fresh Beginning: Starting a New Document

As I mentioned earlier, WordPerfect for Windows displays a new document when you start the program. However, you can start a fresh file anytime you want. Here are the steps to trudge through:

1. Pull down the File menu and select the New command, or press **Ctrl+T**. The New Document dialog box appears, as shown in the following figure.

You can also display the New Document dialog box by clicking on this button in the 6.1 WordPerfect Toolbar.

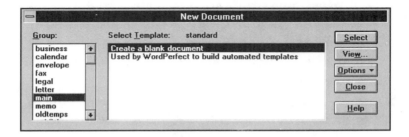

The New Document dialog box shows up when you select the File menu's New command.

2. In the Group list, make sure **main** is highlighted.

3. In the Select Template list, make sure **Create a blank document** is highlighted. (Don't know what a "template" is? Check out Chapter 29, "Ten Great WordPerfect for Windows Ideas," to find out more.)

Press **Ctrl+N** to start a new blank document without opening the New Document dialog box.

4. Choose the Select button. WordPerfect for Windows creates a new document for you.

You can also get a new document by clicking on this button in any Toolbar.

Closing a Document

When you're done with a document, you should close it to make room for other files. All you have to do is pull down the File menu and select the Close command, or press **Ctrl+F4**. It's that simple!

The Least You Need to Know

Now that was a chapter! WordPerfect for Windows sure seems to like complicating such simple tasks as saving and opening documents. Here's a summary of what you need to know:

➤ You should save your documents as often as you can to avoid losing any work. All you have to do is select the Save command from the File menu (or press **Ctrl+S**).

➤ When you save a new document, WordPerfect for Windows asks you to enter a name for the file. Be sure to follow DOS's arcane file-naming rules, or you'll get an error.

➤ If you want to save a document under a different name, use the File menu's Save As command (or press **F3**).

➤ To open a document, select Open from the File menu (or press **Ctrl+O**), and select the file from the Open File dialog box.

➤ To retrieve a file, select the Insert menu's File command.

➤ To close a document, use the File menu's Close command (or press **Ctrl+F4**).

Chapter 8

Day-to-Day Drudgery II: Navigating Documents

In This Chapter

➤ Navigating a document with the keyboard

➤ Using WordPerfect for Windows' Go to command

➤ Navigating a document with a mouse

➤ Using scroll bars

➤ Tales of a thousand-and-one key combos

A lot of what you do in WordPerfect for Windows will be short little letters and memos that'll fit right on-screen. But you'll also be creating longer documents, and what you see in the typing area will only be a small chunk of the entire file. To see the rest of the document, you'll need to learn a few *navigational* skills. Now, I'm not talking about navigating the Baja 500 or anything, but just a few simple skills to help you get around. With this chapter riding shotgun, you'll get through just fine. (To get the most out of this chapter, you should follow along and try each of the techniques as I present them. For best results, open—or create—a document that's larger than the screen.)

Keyboard Navigation Skills

WordPerfect for Windows has a fistful of ways to navigate your documents from the keyboard. In this section, we'll work our way up from short hops between characters and words to great leaps between screens and pages.

Navigating Characters and Words

The simplest move you can make in a document is to use the left and right arrow keys to move left or right one character at a time. If you've got a bit of ground to cover, try holding down the key. After a slight delay, the insertion point starts racing through each line. (Notice that when it hits the end of one line, it starts over at the beginning of the next.)

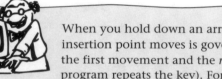

When you hold down an arrow key, the speed at which the insertion point moves is governed by two factors: the *delay* after the first movement and the *repeat rate* (the rate at which the program repeats the key). For the fastest possible keyboard (the shortest delay and the quickest repeat rate), try this: the next time you're in Program Manager, access the **Control Panel** (it should be in the **Main** group) and select the **Keyboard** icon. In the Keyboard dialog box, drag the boxes in both slider bars as far to the right as they'll go. Select **OK** and then exit Control Panel (by selecting Exit from the **Settings** menu). Now start WordPerfect, and your insertion point keys just whizz around the screen.

If you need to jump over a couple of words, hold down the **Ctrl** key and then use the left or right arrow key to move one word at a time. If you're in the middle of a long word, such as "hippopotomonstrosesquipedalian" (which is a very, very long word that means "pertaining to very, very long words") you can use **Ctrl+left arrow** to move quickly to the beginning of the word.

Navigating Lines and Paragraphs

If you need to move up or down one line at a time, use the up or down arrow keys. If you're at the bottom of the screen and you press the down arrow, the text moves up so you can see the next line. (The line that used to be at the top of the screen heads off into oblivion, but don't worry: WordPerfect for Windows keeps track of everything.) A similar thing happens if you're at the top of the screen (unless you're at the top of the document): if you press the up arrow, the text moves down to make room for the next line. (Moving text up or down is called *scrolling* through the document.)

To move to the beginning of the current line, press **Home**. To move to the end of the current line, press **End**. If you need to jump around one paragraph at a time, use **Ctrl+up arrow** (to move up one paragraph) or **Ctrl+down arrow** (to move down one paragraph).

Navigating Screens, Pages, and Documents

For really big documents, you need to know how to cover a lot of ground in a hurry. WordPerfect for Windows, of course, is up to the task:

➤ To move to the top of the screen, press **Page Up**. To move to the bottom of the screen, press **Page Down**. Keep pressing these keys to navigate the document one screenful at a time.

➤ For multipage documents, use **Alt+Page Up** to move to the beginning of the previous page and **Alt+Page Down** to move to the beginning of the next page.

➤ For truly large leaps, press **Ctrl+Home** to move to the beginning of the document, or **Ctrl+End** to move to the end of the document.

As you hop madly through a file, get your bearings by keeping your eyes on the status bar's data. The Pg setting will tell you which page you're on, and the Ln setting tells you where you are on the current page.

Bounding Through a Document with Bookmarks

When they stop reading a book, most people insert a bookmark of some kind (a piece of paper, the phone bill, the cat's tail, whatever) so they know where they left off. You can apply the same idea to your WordPerfect for Windows documents. You can mark special points in your documents with the electronic equivalent of a bookmark, which lets you leap to those points quickly.

Creating a Bookmark

To create a bookmark, follow these steps:

1. Position the insertion point where you want to insert a bookmark.

2. Pull down the Insert menu and select the Bookmark command. The Bookmark dialog box appears.

3. Select the Create button. WordPerfect for Windows displays the Create Bookmark dialog box.

4. The Bookmark Name text box usually shows a few words from the document. You can accept this or enter your own name, as shown in the following figure.

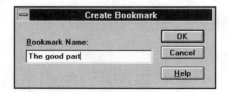

Use the Create Bookmark dialog box to identify your bookmark.

5. Select OK to return to the document.

Finding a Bookmark

Once you've defined your bookmarks, you can use them to jump giddily through your document. All you have to do is select Bookmark from the Insert menu again, highlight the bookmark you want in the Bookmark List, and then select the Go To button. WordPerfect for Windows leaps immediately to the marked spot.

Performing Bookmark Maintenance

Once you've used a bookmark or two, you'll probably find that bookmarks are an indispensable way to get around in massive documents. To help out, here are a few techniques you can use to help keep your bookmark affairs in order:

Moving a bookmark If you insert a bookmark in the wrong place, or if your text changes and you need to update a bookmark, you can easily move it to a new spot. First, move the insertion point to the new location. Then display the Bookmark dialog box, highlight the bookmark you want to move in the Bookmark List, and then select the Move button.

Renaming a bookmark If you give a bookmark the wrong name, changing it to something else is no problem. Just highlight the bookmark in the **Bookmark List** and select the **Rename** button. In the Rename Bookmark dialog box that appears, enter the new name and select **OK**.

Deleting a bookmark Don't need a bookmark any longer? Then you should delete it to make the list of bookmarks easier to navigate. To do this, highlight the expendable bookmark in the **Bookmark List**, select the **Delete** button, and then select Yes when WordPerfect for Windows asks you for confirmation.

Checking Out the Handy QuickMark Feature

If you have a favorite spot in a document, you can label it with a special bookmark called a QuickMark. Just position the insertion point on the spot and press **Ctrl+Shift+Q**. (If, for some reason, you want to do it the hard way, you can also choose **Bookmark** from the Insert menu and select the Set QuickMark button.)

To find the QuickMark, just press **Ctrl+Q**. Now *that's* quick! (Just for the record, the non-quick method is to choose **Bookmark** from the Insert menu, and then select Find QuickMark.) One of the best uses for a QuickMark is to mark your current position before you go traipsing off to another part of the document. If you set up a QuickMark before you go, you just have to press Ctrl+Q to return to where you were.

Navigating with the Go To Command

No document jockey's arsenal of navigation tricks would be complete without WordPerfect for Windows' Go To command. If you select **Go To** from the Edit menu, or press **Ctrl+G**, you'll see the Go To dialog box shown on the following page.

```
┌─────────────────────────────────────────────────┐
│ ─                      Go To                      │
├─────────────────────────────────────────────────┤
│ ○ Position:   ┌─────────────────────┐ ┌────────┐ │
│               │Last Position        │ │   OK   │ │
│               │Previous Table       │ └────────┘ │
│               │Next Table           │ ┌────────┐ │
│               │Top of Current Page  │ │ Cancel │ │
│               │Bottom of Current Page│ └────────┘ │
│               └─────────────────────┘ ┌────────┐ │
│                                       │  Help  │ │
│ ● Page Number: [1           ]  [▲▼]   └────────┘ │
│                                                   │
│ ○ Bookmark:   [QuickMark        ▼]                │
│                                                   │
│ ○ Table:      [                 ▼]                │
│   Cell/Range: [                 ▼]                │
└─────────────────────────────────────────────────┘
```

Use the Go To command to jump strategically through a document.

Using the **G**o To command, you can jump to specific parts of a document at warp speed. Here's a summary of some of the options you can choose from the Go To dialog box:

Position	Select this option and choose to move to Last Position, (where you were before you made your last leap), Top of Current Page, or Bottom of Current Page. (If you've got tables in your document, you can also use the Previous Table and Next Table selections. Wouldn't know a table if you tripped over one? Then pop in on Chapter 26, "Techniques for Terrific Tables," to get the nitty-gritty.)
Page **N**umber	Select this option to move to the top of a specific page. Type the page number or use the spinner controls.
Bookmark	If you've inserted bookmarks, select one from the drop-down list box.

When you've made your selection, choose **OK** to make the jump to hyperspace.

How the Repeat Command Works

You can use the Repeat command to save some legwork. The idea is that you enter a repeat number (8 is the default), and then press a navigation key combination (such as **Alt+Page Down**). WordPerfect for Windows repeats the action the number of times you specified.

To try it out, select Repeat from the Edit menu to display the Repeat dialog box (shown in the following figure). Enter the repeat number in the Number of Times to Repeat Next Action spinner, and then select **OK**. Now just press the key combination you want to repeat. If you leave the repeat number at 8 and you press, say, Page Down, WordPerfect for Windows scrolls down 8 screens.

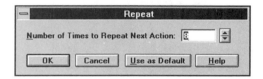

Use the Repeat dialog box to specify how many times WordPerfect for Windows should repeat a key combination.

If you'd like to see another number besides 8 when you open the Repeat dialog box, enter the number, and then select the Use as Default button. WordPerfect for Windows uses that new number from now on.

Navigating a File with the Mouse

Keyboard users, of course, can't have *all* the fun. If you like using a mouse, you can still navigate a document. The most basic technique is simply to click on any visible part of the typing area, and WordPerfect for Windows moves the insertion point to that position. This doesn't do you much good for long documents, however. No, to really get around with a mouse, you have to learn about scroll bars (see the next figure).

Scroll bars are a lot like elevators. They sort of look like elevator shafts, and like your favorite Otis device, they serve a dual purpose: they can tell you where you are, and they can take you somewhere else.

The WordPerfect for Windows scroll bars.

Where Am I? The Scroll Bar Knows

Thanks to my innately lousy sense of direction (I've been known to get lost getting out of bed in the morning), I always seem to lose my way in any document longer than a couple of pages. Fortunately, I have scroll bars to bail me out. The idea is simple: the position of the scroll box in the vertical scroll bar tells me my relative position in the document. So, for example, if the scroll box is about halfway down, I know I'm somewhere near the middle of the file. In this sense, the scroll box is a little like the floor indicator on an elevator.

Can I Get There from Here? Navigating with Scroll Bars

The real scroll bar fun begins when you use them to move around in your documents. There are three basic techniques:

➤ To scroll vertically through a document one line at a time, click on the vertical scroll bar's up or down scroll arrows.

➤ To leap through the document one screen at a time, click inside the vertical scroll bar between the scroll box and the scroll arrows. For example, to move down one screenful, click inside the scroll bar between the scroll box and the down scroll arrow.

➤ To move to a specific part of a document, drag the vertical scroll box up or down to the appropriate position. For example, to move to the beginning of a document, drag the scroll box to the top.

The vertical scroll bar also sports two buttons that make it easier to navigate your documents in page-length leaps. Here's how they work:

➤ To scroll to the top of the next page, click on the Page Down button.

➤ To scroll to the top of the previous page, click on the Page Up button.

It's important to bear in mind that none of these scroll bar techniques actually moves the insertion point. While you're traipsing all over the hills and dales of your document, the insertion point stubbornly remains where it was, keeping the home fires burning, so to speak. Once you've scroll-barred to a spot you like, you have two options. If you want to do some typing or editing in the new location, you can bring the insertion point along just by clicking at the point where you want to type or edit. If you just wanted to check something out, you can return to the insertion point position by pressing one of the navigation keys (left arrow and right arrow are the best bets).

The Least You Need to Know

This chapter concluded our look at document drudgery by examining a few easy navigation techniques. Here's the lowdown:

➤ Use the left and right arrow keys to move left and right one character at a time.

➤ Use **Ctrl+left arrow** or **Ctrl+right arrow** to jump left or right one word at a time.

➤ The up arrow and down arrow keys move you up or down one line at a time.

➤ Pressing **Ctrl+up arrow** moves you up one paragraph and **Ctrl+down arrow** moves you down one paragraph.

➤ Page Up moves you up one screen, while Page Down moves you down one screen.

➤ You can set up bookmarks to mark important places in your documents.

➤ When navigating with a mouse, just click to move to a spot you can see, or use the scroll bars to navigate through the entire document.

Chapter 9

Getting It Down on Paper: Printing Documents

In This Chapter

➤ The basic printing steps

➤ Printing a selection of pages

➤ Printing an unopened document right from your hard disk

➤ Using WordPerfect for Windows' cool Print Preview feature

➤ Selecting a different printer

➤ Miscellaneous mumbo-jumbo that'll have you printing like a pro

Okay, you've managed to peck out a few words on the keyboard, and maybe you've even gotten used to the idea of not pressing Enter at the end of each line. You've struggled through all those pull-down menus and dialog boxes, you've got a few editing skills down pat, and you've even managed to add a bit of formatting to perk things up a bit. Now what? Now you print out your creation for all to see. This is one of my favorite parts because, no matter how much I work with computers, I still feel like it's all hocus-pocus—just a bunch of smoke and mirrors. I don't feel right until I see those pages come slithering out of my printer. To that end, this chapter takes you painlessly through the basics of printing with WordPerfect for Windows.

Basic Printing

Without further ado, let's get right to the basic steps you use to print a document in WordPerfect for Windows.

1. Make sure your printer is ready to go:

   ➤ Is it plugged into both the wall and your computer?

   ➤ Is it turned on?

   ➤ Is it *on line*? (Most printers have an "On Line" light that'll tell you. If the light isn't on, press the **On Line** button.)

   ➤ Is there enough paper loaded in the printer for your document?

2. Once your printer is warm and happy, you need to decide how much of the document you want to print:

   ➤ If you want to print the whole thing, go ahead and skip to step 3.

   ➤ If you want to print only a single page, place the insertion point anywhere on that page.

   ➤ If you want to print a block, select the block. (You select a block by dragging your mouse over the appropriate text, or by holding down **Shift** and using the arrow keys to highlight what you need. See Chapter 11, "Block Partying: Working with Blocks of Text," for details.)

3. Pull down the File menu and select the **Print** command, or press **Ctrl+P**. (If you're using version 6.0, the shortcut key for the Print command is **F5**). You'll see the Print dialog box, shown in the following figure.

    You can also click on this tool in any Toolbar to display the Print dialog box.

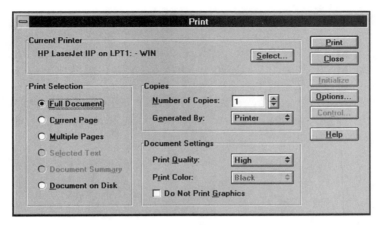

WordPerfect for Windows' Print dialog box contains all the options you need to print your documents.

4. Use the Print Selection group's option buttons to tell WordPerfect for Windows what to print:

Full Document   Prints the entire document.

Current Page   Prints only the current page.

Multiple Pages   Prints a range of pages. See the "Printing Multiple Pages" section later in this chapter.

Selected Text   Prints only the currently selected block.

Document Summary   Prints the document's summary info, if it has any. (See Chapter 27, "A WordPerfect for Windows Miscellany," to get the scoop on document summaries.)

Document on Disk   Prints a document right from the disk without opening it. Read the section "Printing an Unopened Document" to learn how this works.

5. If you need more than one copy, enter the number you want in the Number of Copies text box.

6. Use the Print Quality pop-up list to indicate how nice you want your text to look. If you're printing a final draft, select High for the best looking output. If you're just printing out a copy to see how things look, you can save some ink (or toner, if you have a laser printer) by selecting Medium or even Draft quality.

7. If you want your pages printed in reverse order (which is handy if your printer spits out the pages face up), select the Options button, and in the Print Output Options dialog box that appears, activate the Print in Reverse Order check box. You can also use the dialog box to tell WordPerfect for Windows to print only odd- or even-numbered pages. In the Print Odd/Even Pages pop-up list, select either Odd or Even. When you're done, select OK to return to the Print dialog box.

8. When you've finished picking your options, select the Print button to set everything in motion.

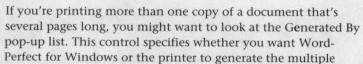

If you're printing more than one copy of a document that's several pages long, you might want to look at the Generated By pop-up list. This control specifies whether you want Word-Perfect for Windows or the printer to generate the multiple copies. For example, suppose you want three copies of a two-page document. If WordPerfect generates the copies, things take a little longer, but the copies are *collated*, which means that each copy of the entire document is printed at one time. If the printer does it, the job will print fast-er, but you'll get 3 copies of page 1, and then 3 copies of page 2, and so on.

Printing Multiple Pages

If you only need to print a few pages from a document, select Print from the File menu, and then select the Multiple Pages option in the Print dialog box. When you select the Print button, the Multiple Pages dialog box appears (see the next figure). Use the Page(s)/Label(s) text box to specify the pages you want printed. The following table shows you how to enter the page numbers (the letters *a*, *b*, and *c* represent page numbers you can enter):

Use	To print
a	Page *a*. For example, entering **3** prints only page 3.
a, *b*, *c*	Pages *a*, *b*, and *c*. For example, entering **1,3,5** prints pages 1, 3, and 5.
a–b	Pages *a* to *b*. For example, entering **2–5** prints pages 2, 3, 4, and 5.

Use	To print
a–	From page *a* to the end of the document. In a 10-page document, for example, entering **5**– prints pages 5 through 10.
–*a*	From the beginning of the document to page *a*. For example, entering **–6** prints pages 1 through 6.
a, b, c–d	Pages *a* and *b*, and pages *c* to *d*. For example, entering **1,3,6–10** prints pages 1, 3, and 6 through 10.

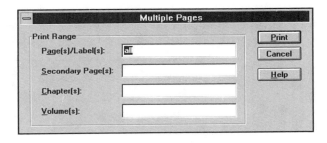

Use the Multiple Pages dialog box to specify the page numbers you want to print.

If you've been using secondary page, chapter, or volume numbers, use the Secondary Page(s), Chapter(s), or Volume(s) text boxes to specify which ones you want to print. (See Chapter 15, "Making Your Pages Look Good," to get the poop on adding secondary page, chapter, and volume numbers to your documents.)

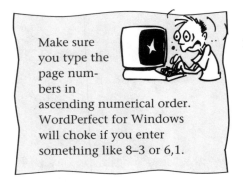

Make sure you type the page numbers in ascending numerical order. WordPerfect for Windows will choke if you enter something like 8–3 or 6,1.

When you're ready to roll, select the Print button.

Printing an Unopened Document

One of WordPerfect for Windows' nice timesaving features is its capability to print an unopened document. This saves you from having to go through the whole hassle of opening the file, printing it, and then closing it again.

In the Print dialog box, select the Document on Disk option. When you select the **P**rint button, you'll see the Document on Disk dialog box appear, as shown in the following figure. Just enter the name of the file you want to print in the Filename text box. (If you're not sure of the name, select the list button beside the Filename box, and then use the Select File dialog box to pick out the file you want. This dialog box is identical to the Open File dialog box we looked at in detail back in Chapter 7, "Day-to-Day Drudgery I: Saving, Opening, and Closing." When you're done, select **OK** to return to the Document on Disk dialog box.) Enter the pages you want to print, if necessary, and then select the **P**rint button.

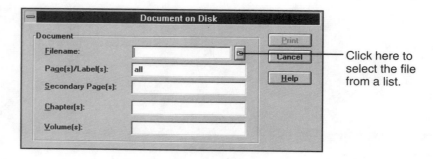

Click here to select the file from a list.

Use the Document on Disk dialog box to print a document without opening it.

Printing Multiple Documents

If you need to print a bunch of documents, you don't have to run a separate Print command for each one. Instead, follow these steps:

1. Pull down the File menu and select Open, or press **Ctrl+O**.

2. Select the appropriate drive and directory, if necessary. (See Chapter 7, "Day-to-Day Drudgery I: Saving, Opening, and Closing," to learn how to do this.)

3. In the Filename list, select the files you want to print using any of the following methods:

   ➤ If the files you need are listed consecutively, click on the first file, hold down **Shift**, and then click on the last file.

➤ To select files randomly, hold down the **Ctrl** key and click on each file.

➤ With your keyboard, highlight the first file, press **Shift+F8**, and then for the other files you want, highlight each one and press the **Spacebar**. When you're done, press **Shift+F8** again.

4. In the File Options pop-up list, select Print. WordPerfect for Windows, ever skeptical, asks if you want to print the selected files. Select Print to crank out your files.

Selecting a Different Printer

If you're lucky enough to have more than one printer, you can switch between them in WordPerfect for Windows fairly easily.

You may have noticed when printing that the Print dialog box shows you the name of the currently selected printer in the Current Printer area. To change this, choose the Select button beside it. This displays the Select Printer dialog box, shown in the following figure. You have two choices:

➤ If you want to use the default printer specified by Windows, activate the **W**indows Default Printer option.

➤ To use any other printer, activate the Specific Printer option, and then choose the printer you want from the drop-down list provided.

When you're done, choose the Select button. Whichever printer you chose, the selection remains in effect for each WordPerfect for Windows session.

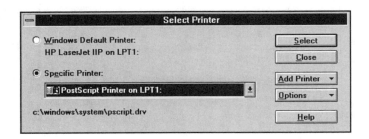

Use the Select Printer dialog box to select a different printer.

Installing a New Printer in WordPerfect for Windows

If the Current Printer area in the Print dialog box says **No Printer Selected**, it means you haven't told WordPerfect for Windows what kind of printer you have. (Technically, it means you haven't told *Windows* what kind of printer you have. It's then Windows' job to let WordPerfect in on what's happening.) On the other hand, suppose you got a new printer for Christmas, and you're wondering what to do because the printer doesn't appear in any of WordPerfect's printer lists.

In both cases, you need to install the appropriate *printer driver* file. (A driver is a tiny program that lets software, such as WordPerfect for Windows, talk to hardware, such as your printer.) Happily, you can do this right from the friendly confines of WordPerfect for Windows by slogging through these steps:

1. In the Print dialog box, choose the Select button to display the Select Printer dialog box.

2. Using the Add Printer pop-up list, select the Windows option. The Printers dialog box appears.

3. Select the Add button to expand the dialog box, as shown in the following figure. (If you haven't already installed at least one printer, the dialog box will already be expanded so you can skip this step).

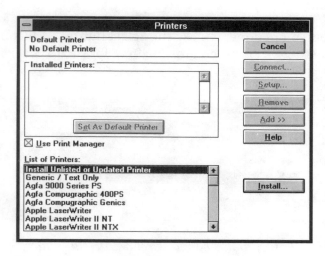

The expanded Printers dialog box.

4. Windows has the goods on dozens of different printers, and they're all shown in the List of Printers box. Find your printer in this list and highlight it. If your printer isn't in the list, you have three choices:

   ➤ Check your printer manual to see if the printer works like (or *emulates*) another printer. If it does, see if you can find the emulated printer in the list.

   ➤ Highlight one of the list's catch-all printers. For example, highlight **Generic/Text Only** for a dot-matrix printer or **PostScript Printer** for, of course, a PostScript printer.

   ➤ If your printer comes with a disk, choose **Install Unlisted or Updated Printer** at the top of the list.

5. Select the Install button. One of these things will happen:

   ➤ If the printer driver is already on your hard disk, the printer name appears in the Installed Printers list.

   ➤ If the printer information *isn't* on your hard disk, Control Panel prompts you to insert one of your Windows installation disks. Place the disk in the appropriate drive (change the displayed drive letter, if it's wrong), and then select **OK**.

   ➤ If you selected **Install Unlisted or Updated Printer**, Control Panel asks you to insert the disk that came with the printer. Insert the disk and select **OK**. Another dialog box appears that shows a list of the printer drivers on the disk. Highlight your printer and select **OK**.

   Note: Depending on which printer you chose, you may be asked to insert another disk for font files or some such nonsense; just follow the directions on-screen. In the end, you're returned to the Printers dialog box.

6. Select the Connect button to display the Connect dialog box.

A **port** is where you plug in the cable for a device, such as a mouse or printer. If you're not sure which port your printer uses, check the printer cable connection at the back of your computer. Some thoughtful computer companies actually label their ports, so look for something like LPT1 or COM2. If there are no labels, your computer manual should tell you. If you're still not sure, just choose LPT1, and cross your fingers.

7. Use the Ports list to select your printer port, and then select **OK**.

8. Repeat steps 4–7 to install any other printer drivers you need.

9. If you've installed multiple drivers, you need to tell Windows which one to use as the default in your Windows applications. To do this, highlight the printer in the Installed Printers list and select the Set As Default Printer button. The printer name appears in the Default Printer box.

10. Select **Close** to return to the Select Printer dialog box.

11. Choose the printer you want to use (as described in the last section), and then choose Select to return to the Print dialog box.

The Least You Need to Know

This chapter showed you how to get hard copies of your WordPerfect for Windows documents. Since you'll likely be doing a lot of printing with WordPerfect for Windows, a quick review of the basics wouldn't hurt:

➤ Before printing, make sure your printer is ready for action. Verify that it's plugged in, the cables are secure, it's turned on (and is on line), and it has enough paper to handle the job.

➤ To print, pull down the File menu and select the Print command (or just press **Ctrl+P**). Enter your options in the Print dialog box, and then select the Print button.

➤ You don't need to print the entire document each time. If you want to, you can print just a block, the current page, or a range of pages. For the latter, select the Multiple Pages option and enter the pages you want to print in the dialog box.

➤ To print an unopened document, select the Document on Disk option from the Print dialog box. When you go to print, WordPerfect for Windows displays a dialog box in which you can enter the name of the file you want printed.

➤ To print multiple documents, select **Open** from the **File** menu (or press **Ctrl+O**), select the files you want to print, and then select **Print** from the **File Options** pop-up list.

➤ To select a different printer, choose the **Select** button in the Print dialog box, highlight the printer you want, and then choose the **Select** button.

Part II
Getting It Right: Editing Stuff

If, as they say, the essence of good writing is rewriting, then word processors ought to make us all better writers because rewriting—or editing—is what they do best. WordPerfect for Windows, in particular, has an impressive array of editing tools (some might say too impressive). The chapters in this section give you the basics of editing your prose in WordPerfect for Windows. You'll learn everything from simply deleting (and, thankfully, undeleting) to shuffling great hunks of text to new locations. I don't know if all this will make you a better writer, but it'll sure make you a heck of a rewriter.

EDITING . . . THE EARLY DAYS.

Chapter 10

Deleting Text (and Undeleting It, Too)

In This Chapter

➤ Deleting one character at a time

➤ Deleting one word at a time

➤ Deleting entire pages

➤ Using the Repeat and Undelete features

➤ A bonanza of techniques for nuking unnecessary text

I moved recently, and it only took me five minutes of packing to realize something: I'm a hoarder. (I said hoar*der*!) I never throw anything away: Old gum wrappers; ticket stubs from every baseball, football, hockey, and basketball game I've ever attended; an ancient (and British!) version of Monopoly; and books! Don't get me started with books!

I have the same trouble throwing things away when I'm writing. As my editor will tell you, I have a hard time deleting *anything*. (I think I just get too attached.) However, that's not WordPerfect for Windows' fault, because it gives you all kinds of ways to nix troublesome text. This chapter will show you how.

Deleting Characters

Did you spell *potato* with an *e* again? (Perhaps you have political aspirations.) Or perhaps you've just seen the Queen on TV, and you're using words like *colour* and *cheque*. Well, not to worry; WordPerfect for Windows makes it easy to expunge individual characters. You have two options:

Before going on any kind of deletion rampage, you should know that there's a section at the end of this chapter called "To Err Is Human, to Undelete Divine." If you wipe out anything you shouldn't have, read ahead to this section to see how to make everything okay again.

➤ Press the **Delete** key to delete the character to the right of the insertion point.

➤ Press **Backspace** to delete the character to the left of the insertion point.

If you'd like to delete several characters in a row, hold down **Delete** or **Backspace** until all the riffraff is eliminated. (Be careful, though. The insertion point really picks up speed if you hold it down for more than a second or two.)

You can also switch to *Typeover mode* by pressing the **Insert** key (you should see the word **Typeover** in the status bar). When you're in Typeover mode, the characters that you type stamp out any existing characters, which means you can wipe out a stretch of bogus text without having to perform an actual delete operation. Just remember to return to *Insert mode*—by pressing **Insert** again—when you're done (you should now see the word **Insert** in the status bar). With Insert mode, your typing is inserted between existing characters, so nothing is deleted.

Deleting Words, Lines, and Paragraphs

To handle any stray words that creep into your documents, Word-Perfect for Windows gives you a way to delete entire words with a single stroke (does that make you feel powerful, or what?). Just position the insertion point anywhere inside the word you want to blow away, and then press **Ctrl+Backspace**.

By the way, if you place the insertion point between two words and press **Ctrl+Backspace**, WordPerfect for Windows deletes the word to the *left* of the insertion point.

WordPerfect for Windows also lets you delete a portion of a line, or even (with just a little extra work) an entire line. For starters, if you just need to delete text from the insertion point to the end of the line, press **Ctrl+Delete**. Deleting an entire line takes an extra step: first place the insertion point at the beginning of the line (by pressing **Home** or by clicking to the left of the line), and *then* press **Ctrl+Delete**. (To learn how to delete entire sentences and paragraphs, see Chapter 11, "Block Partying: Working with Blocks of Text.")

Recall that WordPerfect for Windows places a line across the screen to show you where one page ends and another begins. To be safe, you should scroll down to the bottom of the page before using **Ctrl+Shift+Delete** to make sure you're not going to wipe out anything important.

If you've really made a mess of things, you may need to obliterate great chunks of text. One handy way to do this is to delete everything from the insertion point to the end of the page. You do this by pressing **Ctrl+Shift+Delete**.

Repeat Deleting

The Repeat command comes in handy for speeding up your deletion chores. Just select Repeat from the Edit menu, enter the number of repetitions you want in the Repeat dialog box that appears, and then select **OK**. Now press the appropriate deletion key or key combination, and WordPerfect for Windows repeats it the number of times you specified. For example, if you set the repeat value at 8 and press **Ctrl+Backspace**, WordPerfect will delete the 8 words to the left of the insertion point.

To Err Is Human, to Undelete Divine

Let's face facts: *everybody* deletes stuff accidentally, and one day *you'll* do it, too. It's one of those reality things (like nose hair and paying taxes) that we just can't avoid. The good people at WordPerfect know this, and the gurus in their programming department came up with a way to ease the pain: the Undelete command. This command, as its name implies, miraculously reverses any of your three most recent deletions. (Which, believe me, has saved *my* bacon on more than one occasion.)

101

In computing circles, the **ohnosecond** is defined as the brief fraction of time in which you realize you've just made a real mega-blunder, like wiping out an entire morning's work. (*Ohnosecond*, of course, is supposed to sound like the word *nanosecond*, which means a billionth of a second.)

Here are the steps to follow to undelete something:

1. Get whatever cursing, fuming, and gesticulating you normally do when you've just deleted your last three hours work out of the way first. You need a clear head for what's to come.

2. Select U**n**delete from the **Edit** menu, or press **Ctrl+Shift+Z**. As you can see here, WordPerfect for Windows displays the Undelete dialog box, adds the last deletion back into the text, and highlights it so you can see it clearly.

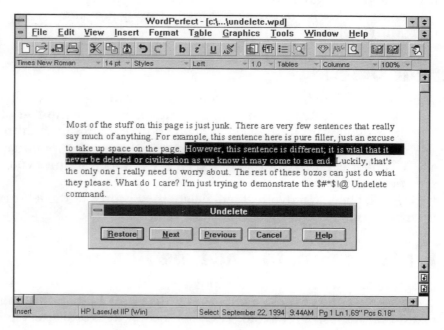

When you select the Undelete command, WordPerfect for Windows adds the last deletion back into the text, and displays the Undelete dialog box.

3. If that's the text you want undeleted, select **Restore**. If it's not, select **Previous deletion** until you see what you want, and then select **Restore**. (Remember that WordPerfect for Windows only stores the last three things you deleted.)

How does Undelete perform its magic? Well, each time you delete something, it might appear to have gone off to some la-la land of deleted text, but that's not quite the case. WordPerfect for Windows sneakily saves each of the last three deletions in a special memory location called a *buffer* that stores not only the text itself, but its original location, as well. Undeleting, then, is a simple matter of restoring the text from the buffer.

The Least You Need to Know

This compact little chapter gave you the scoop on deleting text (and undeleting it too, just in case). Here are few pointers to take with you on your travels:

➤ To delete individual characters, use the **Delete** key (to delete whatever is to the right of the insertion point) or the **Backspace** key (to delete whatever is to the left of the insertion point).

➤ To delete a word, put the insertion point inside the word and press **Ctrl+Backspace**.

➤ Press **Ctrl+Delete** to delete from the current insertion point position to the end of the line.

➤ To delete from the current insertion point position to the end of the page, press **Ctrl+Shift+Delete**.

➤ You can speed up your deleting by using the Repeat command. Just pull down the Edit menu and select the Repeat command to display the Repeat dialog box. Enter a different number, if needed, select **OK** to return to the document, and then press the appropriate deletion key or key combo.

➤ If you delete something by accident, immediately select Undelete from the Edit menu (or press **Ctrl+Shift+Z**). Select **R**estore to undelete the highlighted text, or select **P**revious deletion to see other deleted text.

Block Partying: Working with Blocks of Text

Blocs (as in the "Eastern bloc") may be out, but *blocks* are definitely in. I mean, we have block parents, block parties, block captains. Why even the old *Gumby and Pokey* show (which featured the villainous Block-heads, of course) has made a bizarre comeback of sorts.

WordPerfect for Windows uses blocks, too. In this case, though, a *block* is just a section of text. It could be a word, a sentence, two-and-a-half paragraphs, or 57 pages—whatever you need. The key is that WordPerfect for Windows treats a block as a single entity: a unit. And what does one do with these units? Well, you name it—they can be copied, moved, deleted, printed, formatted, spell-checked, taken to lunch, whatever. This chapter not only shows you how to select a block, but it also takes you through a few of these block tasks.

Selecting a Block of Text

WordPerfect for Windows, bless its electronic heart, gives you no less than three ways to select a block of text: you can use your keyboard, your mouse, or the handy Select command.

Selecting Text with the Keyboard

To select some text with your keyboard, begin by positioning the insertion point at the beginning of the text. Now hold down the **Shift** key and use the arrow keys to move through the text you want to include in the block. As you do, the selected characters become highlighted (they appear white on a black background), as you can see in the next figure. If you decide you don't want to select the text after all, just press **Esc**.

A block of selected text

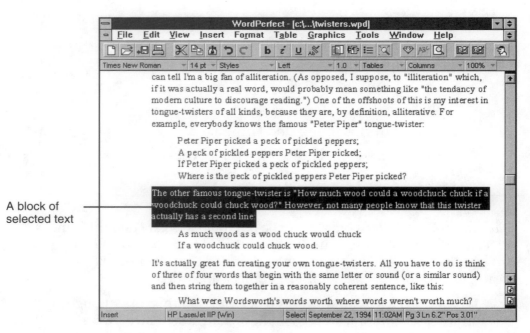

When you select text, WordPerfect for Windows displays the highlighted characters as white text on a black background.

For more fine-tuned selecting, this table presents some key combinations you can use to select text.

Press	To select text through
Ctrl+Shift+right arrow	The next word
Ctrl+Shift+left arrow	The previous word
Shift+End	The end of the line
Shift+Home	The beginning of the line
Ctrl+Shift+down arrow	The end of the paragraph
Ctrl+Shift+up arrow	The beginning of the paragraph
Shift+Page Down	The bottom of the screen
Shift+Page Up	The top of the screen
Ctrl+Shift+End	The bottom of the document
Ctrl+Shift+Home	The top of the document

The sharp-eyed will have noticed that the key combinations you use to select text bear a remarkable resemblance to the navigation keys you struggled with back in Chapter 8, "Day-to-Day Drudgery II: Navigating Documents." Hey, you get an extra dessert tonight—because, yes, they're exactly the same! In fact, you can use any of the stuff from that chapter (including the handy **G**o To command) to select text.

Selecting Text with the Mouse

Mouse users, forget the keyboard; selecting text with the little rodent guy is *way* easier. All you have to do is position the pointer at the beginning of the block, press and hold down the left button, and then drag the mouse over the text you want to select. That's it! No unsightly key combinations!

If you have version 6.1, you'll notice that WordPerfect for Windows selects text word by word instead of character by character. This affects your block selecting in two ways:

➤ If you start the block in the middle of a word, WordPerfect for Windows selects only characters at first. But once you move past the word (once you include a space either to the right or to the left or the word), the program automatically selects the entire word.

➤ If you start the block at the beginning of a word, once again WordPerfect for Windows only selects the text character by character. But as soon as you include even a single letter from another word in the block, the program includes the entire word as part of the selection.

If you don't like this word by word stuff, I'll show you how to turn it off in Chapter 28, "Customizing WordPerfect for Windows."

Triple-clicking, as you may have guessed by now, means you quickly press and release the left mouse button three times in succession. **Quadruple-clicking** is a real workout: you quickly press and release the left mouse button four— count 'em, four times—in succession. (Don't worry: there's no such thing as quintuple-clicking—yet.)

What's that? You've got a ton of text to select? In that case, just click at the beginning of the text, hold down the **Shift** key, and then click at the end of the text. WordPerfect for Windows automatically selects everything in between. But wait, there's more! You can also use the following mouse techniques for even more block fun:

To select	Do this
A word	Double-click on it.
A sentence	Triple-click on it, or click beside the sentence in the left margin.
A paragraph	Quadruple-click on it, or double-click beside the paragraph in the left margin.

Using the Select Command

WordPerfect for Windows' Select command makes it easy to select single sentences, paragraphs, pages, or even the entire document. Just position the insertion point in the appropriate sentence, paragraph, or page (if that's what you want to select), and then choose the Edit menu's Select command. You'll see a cascade menu with several options, including the following:

Sentence	This command selects the current sentence.
Paragraph	This one selects the current paragraph.
Page	This command selects the current page.
All	This one selects the entire document—lock, stock, and barrel.

You can also take advantage of the right mouse button to select a sentence, paragraph, page, or document easily. First, click inside the sentence, paragraph, or page you want to select (unless, of course, you're selecting the entire document). Now right-click anywhere in the left margin to display the QuickMenu. Then simply click on Select Sentence to select the current sentence, Select Paragraph to select the current paragraph, Select Page to select the current page, or Select All to select—you guessed it—the entire document.

Selecting Text with Bookmarks

Bookmarks (as you saw in Chapter 8, "Day-to-Day Drudgery II: Navigating Documents") provide a handy way to get around a document. But you can also use them to mark blocks so you can reselect them quickly. Follow these steps to check out this feature:

1. Select the block you want to mark.

2. Select the Insert menu's Bookmark command, and when the Bookmark dialog box appears, select the Create button.

3. Enter a name for the selection, and then choose **OK**.

4. To reselect the block later, select the Bookmark command again, highlight the bookmark in the Bookmark List, and then select the Go To & Select button. WordPerfect for Windows obligingly reselects the entire block.

As if all this weren't enough, you can also use the Go To command to select—or, in this case, reselect—text. Just select Go To from the Edit menu (or press **Ctrl+G**) and, in the Position list, choose **Reselect Last Selection**. Select OK, and WordPerfect for Windows returns you to the document that contains the last block you selected.

Copying a Block

One of the secrets of computer productivity is a simple maxim: "Don't reinvent the wheel." In other words, if you've got something that works, and you need something similar, don't start from scratch. Instead, make a copy of the original, and then make whatever changes are necessary to the copy. (Text that you use over and over is called *boilerplate* by those in the know.)

Chapter 7, "Day-to-Day Drudgery I: Saving, Opening, and Closing," showed you how to use the Save As command to make a copy of an entire document. In most cases, though, your requirements won't be so grandiose; you'll usually only need to make a copy of a few sentences or a few paragraphs. Happily, WordPerfect for Windows makes it easy to copy these smaller clumps of prose. In fact, you get two methods: the Copy command and something called "drag-and-drop."

Using the Copy Command

Once you've selected the block you want to copy, all you have to do is pull down the Edit menu and select the Copy command, or press **Ctrl+C**. You then position the insertion point where you want to place the copy and select **Paste** from the Edit menu, or press **Ctrl+V**. A perfect copy of your selection appears instantly. If you need to make other copies, position the insertion point appropriately, and select the Paste command again.

 You can click on this button in any Toolbar to copy a block.

 For easy block pasting, you can also click on this button in any Toolbar.

Copying with Drag-and-Drop

WordPerfect for Windows' *drag-and-drop* technique is one of my favorite features. The idea is that you use your mouse to physically drag a copy of a block from one part of a document to another. Here's how it works:

1. Select the block you want to copy.

2. Position the mouse pointer anywhere inside the block (the pointer will change to an arrow), hold down the **Ctrl** key, and then press and hold down the left mouse button. The mouse pointer should now look like this:

3. Move the mouse until the insertion point is where you want the copy to appear (this is the "dragging" part).

4. Release the mouse button (this is the "dropping" part), and then release **Ctrl**.
   WordPerfect for Windows copies the block, as pretty as you please.

> You can also use the QuickMenus for your copying chores. When you've selected the block, right-click anywhere inside the page, and then select Copy from the QuickMenu. Now position the insertion point where you want the copy to go, right-click inside the page again, and this time select **Paste** from the QuickMenu.

Moving a Block

One of the all-time handiest word processor features is the capability to move stuff from one part of a document to another. This is perfect for rearranging everything from single sentences to humongous chunks of text.

Now, you might think you'd do this by making a copy, pasting it, and then going back and deleting the original. Well, you *could* do it that way, but your friends would almost certainly laugh at you. Why? Because there's an easier way. WordPerfect for Windows lets you *cut* a selection right out of a document, and then paste it somewhere else. And (as with copying) you get to choose from two methods.

Moving with the Cut Command

Once you've selected what you want to move, pull down the Edit menu and select the Cut command, or press **Ctrl+X**. Your selection disappears from the screen, but don't panic: WordPerfect for Windows is saving it for you in a secret location. Now position the insertion point where you want to move the selection, and choose **Paste** from the Edit menu. Your stuff miraculously reappears in the new location. If you need to make further copies of the selection, just reposition the insertion point and select **Paste** again.

 Cutting chores can also be handled by clicking on this button in any Toolbar.

If you cut a selection accidentally, immediately select Undo from the Edit menu, or press **Ctrl+Z**. For more Undo info, see the section titled "The Life-Saving Undo Command" later in this chapter.

Moving with Drag-and-Drop

Yes, our old friend drag-and-drop can move text, too. This is very similar to copying, as you'll see here:

 Yes, you can use the QuickMenus for moving, too. With a block selected, right-click anywhere inside the page, and then select Cut from the QuickMenu. Position the insertion point where you want to move the text, right-click again, and select Paste from the QuickMenu.

1. Select the block you want to move.

2. Position the mouse pointer anywhere inside the block, and then press and hold down the left mouse button. The mouse pointer will change into this:

3. Drag the mouse to where you want to move the text.

4. Release the mouse button. WordPerfect for Windows moves your text to the new location.

Saving a Block

If you've just written a block of some particularly breathtaking prose, you might want to save it in a file all its own. No sweat. Just select it, pull down the File menu, and choose the Save command. WordPerfect for Windows displays the Save dialog box shown below. Make sure the Selected Text option is activated and select **OK**. You'll see the Save As dialog box on-screen. Just enter the information as though you were saving a file. (See Chapter 7, "Day-to-Day Drudgery I: Saving, Opening, and Closing," for details.)

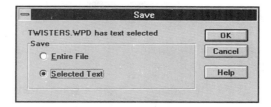

Use this Save dialog box to save a highlighted block to a file.

Deleting a Block

Deleting a block of text is a no-brainer. Just make your selection, then press either **Delete** or **Backspace**. Remember that if you delete anything accidentally, you can always fall back on WordPerfect for Windows' Undelete command. See Chapter 10, "Deleting Text (and Undeleting It, Too)," for the skinny on Undelete.

The Life-Saving Undo Command

Every WordPerfect for Windows user—from the rawest novice to the nerdiest expert—ends up at some time or other doing something downright silly. It may be cutting when you should have been copying, or just pasting a chunk of text in some absurd location.

Fortunately, WordPerfect for Windows has an Undo feature to get you out of these jams. The Undo command restores everything to the way it was before you made your blunder. (I've had some relationships where an Undo command would have come in *real* handy.) All you have to do is pull down the Edit menu and select Undo, or press **Ctrl+Z**.

Mouse mavens can delete stuff quickly, too. Simply select the block you want to blow away, right-click inside the page, and then select **Delete** from the QuickMenu that appears.

 You can also undo your last action by clicking on this button in any Toolbar.

If you're using version 6.0 or earlier, WordPerfect for Windows can only reverse your last action, so make sure you select the Undo command *immediately* after making your mistake. If you do anything else in the meantime, you may not be able to recover.

If you have version 6.1, however, you get the added bonus of multiple levels of Undo. This means you can undo not only your last action, but the one before it and the one before that. In fact, it's possible to undo up to 300 operations for each of your documents! The following steps show you how it works:

1. Pull down the **Edit** menu and select the Undo/Redo **History** command. WordPerfect for Windows displays the Undo/Redo History dialog box.

2. The Undo list shows the last 10 operations you performed on the document (the most recent is at the top of the list). Highlight the action you want to undo. Note: WordPerfect for Windows automatically highlights all the actions above the one you choose. Why does it do this? Well, WordPerfect for Windows can't undo a single action (unless, of course, it's the last action you performed). Instead, it has to undo every action up to and including the one you've highlighted.

"Hey, what gives? You said we could undo up to 300 actions." You can, but WordPerfect for Windows uses 10 as the default. To change this, select the **Options** button to display the Undo/Redo Options dialog box. Enter the number you want in the Number of Undo/Redo Items spinner, and then select **OK**.

3. Select the Undo button. WordPerfect for Windows reverses each operation, and then adds it to the Redo list (see the following figure).

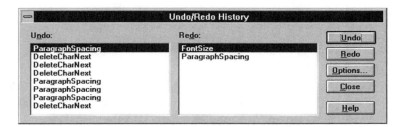

When you undo an operation, it appears in the Redo list.

4. If you change your mind about undoing an operation, highlight it in the Redo list and select the **R**edo button.

5. When you've finished playing, select Close to return to the document.

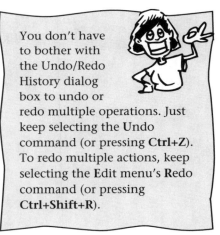

Keep clicking this button in any Toolbar to undo multiple actions one at a time.

To redo actions you've undone, keep clicking this button in any Toolbar.

You don't have to bother with the Undo/Redo History dialog box to undo or redo multiple operations. Just keep selecting the Undo command (or pressing **Ctrl+Z**). To redo multiple actions, keep selecting the Edit menu's Redo command (or pressing **Ctrl+Shift+R**).

The Least You Need to Know

This chapter led you through the basics of working with WordPerfect for Windows' text blocks. We really only scratched the surface here, because there's plenty more you can do with blocks. However, I'll save all that rot for the chapters to come. For now, here's a rehash of what just happened:

➤ A block is a selection of text you can work with as a unit.

➤ To select text with the keyboard, hold down the **Shift** key and use WordPerfect for Windows' navigation keys to highlight the text you want.

➤ Selecting text with a mouse is even easier. Position the pointer at the beginning of the text, and then drag the mouse over the area you want to select.

➤ To copy a block, select Copy from the Edit menu, position the insertion point, and select Paste. Alternatively, hold down **Ctrl** and use your mouse to drag a copy of the block to the new location.

➤ To move a block, pull down the Edit menu and select Cut, position the insertion point, and then select Paste from the Edit menu. You can also simply drag the block to its new locale with your mouse.

➤ To delete a block, just press **Delete** or **Backspace**.

➤ To reverse a blunder, immediately select Undo from the Edit menu.

Chapter 12

Search and Ye Shall Replace

In This Chapter

➤ Searching for text, the basic technique

➤ Searching for and selecting a text block

➤ Searching for and replacing text

➤ Superior search strategies guaranteed to save you oodles of time

Oh where, oh where has my little text gone?

Oh where, oh where can it be?

If you've ever found yourself lamenting a long-lost word adrift in some humongous megadocument, the folks at WordPerfect for Windows can sympathize (probably because it's happened to them a time or two). They were even kind enough to build a special Find feature into WordPerfect for Windows to help you search for missing text. And that's not all: you can also use the related Replace feature to seek out and replace every instance of one word with another. Sound like fun? No? Well, okay, but it is handy, so you might want to read this chapter anyway.

Finding a Text Needle in a Document Haystack

If you need to find a certain word or phrase in a short document, it's usually easiest just to scroll through the text. But if you're dealing with more than a couple of pages, don't waste your time rummaging through the whole file. WordPerfect for Windows' Find feature will do the dirty work for you.

Searching: The Basic Steps

Here are the steps you need to follow to search for a piece of text (it could be a single word or a phrase):

1. Pull down the Edit menu and select the Find and Replace command, or press **F2**. The Find and Replace Text dialog box appears, as shown below.

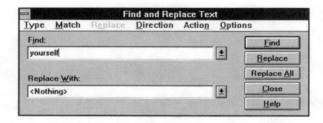

Use the Find and Replace Text dialog box to hunt for text in a document.

2. In the Find text box, type the text you want to find. If you'd like to repeat a recent search, click on the downward-pointing arrow to the right of the Find text box, and choose one of the last 10 search phrases you entered.

3. WordPerfect for Windows normally searches from the current insertion point position to the end of the document. If you suspect the search text lies somewhere above the current insertion point position, pull down the Direction menu and activate the Backward command.

4. Select the Find button. If WordPerfect for Windows finds a match, it selects the match and displays it on-screen. If WordPerfect does not find a match, it displays a message to that effect (which you can remove from the screen by selecting **OK**). In both cases, you end up back in the Find and Replace Text dialog box.

5. Repeat steps 2–4 to resume the search, or select the Close button to return to the document.

Sometimes the text that WordPerfect for Windows finds is not the particular instance you want. If you've exited the Find and Replace Text dialog box, you can continue the search simply by repeating the steps from the last section. Note, however, that WordPerfect for Windows is smart enough to remember your last search text, and displays it automatically in the Find

The fastest way to continue searching is to press **Shift+F2** to search forward or **Alt+F2** to search backward.

text box. So when the Find and Replace Text dialog box appears, simply select the Find button to find the next example of the text.

Using Find to Select a Text Block

One handy use for the Find feature is to select a text block from the insertion point's current position down to the next occurrence of a word or phrase. (Head back to Chapter 11, "Block Partying: Working with Blocks of Text," if you need to learn more about text blocks.)

To try this out, follow these steps:

1. Move the cursor to the beginning of the text you want to select.

2. Select the Edit menu's Find and Replace command to display the Find and Replace Text dialog box.

3. In the Find text box, enter the word or phrase that marks the end of the text block you want to select.

4. Pull down the Action menu and select the Extend Selection command.

5. Select Find. WordPerfect for Windows creates a text block from the insertion point down to the first occurrence of the search text. To extend the selection even further, keep pressing Find.

Some Notes on Searching

Searching for text is a fairly straightforward affair, but it wouldn't be WordPerfect for Windows if there weren't five thousand other ways to confuse the heck out of us. To make things easier, here are a few notes that'll help you get the most out of your text searches:

➤ For best results, don't try to match entire sentences. A word or two is usually all you really need. Trying to match long phrases or even entire sentences can be a problem because you increase your chances of misspelling a word or accidentally leaving a word out of the search text. (For example, if you want to search for "It's a wonderful day in the neighborhood" and you enter "It is a wonderful day in the neighborhood," WordPerfect will scoff at your efforts because the beginning of the two sentences don't match.) And besides, it takes longer to type in a lengthy phrase or sentence than it does to type in a few words.

➤ If you're not sure how to spell a word, just use a piece of it. WordPerfect for Windows will still find *egregious* if you search for *egre* (although, efficient beast that it is, it will also find words like *regret* and *degree*).

➤ As you can tell from the last point, WordPerfect will happily find a chunk of text that sits in the middle of a word (such as the *egre* in *regret* and *degree*). To find only words that *begin* with your search text, add a space to the beginning of the text.

➤ So that you don't have to fumble around and search both forward and backward, WordPerfect for Windows gives you two commands on the **Options** menu in the Find and Replace Text dialog box. Activate the **Begin** Find At Top of Document command to always start searching from the top. Activate the **Wrap** at Beg./End of Document command to force WordPerfect for Windows to continue searching at the top of the document once it reaches the bottom (if you're searching forward, that is. If you're searching backward, the program will continue searching at the bottom of the document once it reaches the top).

➤ If you need to differentiate between, say, *Bobby* (some guy) and *bobby* (as in a *bobby* pin or an English *bobby*), activate the **Case** command from the **Match** menu in the Find Text dialog box. This tells WordPerfect for Windows to match not only the letters, but also whatever uppercase and lowercase format you use.

➤ If you search for, say, *gorge*, WordPerfect for Windows may find not only the word *gorge*, but also *gorged*, *gorgeous*, and *disgorge* as well. If all you want is *gorge*, select the **Match** menu's **Whole** Word command.

Replacing Found Text with Something More Sensible

If you do a lot of writing, one of the features you'll come to rely on the most is *find and replace*. This means that WordPerfect for Windows seeks out a particular bit of text and then replaces it with something else. This may not seem like a big deal for a word or two, but if you need to change a couple of dozen instances of *irregardless* to *regardless*, it can be a real timesaver.

Find and Replace: The Basic Steps

Finding and replacing is, as you might imagine, not that different from plain old finding. Here's how it works:

1. Select the Find and Replace command from the Edit menu (or press **F2**) to display the Find and Replace Text dialog box.

2. In the Find text box, enter the text you want to find.

3. In the Replace With text box, enter the text you want to use as a replacement.

4. If you want to find and replace backwards, pull down the Direction menu and select the Backward command.

5. If you're sure you want to replace every instance of the text in the Find box, select the Replace All button. If you'd like to verify the replacements, select Find instead.

6. If you chose the Replace All button, WordPerfect for Windows merrily chugs along replacing everything in sight. When it's done, it displays a message to that effect. Select **OK** to return to the Find and Replace Text dialog box.

   If you selected Find, and WordPerfect for Windows finds a match, it highlights the text and displays it on-screen. Select Replace to perform the replacement, or select Find to look for the next match. (You could also select Replace All to let WordPerfect go crazy.)

   If WordPerfect for Windows doesn't find a match, a message appears to tell you the bad news. Select **OK** to return to the dialog box.

7. Keep repeating step 5 until you're done. Then select Close to return to the document.

To keep your find-and-replace operations focused, you can first select a block (glance back at Chapter 11 "Block Partying: Working with Blocks of Text," if you need to learn block basics). This tells WordPerfect for Windows to find and replace *only* within the block.

Replacing Word Forms

Find and Replace is certainly a handy feature, and you'll probably use it regularly. However, you'll eventually notice that it often runs smack into the huge wall that is the complexity of the English language. For example, suppose you've written a document that uses the verb *to grab* in various forms: grab, grabbing, grabbed, and so on. You decide that *to grab* is a little too jaunty, so you want to replace it with the more sedate verb *to take*. So you run a Find and Replace command to replace every instance of *grab* with *take*. This works like a charm for the word *grab*, but *grabbing* is replaced with *takebing*, and *grabbed* is replaced with *takebed*. Bummer.

The problem, of course, is that English is just plain weird. The various verb forms are created in too many strange ways for a simple find-and-replace operation to handle. Sometimes you add letters (as in going from *grab* to *grabbing*, for example), sometimes you drop letters (such as going from *take* to *taking*), and sometimes you have multiple choices (the past tense of *take* can be *took* or *taken*, for example).

Does this mean you're stuck running a bunch of different Find and Replace commands to try to get things right? Not if you have WordPerfect for Windows version 6.1. This upgrade uses a new "PerfectSense" technology that allows a Find and Replace operation to handle the different forms of a word. To use it, pull down the Type menu in the Find and Replace Text dialog box, and select the Word Forms command. Use the Find text box to enter the basic form of the search word (*grab*), and use the Replace With text box to enter the replacement word (*take*). Then run the replace operation as you normally would. The PerfectSense technology replaces all the forms of the search text with the proper forms of the replacement text. If a choice of replacement words exists (such as *took* or *taken*), one of two things will happen:

➤ If you chose the Replace All button, the Word Form dialog box appears, as shown in the following figure. Highlight the form you want from the Word Forms list, and then select **R**eplace. (You can also choose **S**kip to move on, or **U**se Always to tell WordPerfect for Windows to always use the highlighted word form.)

If a word has multiple forms, you'll see the Word Form dialog box so you can choose which one you want.

➤ If you chose the Find button, WordPerfect for Windows displays the available forms in a list below the Replace **W**ith text box. Select the form you want from the list, and then proceed with the replacement.

Find and Replace Options

To get the most out of the powerful find-and-replace stuff, you'll probably want to test-drive a few options. Here's what's available in the Find and Replace Text dialog box:

➤ Sometimes, you want to replace only the first few occurrences of a piece of text. In this case, select the Limit **N**umber of Matches command from the **O**ptions menu to display the Limit Number of Changes dialog box. Enter the limit in the **N**umber spinner (enter 0 to place no limit on the number of replacements). When you're done, select **O**K.

➤ WordPerfect for Windows normally preserves the case of whatever text it replaces. For example, suppose your search text is *bobbie* and your replacement text is *bobby*. If WordPerfect for Windows finds *Bobbie*, it will replace it with *Bobby*. If you want to force the program to use the case you enter in the Replace With text box, pull down the Replace menu and activate the Case command. (Note: the Replace menu is only active when you're inside the Replace With text box.)

➤ If you want to search and *delete* text, just leave the Replace With text box blank and proceed normally (although, in this case, it's probably a good idea to avoid the Replace All button).

The Least You Need to Know

This chapter introduced you to WordPerfect for Windows' handy Find and Replace feature. Here's a fond look back:

➤ To find some text, select the Edit menu's Find and Replace command (or press **F2**), enter the search text, and then select the Find button.

➤ To search for text backwards through the document, pull down the Direction menu in the Find and Replace Text dialog box and select the Backward command.

➤ If you're searching for proper names and other things where case matters, make sure you activate the Case command from the Match menu.

➤ To find some text and replace it with something else, select Find and Replace from the Edit menu (or press **F2**), enter your search text in the Find text box, enter the replacement text in the Replace With text box, and then select the Find, Replace, or Replace All button.

Part III
Looking Good: Formatting Stuff

"The least you can do is look respectable." That's what my mother always used to tell me when I was a kid. This advice holds up especially well in these image-conscious times. If you don't look good up front (or if your work doesn't look good), you'll often be written off without a second thought.

When it comes to looking good—whether you're writing a memo, slicking up a report, or polishing your résumé—WordPerfect for Windows gives you a veritable cornucopia of formatting options. The chapters in this part give you the skinny on these various options, including lots of hints about how best to use them.

Chapter 13

Making Your Characters Look Good

In This Chapter

➤ Applying character attributes such as bold and italics

➤ Using different character sizes

➤ Converting letters between uppercase and lowercase

➤ Working with different fonts

➤ Adding WordPerfect for Windows' symbols to your documents

➤ Frighteningly fun formatting frolics

The first step on our road to looking good is the lowly character. I know, I know, you want to try out some really *big* stuff, but don't forget all that blather about the longest journey beginning with a single step. Besides, working with characters *can* make a big difference. Why, just a little bit of bold here, a couple of italics there, throw in a font or two, and suddenly that humdrum, boring memo becomes a dynamic, exciting thing of beauty. People from all over will be clamoring to read your stuff. You will be, in short, a star.

Working with Fonts

Until now, you may not have given much thought to the individual characters that make up your writings. After all, an *a* is an *a*, isn't it? Well, WordPerfect for Windows will change all that. When you start working with different fonts, you'll see that not all *a*'s are the same.

Fonts are to characters what architecture is to buildings. In architecture, you look at certain features and patterns; if you can tell a geodesic dome from a flying buttress, you can tell whether the building is Art Deco or Gothic or whatever. Fonts, too, are distinguished by a set of unique design characteristics. Specifically, there are four things to look for: typeface, type style, type size, and type position.

The Typeface

Anyrelated set of letters, numbers, and other symbols has its own distinctive design called the *typeface*. Typefaces, as you can see in the following figure, can be wildly different depending on the shape and thickness of the characters, the spacing, and what the designer had for breakfast that day.

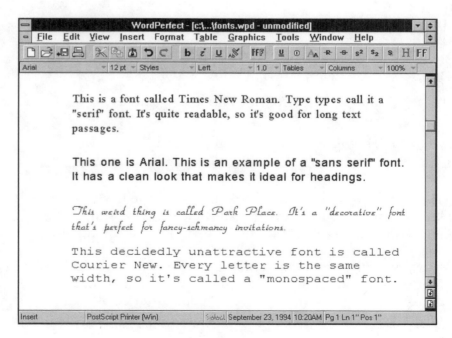

As these examples show, typefaces can be very different.

Typefaces come in three flavors: *serif*, *sans-serif*, and *decorative*. A serif typeface contains fine cross strokes—typographic technoids call them *feet*—at the extremities of each character. These subtle appendages give the typeface a traditional, classy look. Times New Roman (shown in the previous figure) is an example of a common serif typeface.

A sans serif typeface doesn't contain these cross strokes. As a result, serif typefaces usually have a cleaner, more modern look (check out Arial in the figure).

Decorative typefaces are usually special designs used to convey a particular effect. So, for example, if your document really needs a sophisticated look for a wine-and-cheese invitation or something, Park Place (also shown in the figure) would be perfect.

In case you're wondering, the Park Place font—unlike Times New Roman, Arial, and Courier New—does *not* come with Windows. To get it, I had to buy a *TrueType font collection*. These collections (there are lots of them on the market these days) usually consist of a few dozen unusual—but often highly useful—fonts. They cost around a dollar a font, and they're worth it if you use WordPerfect for Windows for lots of different documents (invitations, newsletters, flyers, and so on).

You can also classify typefaces according to the space they allot for each character. This is called the *character spacing* of a font, and it can take two forms: *monospaced* or *proportional*. Monospaced fonts reserve the same amount of space for each character. For example, look at the Courier New font shown earlier. Notice that skinny letters, such as "i" and "l," take up every bit as much space as wider letters, such as "y" and "w." While this is admirably egalitarian, these fonts tend to look like they were produced with a typewriter (in other words, they're ugly). By contrast, in a proportional font (such as Arial or Times New Roman), the space allotted to each letter varies according to the width of the letter.

The Type Style and Size

The *type style* of a font usually refers to whether the characters are **bold** or *italic*. WordPerfect for Windows also lets you set character attributes like <u>underlining</u> and ~~strikeout~~ (sometimes called "strikethrough"). These styles are normally used to highlight or add emphasis to sections of your documents.

The *type size* measures how tall a font is. The standard unit of measurement is the *point*, in which 72 points make up an inch. For example, the individual letters in a 24-point font would be twice as tall as those in a 12-point font. (In case you're wondering, this book is printed in a 10-point font.)

Technically, type size is measured from the highest point of a tall letter such as "f" to the lowest point of an underhanging letter such as "g".

Using different character sizes and styles is an easy way to fool people into thinking you're a competent professional. For example, you can make your titles and section headings stand out by using bold characters that are larger than your regular text. Italic is good for things like company names and book titles, and you can also use it to emphasize important words or phrases.

The Type Position

Characters normally follow each other along each line. However, you can also format the relative *position* of characters to get superscripts (slightly higher than normal) or subscripts (slightly lower than normal), as shown in the following figure.

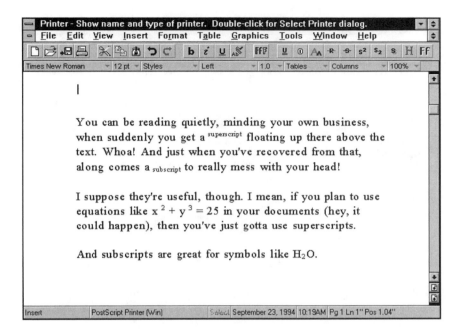

WordPerfect for Windows lets you change the relative position of characters to get superscripts and subscripts.

Selecting Different Fonts

Okay, enough theory. Let's get down to business and see how you go about selecting different fonts for your documents. To begin with, select the block of text you want to format (by dragging your mouse over the text, or by holding down **Shift** and using the arrow keys; see Chapter 11, "Block Partying: Working with Blocks of Text," for details). You then need to access the Font dialog box using one of the following three methods (depending on your mood):

➤ Pull down the Format menu (or the Layout menu, if you're using version 6.0) and select the Font command.

➤ Press **F9**.

➤ Right-click inside the typing area and select Font from the QuickMenu.

In each case, you'll see the Font dialog box (shown in the following figure).

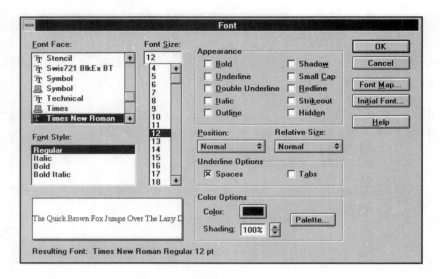

Use the Font dialog box for your character formatting chores.

From here, selecting the font you want is easy:

➤ Use the Font Face list to pick out a typeface.

➤ For the type style, you can use the Font Style list, or you can select individual attributes from the check boxes in the Appearance group.

➤ Use the Font Size list to select the type size. If you're not sure which point size you need, you can also use the Relative Size pop-up list to pick a size that's a percentage of the regular font size (see the section "Working with Initial Fonts" later in this chapter to learn how to change the regular font). Your choices are Fine (60% of the regular type size), Small (80%), Large (120%), Very Large (150%), or Extra Large (200%).

➤ Use the Position pop-up list to select either Subscript or Super-script.

➤ If you feel like adding a dash of color to your document, select the Color button, and then choose a color from the box (or *palette*, as it's called) that appears. (Note, however, that to print colors you need a color printer.)

When you make your selections in the Font dialog box, keep an eye on the Resulting Font box. This gives you an idea of what your font will look like. When you're done, select **OK** to return to the document.

Instead of changing existing text, you might prefer to have any *new* text you type appear in a certain font. This is even easier; just select the font options you want from the Font dialog box, select **OK**, and then start typing. WordPerfect for Windows displays subsequent characters in the font you chose.

Finagling Fonts from the Toolbar and Power Bar

If you do a lot of work with fonts, you'll really appreciate the push-button convenience of the font-related buttons on the Toolbar and the Power Bar. First of all, every Toolbar has buttons that can apply the three most common type styles and effects:

Click	To apply
b	Bold
i	Italic
<u>u</u>	Underline

Note that these buttons are all *toggles*, which means they not only turn an attribute on, but turn it off, as well. For example, if you select a block and then click on the Bold button, the text is bolded, and the Bold button remains "pressed." If you click the button again, WordPerfect for Windows removes the bold and returns the button to its normal state.

You can also use the following shortcut keys for character formatting: **Ctrl+B** for bold, **Ctrl+I** for italic, and **Ctrl+U** for underline.

For more ambitious character formatting, you'll need the buttons on the Font toolbar. To display this toolbar, right-click on the current Toolbar, and then select **Font** from the QuickMenu. Here's a rundown of the new buttons you get:

Click	To
[FfF]	Display the Font dialog box
[U]	Toggle double underlining
[O]	Toggle the outlining effect
[Aa]	Toggle small capitals
[R]	Toggle the redline effect
[S]	Toggle the strikeout effect
[s²]	Toggle the superscript position
[s₂]	Toggle the subscript position
[s]	Toggle the shadow effect
[H]	Toggle hidden text
[Ff]	Add sample text for each typeface to the current document

What's the deal with this hidden text stuff? Well, it means you can designate certain passages in your document as "hidden," and then you can hide or display those passages at will. How? By pulling down the View menu and deactivating the Hidden Text command (to hide the text), or activating the Hidden Text command (to display the hidden text). For example, suppose your document contains the text of a presentation you're making. Instead of scribbling your own notes on your hard copy, you could add them to the document, format them as hidden, and then hide them before you print out the distribution copies.

The Power Bar also has a couple of lists that make character formatting a breeze: Font Face and Font Size (see below). Font Face is just a list of all the typefaces installed on your computer. Font Size is a list of the available type sizes for the selected typeface.

Font Face list   Font Size list

Working with Initial Fonts

Every document has what WordPerfect for Windows calls an *initial font*. This is just the default font that appears before you've selected any font options. If you want your regular text to appear in a different font, you can change the initial font to whatever you like (although you only get to choose a different typeface or type size, and your type styles are limited to bold and italic).

To change the initial font for the current document, display the Font dialog box, select the Initial Font button, and then select your font options from the Document Initial Font dialog box that appears. Select **OK** to return to the Font dialog box, and then select **OK** again to return to your document with the new font in effect.

> You can display the Font dialog box by double-clicking either the Font Face or Font Size list in the Power Bar.

To change the initial font for every new document you create, select the **File** menu's **Print** command, and then choose the **Select** button in the Print dialog box. In the Select Printer dialog box that appears, make sure the printer you normally use is highlighted, and then select **Initial Font** from the **Options** pop-up list. (In version 6.0, just select the Initial Font button.) Use the Printer Initial Font dialog box to select your font, and then select **OK**. Select Close to return to the Print dialog box, and then select Close again to return to the document. (If you need more info about selecting different printers, see Chapter 9, "Getting It Down on Paper: Printing Documents.")

Avoiding the Ransom Note Look

The downside to WordPerfect for Windows' easy-to-use character attributes and fonts is that they can sometimes be *too* easy to use. Flushed with your newfound knowledge, you start throwing every font formatting option in sight at your documents. This can turn even the most profound and well-written documents into a real dog's breakfast. (It's known in the trade as the *ransom note look*.) Here are some tips to avoid overdoing your formatting:

➤ Never use more than a couple of fonts in a single document. Anything more looks amateurish and will only confuse the reader.

➤ If you need to emphasize something, bold or italicize it in the *same* font as the surrounding text. Avoid using underlining for emphasis.

➤ Use larger sizes only for titles and headings.

➤ Avoid bizarre decorative fonts for large sections of text. Most of those suckers are hard on the eyes after a half dozen words or so. Serif fonts are usually very readable, so they're a good choice for long passages. The clean look of sans serif fonts makes them a good choice for headlines and titles.

State Your Case: Converting Uppercase and Lowercase Letters

On most keyboards, the Caps Lock key is just above the Shift key and right beside the *A* key. Inevitably, in the heat of battle, I end up hitting Caps Lock by mistake a few times a day. The result: anything from a few words to a few lines all in uppercase! Fortunately, WordPerfect for Windows lets me off the hook easily with its case-conversion feature. You can change uppercase to lowercase, you can change lowercase to uppercase, and you can even get it to convert only the initial letter in each word to uppercase (to change *alphonse* to *Alphonse*, for example).

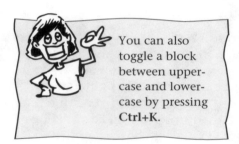

You can also toggle a block between uppercase and lowercase by pressing **Ctrl+K.**

To convert case, select the appropriate block, pull down the Edit menu, and select the Convert Case command. In the cascade menu that appears, select Uppercase, Lowercase, or Initial Capitals.

Adding Silly Symbols

Were you stumped the last time you wanted to write Dag Hammarskjöld because you didn't know how to get one of those ö thingamajigs? I thought so. Well, you'll be happy to know that in WordPerfect, you aren't restricted to using just the letters, numbers, and punctuation marks you can eyeball on your keyboard. In fact, WordPerfect for Windows comes with all kinds of built-in characters that will supply you not only an ö, but a whole universe of weirdo symbols.

To start, position the insertion point where you want to insert the symbol. Now pull down the Insert menu and select the Character command, or press **Ctrl+W**. A dialog box called WordPerfect Characters appears on-screen, as shown in the following figure.

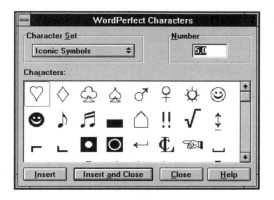

Use the WordPerfect Characters dialog box to insert strange and unusual symbols in your documents.

The layout of this dialog box is pretty simple: the Characters area shows you all the symbols available for whatever character set is selected in the Character Set pop-up list. If you select a different character set, a whole new set of symbols appears.

A **character set** is just a collection of related characters.

To use a symbol from a character set, move into the Characters area and use the arrow keys to highlight the symbol, or just click on it. You then have two choices:

➤ If you want to pick several symbols, select the Insert button for each one.

➤ To add the symbol and then return to the document, select the Insert and Close button.

The Least You Need to Know

This chapter was the first stop on our journey toward looking good on paper. You learned all about fonts and how to format characters with different typefaces, type styles, and so on. Here's the condensed version of what happened:

➤ Fonts are distinctive character designs. They're characterized by four attributes: typeface, type style, type size, and relative position.

➤ To select a different font, choose Font from the Format menu (or press **F9**) and pick out what you need from the Font dialog box.

➤ If you need to convert a block of text from upper- to lowercase (or vice versa), select Convert Case from the Edit menu, and choose the appropriate command.

➤ WordPerfect for Windows comes with various built-in character sets. These sets can give you international characters, scientific symbols, and more. Select the Character command from the Insert menu.

Chapter 14

Making Your Lines and Paragraphs Look Good

In This Chapter

- ➤ Setting and deleting tab stops in a paragraph
- ➤ Left-justifying, centering, and right-justifying text
- ➤ Adjusting the line spacing
- ➤ Indenting paragraph text
- ➤ Working with paragraph margins
- ➤ The usual motley collection of trenchant tips and topical tirades

The last chapter showed you how to format characters, so now we'll bump things up a notch and look at formatting lines and paragraphs. How will this help you look good on paper? Well, all the character formatting in the world won't do you much good if your lines are all scrunched together and if the various pieces of text aren't lined up like boot-camp recruits. Documents like these look cramped and uninviting and will often get tossed in the old circular file without a second look. This chapter will help you avoid such a sorry fate.

A Quick Note About Line and Paragraph Formatting

The way WordPerfect for Windows formats lines and paragraphs can be hopelessly confusing, even for experienced word processing hacks. So, to soften the blow a little, here are some things to keep in mind when working with this chapter's formatting options:

➤ If you select a format option *without* selecting a block, WordPerfect for Windows formats everything from the current paragraph to the end of the document.

➤ If you select a block (even a single character), WordPerfect for Windows formats only the paragraph that contains the block.

Working with Tab Stops

Documents look much better if they're properly indented, and if their various parts line up nicely. The best way to do this is to use tabs instead of spaces whenever you need to create some room in a line. Why? Well, a single space can take up different amounts of room, depending on the font and size of the characters you're using. So your document can end up looking pretty ragged if you try to use spaces to indent your text. Tabs, on the other hand, are fastidiously precise. When you press the **Tab** key, the insertion point moves ahead exactly to the next tab stop, no more, no less. (If you want to arrange text or numbers in columns and rows, it might be easier to set up a *table*, instead. See Chapter 26, "Techniques for Terrific Tables," to find out what tables are all about.)

If things somehow go haywire as you're working through this chapter and your document ends up all askew, you need to do two things. First, start chanting the following mantra in your head: "This is not my fault, this is WordPerfect's fault. This is not my fault..." Second, select Undo from the Edit menu, or press **Ctrl+Z** to reverse the mayhem.

To begin, pull down the Format menu (or the Layout menu in version 6.0), select **Line**, and then select Tab Set. This displays both the Tab Set dialog box and the Ruler Bar. (That's right, *another* bar. It seems like WordPerfect for Windows has more bars than Hershey's.) The Ruler Bar shows you where the current tabs are set. (The numbers measure the distance in inches from the left edge of the page.) Each of the strangely shaped black marks represents a tab stop.

You can also access the Tab Set dialog box by clicking on this button in the Format Toolbar.

Checking Out WordPerfect for Windows' Tab Types

As you can see in the next figure, WordPerfect for Windows has a tab for your every mood. The following summary describes these types:

Tab Type	How It Affects Your Characters
Left	Text lines up with the tab on the left.
Right	Text lines up with the tab on the right.
Center	Text is centered on the tab.
Decimal	Numbers line up with the tab at their decimal places.
Dot	The tab is preceded by a bunch of dots. These tabs can line up on the left, center, right, or decimal.

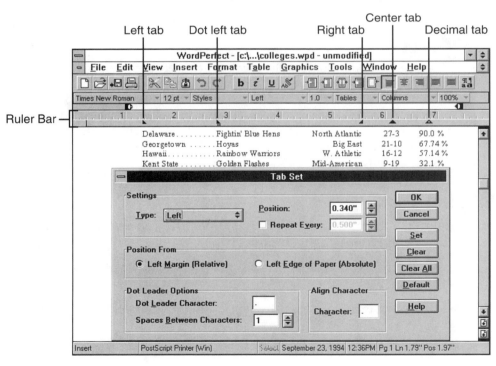

The Tab Set dialog box with example tab types.

Setting Tabs

Once you've displayed the Tab Set dialog box, you can set your tabs by following these steps:

Tabs preceded by dots are called **dot leaders**.

1. Select a tab type from the Type pop-up list.

2. Use the **Position** spinner to enter a location for the tab. If you want to enter multiple tabs at regular intervals, activate the Repeat Every check box and enter the interval in the spinner beside it.

3. Select the **Set** button. The tab stop appears in the Ruler Bar.

4. Repeat steps 1–3 to set other tab stops.

5. When you're done, select **OK**.

You can also make your tab stops *absolute* or *relative*. Absolute tab stops are measured from the left edge of the page. They're rock solid; they wouldn't change position in a hurricane. Set an absolute tab stop by activating the Left Edge of Paper (Absolute) option. Relative tab stops are more laid back. They're measured from the left margin, so if you change the margin position (which I'll show you how to do in the next chapter), they're happy to move right along. Set a relative tab stop by activating the Left Margin (Relative) option. In general, it's best to stick with relative tab stops.

Deleting Tabs

If you'd like to get rid of a tab or two, open the Tab Set dialog box and use any of the following techniques:

➤ To delete a single tab, enter its position in the **Position** spinner, and then select the Clear button.

➤ If you want to delete all the tabs and give yourself a fresh start, select the Clear All button.

➤ If you'd like to revert to WordPerfect for Windows' default tabs (a left tab every half inch), select the **Default** button.

Setting Tabs with the Ruler Bar

Setting tabs with the Tab Set dialog box is a bit of a pain because not only do you have to work all kinds of controls, but if you don't like your tabs, you have to open it up and go through the whole process again. (And when you throw in all that rot about "absolute" versus "relative" tabs, well, forget about it.) What the world needs is a simple way to set tabs; one where you could just point and say "By Jove, I want a decimal tab right here!"

Well, it's my pleasure to report that indeed there *is* a simple way to set tabs: the Ruler Bar. Yes, it's the same Ruler you saw earlier when you ran the **Tab Set** command. Only this time, once you're freed from the shackles of the Tab Set dialog box, you'll see that this handy tool makes setting tabs as easy as clicking your mouse.

First things first, however. To view the Ruler, pull down the **View** menu and select the **R**uler Bar command, or press **Alt+Shift+F3**. Right-click on the lower half of the Ruler Bar and select the type of tab you want (**Left, Center**, and so on) from the QuickMenu that appears. Then move the mouse pointer into the lower half of the Ruler Bar and click on the position where you want the tab to appear. WordPerfect for Windows sets the tab.

The Ruler Bar combination is good for more than just setting tabs. Check this out:

➤ To move a tab, you can drag it along the Ruler Bar with your mouse. To do so, place the mouse pointer over the tab, press and hold down the left mouse button, and then move the mouse to the left or right. (Don't move down, though, or you'll delete the tab!) As you drag, WordPerfect for Windows thoughtfully displays a dashed line down the screen so you can see how things will line up. It also shows the tab type and your current position in the status bar (see the following figure).

Drag the tab markers to move them.

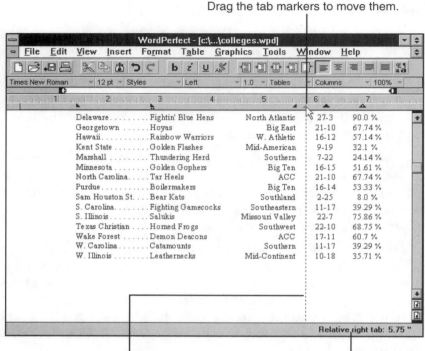

The dashed line shows the new tab position.   The tab info appears here.

As you drag a tab, WordPerfect for Windows displays a dashed line so you can see where the tab will line up.

➤ To clear a tab, drag it below the Ruler Bar.

➤ To clear all the tabs, right-click on the Ruler Bar and then select Clear All Tabs from the QuickMenu.

Justifying Your Text

Justifying your text has nothing to do with defending your ideas (luckily for some of us!). Rather, it has to do with lining up your paragraphs so they look all prim and proper. Here's an example document, showing the various justification options.

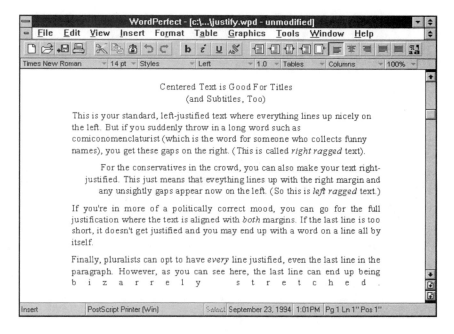

Some text justification examples.

To justify your text, pull down the Format menu (or the Layout menu in version 6.0), select Justification, and choose the command you want from the cascade menu that appears. The following table summarizes the available commands and shows you the appropriate buttons to select from the Format Toolbar. (To display the Format Toolbar Button Bar, right-click the current Toolbar and select **Format** from the QuickMenu.)

Command	Button	Description
Left		Justifies each line on the left margin.
Center		Centers each line between both margins.
Right		Justifies each line on the right margin.
Full		Justifies each line on both margins. Ignores the last line in a paragraph if it's too small.
All		Justifies every line in a paragraph on both margins.

The Power Bar gives you yet another method of justifying your paragraphs. Click on the Justification button (see the figure below), and then select a justification option from the list that appears.

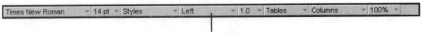

The Justification button

Left-justified text is said to be **right-ragged** because the right side of each line doesn't line up. Similarly, right-justified text is called **left-ragged**.

Just to make things confusing, WordPerfect for Windows also gives you a way to justify individual lines. To check this out, place the insertion point anywhere in the line and select the **Line** command from the Format menu (or the Layout menu in version 6.0). If you want to center the line, select the Center command from the cascade menu or press **Shift+F7**. To right justify the line, select the Flush Right command or press **Alt+F7**.

Changing the Line Spacing

Typewriters have little levers or buttons you can maneuver to alter the line spacing. Well, anything a typewriter can do, WordPerfect for Windows can do better. So, whereas you can only set up double- or triple-spacing on a typewriter, you can set up just about any number of spaces—and even decimals!—in WordPerfect for Windows. (Anybody need *four-point-two-five*-ple-spacing?)

To set your line spacing, pull down the Format menu (or the Layout menu in version 6.0), select Line, and then select Spacing. In the Line Spacing dialog box (shown in the following figure), use the Spacing spinner to enter the number of spaces you want. When you're ready, select **OK**.

The document shows you what the new spacing will look like.

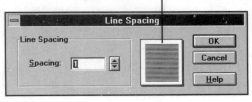

Use the Line Spacing dialog box to mess around with your document's line spacing.

You can also use the ever-handy Power Bar to set your line spacing. Click on the **Line Spacing** button (see below), and then select a number from the list that appears. If you don't see a number you want, select **Other** to access the Line Spacing dialog box.

The Line Spacing button

Indenting Text

If you need to indent a whole paragraph from the margin, don't do it with tab stops. Instead, WordPerfect will indent an entire paragraph for you. You have four options: indenting from the left margin; indenting from both margins; indenting all but the first line from the left margin (a *hanging indent*); and outdenting the first line of the paragraph. (*Outdenting*, also called a *back tab*, means to move something outside the margin.) You can also indent the first line of a paragraph; see "Setting Paragraph Margins," later in this chapter. The figure below shows examples of each type of indentation.

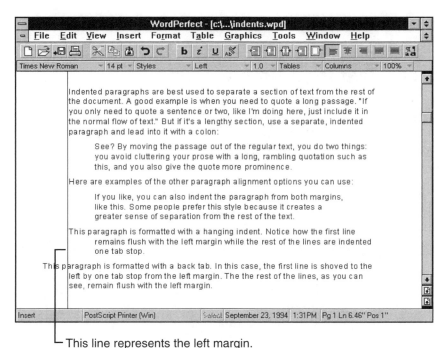

This line represents the left margin.

Examples of the four kinds of indentation.

Indenting a Paragraph from the Left Margin

To indent a paragraph from the left margin, place the cursor at the beginning of the paragraph (you don't need to select a block this time—didn't I tell you this was confusing?), pull down the Format menu (or the Layout menu in version 6.0), select Paragraph, and then select the Indent command from the cascade menu. As an alternative, you can simply press **F7**. WordPerfect indents each line in the paragraph to the first tab stop.

 Click on this button in the Format Toolbar to indent the current paragraph from the left margin.

Creating a Hanging Indent

Hanging indents are useful for a series of point-form paragraphs, or for the items in a bibliography. To create a hanging indent, place the cursor at the beginning of the paragraph, pull down the Format menu (or the Layout menu in version 6.0), select Paragraph, and then select the Hanging Indent command. As an alternative, you can simply press **Ctrl+F7**.

 Click on this button in the Format Toolbar to create a hanging indent.

Indenting Text from Both Margins

If you need to indent a paragraph from *both* margins, place the cursor at the beginning of the paragraph, select Paragraph from the Format menu (or the Layout menu in version 6.0), and then choose the Double Indent command. Or, you can avoid the menus altogether by pressing **Ctrl+Shift+F7**.

 Click on this button in the Format Toolbar to indent the current paragraph from both margins.

Creating a Back Tab

Back tabs are similar to hanging indents, except that the first line is outdented to the left of the left margin by one tab stop; the other lines in the paragraph remain flush with the left margin. To create a back tab indent, pull down the Format menu (or the Layout menu in version 6.0), select Paragraph, and then select Back Tab (or you can press **Shift+Tab**).

Setting Paragraph Margins

Every page in a document has a margin around each side. I'll show you how to work with these margins in the next chapter, but as a warm-up, let's see how you format a paragraph's margins. A *paragraph's* margins? Yup. This just refers to the white space above and below a paragraph (the spacing between paragraphs) and to the left and right of a paragraph (between the paragraph and the left and right page margins). As an added bonus, you can also indent the first line of a paragraph. Here's how it's done:

1. Select a block in the paragraph you want to work with.

2. Pull down the Format menu (or the Layout menu in version 6.0), select Paragraph, and then select Format from the cascade menu. You'll see the Paragraph Format dialog box, shown in the following figure.

    You can also access the Paragraph Format dialog box by clicking on this button in the 6.1 WordPerfect Toolbar.

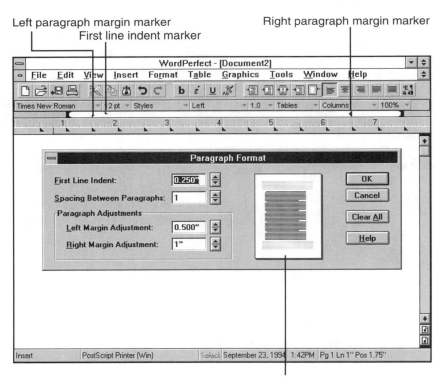

Left paragraph margin marker

First line indent marker

Right paragraph margin marker

Your margin adjustments appear in the sample page.

3. Use the spinners to select your paragraph formatting options, and keep an eye on the sample page to preview how your adjustments will affect the paragraph. You should also note three things here:

➤ First Line Indent adjusts the first line of the paragraph relative to the left paragraph margin.

➤ Spacing Between Paragraphs adjusts the number of spaces above and below the paragraph.

➤ The Left Margin Adjustment and Right Margin Adjustment are relative to the current page margins. So if you enter **1"** and the page margins are 1 inch, the paragraph will be indented 2 inches from the left edge of the page.

4. When you're done, select **OK** to return to the document.

Adjusting Paragraph Format with the Ruler Bar

If you prefer a more visual approach to paragraph formatting, you can use the Ruler Bar to adjust both the left and right paragraph margins, as well as the first line indent, with a simple drag of the old mouse. To see how to do this, display the Ruler Bar (by selecting **Ruler Bar** from the **View** menu, or by pressing **Alt+Shift+F3**) and look inside the open area just above the Ruler's numbers. Inside, you'll see two small triangles on the left and one slightly larger triangle on the right. (Yes, they *are* hard to see at first. To help out, the previous figure shows each triangle moved out from the edges.) They're called *paragraph markers*, and here's how you use them to format your paragraphs:

Once you have the Ruler Bar on-screen, you can also use it to display the Paragraph Format dialog box quickly. Either double-click on a paragraph marker, or right-click on the Ruler and select the **Paragraph Format** option from the QuickMenu.

➤ To adjust the left paragraph margin, drag the bottom triangle of the two on the left. Both paragraph markers will move; this is perfectly normal.

➤ To adjust the right paragraph margin, drag the right triangle.

➤ To adjust the first line indent, drag the top triangle on the left.

The Least You Need to Know

This chapter walked you through some of WordPerfect for Windows' line and paragraph formatting options. They are, as I said, somewhat confusing at times, so I think a brief recap is in order:

➤ If you want to format a paragraph, block off some text in the paragraph (a letter or two will do). Otherwise, WordPerfect for Windows formats everything from the insertion point position down.

➤ To set tab stops, pull down the Format menu, select Line, and then select Tab Set. Use the Tab Set dialog box to enter your tabs.

➤ To justify text, pull down the Format menu, select the Justification command, and choose the justification option you need from the cascade menu that appears.

➤ To change the spacing between the lines in a paragraph, select the Format menu's Line command, and then select Spacing. In the Line Spacing dialog box, enter the number of spaces you want in the Spacing spinner.

➤ You can indent text from either the left margin or from both margins. Just select the Paragraph command from the Format menu, and select the appropriate option from the cascade menu.

➤ To set paragraph margins, pull down the Format menu, select Paragraph, and then select Format. Enter your new margin values in the Paragraph Format dialog box.

Chapter 15

Making Your Pages Look Good

In This Chapter

➤ Making adjustments to the page margins

➤ Creating your own page breaks

➤ Using WordPerfect for Windows' new Page mode

➤ Adding and formatting page numbers

➤ Defining headers and footers

➤ Sad stories of widows and orphans

Well, let's see: we've looked at formatting characters, lines, and paragraphs. And since logic is an occasionally useful tool that I succumb to from time to time, we'll now graduate to full-fledged *page formatting*. This is the stuff—we're talking margin adjustments, page numbers, headers, and footers—that can add that certain *je ne sais quois* to your documents. (Of course, adding fancy foreign terms in italics also helps, but I'll leave that up to you.) This chapter takes on these topics and more.

As usual, if any of this formatting stuff gets out of hand, immediately select the Edit menu's Undo command (or press **Ctrl+Z**) to bring everything back in line.

Views à la Mode: A Note About View Modes

This is as good a place as any to talk about WordPerfect for Windows' *view modes*. The view modes determine how your pages look on the screen. Here's a summary of the options, which you can select from the View menu:

➤ **Page mode**   This is the default view. It shows you exactly what your page will look like when you print it. This includes the document's margins, headers, footers, page numbers, footnotes, and endnotes. You name it, Page mode shows it.

➤ **Draft mode**   This mode hides the top and bottom margins, as well as page formatting such as headers, footers, and page numbers. You don't see your exact page, but it makes scrolling through the document a lot faster.

Press **Ctrl+F5** to switch to Draft mode, and press **Alt+F5** to return to Page mode.

➤ Two Page mode   This mode shows you the big picture by displaying two full pages on the screen at once. You can still work with the pages normally (although you may need a magnifying glass to see what you're doing).

Keep these modes in mind as you work through this chapter, especially when we talk about stuff like headers and footers.

Adjusting Page Margins

Page margins are the white space that surrounds text on a page. There are four margins altogether: at the top and bottom of the page, and on the left and right sides of a page. By default, WordPerfect for Windows decrees each of these margins to be one inch, but you can override that. Why would you want to do such a thing? Here are a few good reasons:

➤ If someone else is going to be making notes on the page, it helps to include bigger left and right margins (to give them more room for scribbling).

➤ Smaller margins all around mean that you get more text on a page. On a really long document, this could save you a few pages when you print it out.

➤ If you have a document that's just slightly longer than a page (say by only a couple of lines), you could decrease the top and bottom margins just enough to fit the wayward lines onto a single page.

Before changing the margins, you need to decide how much of the document you want to affect. (If you just want to change the margins for a single paragraph, refer to Chapter 14, "Making Your Lines and Paragraphs Look Good," for the appropriate steps.) To adjust the margins from a particular paragraph to the end of the document, position the cursor inside that particular paragraph. If, for example, you want to adjust the margins for the entire document, place the cursor at the top of the first page (by pressing **Ctrl+Home**). However, if you want to adjust the margins for only certain (consecutive) paragraphs, select a block that includes some text from each paragraph.

When you're ready, pull down the Format menu (or the Layout menu in version 6.0) and select the **Margins** command, or press **Ctrl+F8**. The Margins dialog box appears, as shown in the following figure.

 Clicking on this button in the Format Toolbar will also display the Margins dialog box.

Use the Margins dialog box to set your page margins.

You use the four spinners (sounds like a singing group, doesn't it?) to set your margins. For example, to adjust the left margin, enter a number in the Left spinner. Note that these numbers are measured in inches from the edge of the page. You don't have to bother with the inch sign (") though; WordPerfect for Windows adds it for you automatically.

If you plan to print a document on a laser printer, keep in mind that most lasers can't print anything that's closer than a quarter of an inch or so to the edge of the page.

155

The Margins dialog box also displays a sample page that shows you what havoc your new settings will wreak on your unsuspecting pages. When you're good and ready, select **OK**.

When you adjust your margins, you'll notice that the status line's Ln and Pos indicators change as well. For example, if you set the top margin to two inches, the Ln indicator displays **2"** when you're at the top of a page.

Setting the Left and Right Margins with the Ruler Bar

Our old friend the Ruler Bar makes it easy to adjust the left and right margins. First, display the Ruler Bar by selecting **R**uler Bar from the View menu, or by pressing **Alt+Shift+F3**. Look at the thin strip just above the Ruler's numbers, and you'll see two black shapes that look like rectangles someone has taken a bite out of. (This is, admittedly, an obscure description. To help, I've pointed out these mysterious shapes in the figure below.) These are called the *margin markers*, and they work like this:

➤ To adjust the left page margin, drag the left margin marker.

➤ To adjust the right page margin, drag the right margin marker.

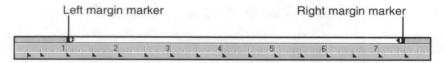

Left margin marker   Right margin marker

You can adjust your page margins by dragging the Ruler Bar's margin markers.

Once you have the Ruler Bar displayed, you can also use it to crank up the Margins dialog box. You can either right-click on the Ruler Bar and select **Margins** from the QuickMenu, or you can double-click in the margin marker area.

Dealing with WordPerfect for Windows' Page Breaks

As you may know by now, WordPerfect for Windows signals the start of a new page by running a line across the screen (it's called a *page break*). Text that appears above the line prints on one page, and text

below the line prints on the next page. This
text arrangement is not set in stone, of
course. If you insert a new paragraph or
change the margins, the text on both sides
of the page break moves accordingly.

Page breaks that
are inserted by
WordPerfect and
that adjust them-
selves automatically
are **soft page breaks.**
Page breaks that you
insert manually and that don't
move are **hard page breaks.**

But what if you have a line or paragraph that *has to* appear at the top of a
page? You could fiddle around by pressing
Enter enough times, but WordPerfect for
Windows gives you an easier way. Just
position the insertion point where you
want the new page to begin, pull down the Insert menu, and select the
Page Break command (or press **Ctrl+Enter**).

Here's a good example of when it's better to be in Draft mode
while you're putting a document together. If you insert a hard page
break in Page mode, WordPerfect for Windows actually sticks in a
whole page, which makes it both slower and more confusing to scroll
through the document. To overcome this, switch to Draft mode (as
described earlier in this chapter). The hard page break will appear as a
double line (as opposed to the single line of a soft page break), and
you'll be able to just scroll past it normally.

To delete a hard page break, you have two options:

➤ Position the insertion point at the beginning of the line below the
break and press **Backspace.**

➤ Position the insertion point at the end of the line above the break
and press **Delete.**

Keeping Yourself (and Your Text) Together

When the last line of a paragraph appears by itself at the top of a page,
it's called (sadly) a *widow*. If the first line of a paragraph appears by
itself at the bottom of a page, it's called an *orphan*. (No, I don't know
who comes up with these names.) With WordPerfect for Windows, you
can prevent these pathetic creatures from inhabiting your documents.
Just pull down the Format menu (or the Layout menu in version 6.0),

select **Page**, and select **Keep Text Together**. In the Keep Text Together dialog box (see the figure below), activate the check box in the Widow/Orphan group.

 You can also click on this button in the Page Toolbar to access the Keep Text Together dialog box.

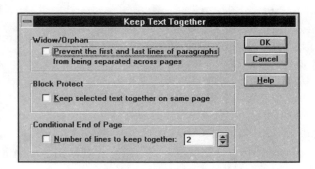

Use the Keep Text Together dialog box to, well, keep your text together.

While we're on the subject, here's a quick description of the other two (occasionally useful) options in this dialog box:

➤ If you have a block of text that you don't want broken up by an unruly page break, activate the check box in the Block Protect group. (You need to have the appropriate block selected beforehand, of course.)

➤ If you want to keep a certain number of lines together, activate the check box in the Conditional End of Page group and enter the number in the spinner. (You need to position the cursor at the beginning of the first of these lines before doing this, though.)

Adding Page Numbers

WordPerfect for Windows' status bar tells you which page you're on when you ramble through a document on-screen, but what happens when you print it out? To avoid getting lost in large document printouts, you should add page numbers that'll appear on the hard copies. Once you tell WordPerfect for Windows that you want page numbers, the program tracks the entire kit and kaboodle for you.

Everything happens inside the Page Numbering dialog box, so you need to display that first. Just select the **P**age command from the Fo**r**mat menu (or the Layout menu in version 6.0), and then select the **N**umbering option.

 Click on this button in the Page Toolbar to access the Page Numbering dialog box.

Once you've finished setting up all your page numbering options (which are described in the following sections), select **OK** in the Page Numbering dialog box to return to your document. To see your page numbers in action, make sure you're in Page mode.

Positioning the Page Numbers

The first decision you have to make is where you want your numbers to appear on the page. WordPerfect for Windows, ever eager to please, gives you no less than eight (that's right, *eight*) possibilities. To check them out, select the **P**osition pop-up list.

As you can see, most of the options are straightforward. You can position the numbers on the top or bottom of the page, and in each case you can choose from the left, center, or right side of the page. Two other choices—Alternating Top and Alternating Bottom—may require a bit more explanation. If you choose one of these options, WordPerfect for Windows will switch the position of the numbers depending on whether the page is odd or even. For example, the Alternating Top option places the numbers on the top right for odd pages and the top left for even pages (which is, you'll notice, the way this book is formatted).

After you've marveled at the sheer wealth of choices available to you, pick the one you want, and WordPerfect for Windows shows what your choice will look like in the sample pages.

Setting Page Number Options

Select the Options button in the Page Numbering dialog box and you'll get yet another dialog box: Page Numbering Options (shown in the following figure).

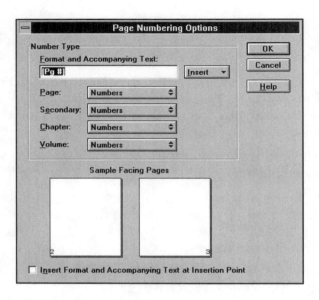

*Use the Page Numbering Options dialog box to set up your page numbers
the way you want.*

Instead of using a number all by itself, you can use the Format and
Accompanying Text text box to add some text to go along with your
page numbers. So, for example, you could add the word *Page* or even
something like *My Great American Novel*. It's usually best to insert the
text before the [Pg #] code that's already in there. (This code tells
WordPerfect for Windows to insert a page number.)

You can display your page numbers not only as numbers, but as
letters and Roman numerals (in either upper- or lowercase). Select the
Page pop-up list and pick out a format that strikes your fancy.

As a rule, you shouldn't work with documents any larger than a
couple of dozen pages or so. Not only might you run out of memory,
but humongous documents are a pain to work with. Ideally, you
should break monster projects into manageable chunks—a chapter per
document is usually okay. Happily, WordPerfect for Windows includes
lots of page numbering options that are great for keeping track of these
large projects. For example, you can include chapter numbers in your
documents. In the Page Numbering Options dialog box, choose the
Insert pop-up list and select Chapter Number. A new code—**[Chp #]**—
appears. Add some text so you know which number is which, like so:

Chapter [Chp #] Page [Pg #]

WordPerfect for Windows won't increment these chapter numbers automatically, so you'll need to add them by hand (see the next section). If your project is a multi-volume deal (my, you *are* prolific, aren't you?), you can do the same thing with volume numbers.

When you're done with the Page Numbering Options dialog box, select **OK** to return to the Page Numbering dialog box.

Setting the Page Number

Most of the time you'll just start your page numbers at 1 and go from there. However, you're free to start the numbers at whatever value you like. This is great if your document is a continuation of an existing project (such as a new chapter in a book). If the rest of the project has 100 pages, then you'd start this document at page 101.

In the Page Numbering dialog box, select the **Value** button. The Numbering Value dialog box appears. In the Page Settings group, use the New **Page** Number spinner to enter the number you want to start with. (You can also use this dialog box to manually adjust your chapter and volume numbers, if you have any.) Select **OK** to return to the Page Numbering dialog box.

Formatting the Page Number Font

For truly fancy page numbering, you can format the font just like any other text. Select the **Font** button in the Page Numbering dialog box, and then fill in the options you want in the Page Numbering Font dialog box. When you're done, select **OK** to return to the Page Numbering dialog box.

Centering Text Between the Top and Bottom

If you've read Chapter 14, "Making Your Lines and Paragraphs Look Good," you know how to center text between the left and right margins. WordPerfect for Windows also lets you center between the top and bottom margins, which is great for things like title pages, résumés, and short business letters.

From the Format menu (or the Layout menu in version 6.0), select **Page** and then **Center**. In the Center Page(s) dialog box, select the option you want (such as Current **Page**) and then select **OK**.

Clicking this button in the Page Toolbar displays the Center Page(s) dialog box.

Setting Up Headers and Footers

Take a look at the top of the page you're reading now. Above the line that runs across the top you'll see a page number and some text (on the even pages, you see the part number and part name; on the odd pages, it's the chapter number and chapter name). These are examples of *headers*—sections of text that appear at the top margin of every page.

WordPerfect for Windows lets you include headers in your documents, just like the pros. You can put in the usual stuff—page numbers (as described in the last section), chapter titles, and so on—but you're free to add anything you like: your name, your company's name, your dog's name, whatever. And you can even do *footers*, as well. A footer is the same as a header, only it appears at the bottom of each page (makes sense).

To add a header or footer, follow these steps:

1. When you add a header or footer, WordPerfect for Windows uses it for all the pages from the current page to the end of the document. So the first thing you need to do is position the insertion point somewhere in the first page you want to use.

2. Pull down the Format menu (or the Layout menu in version 6.0) and select the Header/Footer command. The Headers/Footers dialog box appears.

3. You can define up to two headers or footers (A and B) per page. For example, you could have one header on the left (to show, say, the name of the document) and a second one on the right (showing the page number, for instance). So you now need to select which header or footer to add. For example, to define header A, activate the Header A option.

4. Select the Create button. WordPerfect for Windows, as you can see in the following figure, creates a new header or footer area, and yes, another bar: the Header/Footer feature bar.

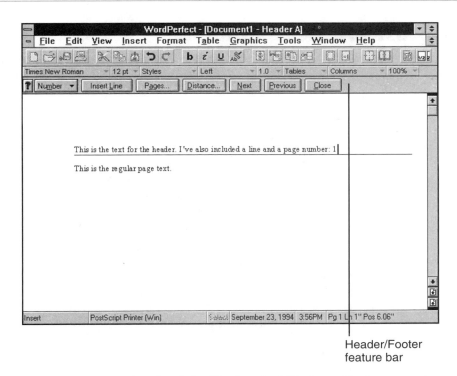

Header/Footer
feature bar

When you create a header, WordPerfect for Windows displays a typing area for the header and the Header/Footer feature bar.

5. Type in the header or footer text you want to use. Feel free to use any character or line formatting options (fonts, bold, justification, and so on). You also use the feature bar buttons (you can either click on a button, or you can hold down the **Alt** and **Shift** keys and press the button's underlined letter):

   Number   Displays a list of page numbering options.

   Insert Line   Draws a line between the header or footer and the regular text.

   Pages   Displays the Pages dialog box so you can choose where you want the header to appear (Odd Pages, Even Pages, or Every Page).

   Distance   Displays the Distance dialog box, in which you enter the distance to leave between the header or footer and the regular text.

6. When you're done, select Close in the feature bar.

The Least You Need to Know

This chapter walked you through some of WordPerfect for Windows' page formatting options. Here's a recap of what you really need to know to make your life complete:

➤ To see formatting options such as page numbers, headers, and footers, switch to Page mode by selecting the **Page** command from the View menu.

➤ To adjust the page margins, pull down the Format menu, select the **Margins** command, and then enter the new margin values in the Margins dialog box.

➤ To add a *hard page break* (one that remains in position even if you enter text above it or change the margins), position the insertion point and press **Ctrl+Enter**.

➤ To add page numbers to a document, open the Format menu, choose **Page**, and select **Numbering**. Use the Page Numbering dialog box to set up your page numbers.

➤ If you need to add headers or footers to a document, select the **Header/Footer** command from the Format menu, select which header or footer you want to add, select **Create**, and then add the header or footer.

Chapter 16

Looking Good with Envelopes and Labels

In This Chapter

- ➤ Defining an envelope
- ➤ Printing an envelope
- ➤ Working with envelope options such as POSTNET bar codes
- ➤ Defining labels and entering label text
- ➤ Envelope and label basics and some smart shopping tips

While waiting in a bookstore checkout line a few years ago, I happened to notice a woman standing in the paperback bestsellers section. She had a book in each hand and was clearly trying to figure out which one to buy. She stared intently at the covers, read the blurbs on the back, and checked out the price, but she just couldn't decide. Finally, she put the two books spine-to-spine and chose the thicker one!

I tell this story to remind you that most people look at the whole package when they evaluate something. If you're going to be mailing your documents, applying all the fancy formatting techniques we've been looking at is only the start. Your package might not even be opened if it arrives in a sloppily addressed envelope (or, if it is opened, your careful prose will almost certainly be read with a jaundiced eye). This chapter helps you avoid such a sorry fate by showing you how easy it is to create great-looking envelopes and labels in WordPerfect for Windows.

Printing Addresses on Envelopes

For a true professional touch, you can persuade WordPerfect for Windows to print mailing and return addresses on an envelope of just about any size. Just think how impressed your recipients will be when they see their names and addresses all slick and neat, smack-dab in the middle of an envelope. Is it hard? Not a chance! All you do is tell WordPerfect for Windows the mailing and return addresses you want to use, tell WordPerfect to print the envelope, and then shove the envelope into your printer. It's all quite civilized, really. (It's also a lot faster than trying to type an address directly on an envelope using that rickety old Selectric you keep hidden in the corner.) The next few sections take you through the basic steps for creating an envelope: setting up, defining the envelope, and printing the darn thing.

Getting Your Document Ready for This Envelope Stuff

Getting your document ready for creating an envelope is pretty straightforward. There are only two things you need to do: select a printer and enter the mailing address.

The first order of business is to make sure you've selected the printer you're going to use to print the envelope. For each printer you've installed, WordPerfect for Windows comes with one or more *envelope definitions* that ensure the envelope is printed like an envelope (and not like, say, an 8 1/2" by 11" sheet of paper). To see which printer is currently selected, pull down the File menu and select the Print command (or press **Ctrl+P**). In the Print dialog box that appears, the Current Printer box at the top shows you the name of the currently selected printer. If this isn't the one you'll be using for your envelope, go ahead and select the correct one. (If you're not sure how to go about this, trudge back to Chapter 9, "Getting It Down on Paper: Printing Documents," to learn everything you need to know.)

In case you're wondering, each envelope definition covers a number of characteristics. These include the dimensions of the envelope, the *orientation* of the text (either *landscape*—the text runs parallel to the long side of the envelope—or *portrait*—the text runs parallel to the short side of the envelope), where you'll be loading the envelope into the printer (this is usually "manual feed"), and any position adjustments that the program will need to get the addresses printing correctly.

With your printer selected, the only other task you need to perform is adding the mailing address to the document. (If you like, you can bypass this step; you can also enter the mailing address when you define the envelope, as you'll see in the next section.) This is no big deal: you can plop the address just about anywhere that makes sense. Remember, however, that what you type is exactly what will appear on the front of the envelope. So make sure the address is complete (including the ZIP or postal code) and that it contains no spelling mistakes (see the figure below).

Mailing address

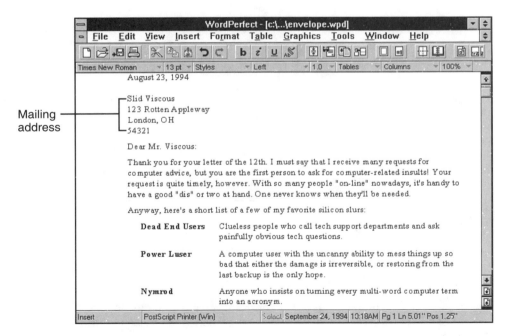

Make sure you enter the mailing address exactly as you want it printed on the envelope.

Defining the Envelope

The next step is to define the envelope itself. This includes entering the return address, selecting the envelope size you'll be using, and a couple of other things. The following steps show you what to do.

1. If you entered the mailing address in the document, select it. If you pressed **Enter** twice after the mailing address, however, WordPerfect for Windows finds the address automatically; you don't have to select it. The only exception to this is if your document contains more than one address; in this case, you have to select the address you want to use.

2. Pull down the Format menu (or the Layout menu in version 6.0) and select the Envelope command. WordPerfect for Windows displays the Envelope dialog box, shown in the following figure.

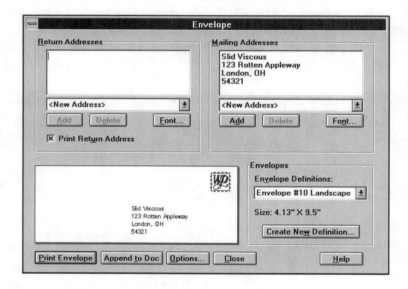

Use the Envelope dialog box to define your envelope.

Depending on which printer you selected, WordPerfect for Windows may ask if you want to create an envelope definition. Select Yes to display the Create Envelope Definition dialog box. Enter a name in the **P**aper Name text box, select an envelope size from the **S**ize drop-down list, and then select **OK**. WordPerfect for Windows then displays the Envelope dialog box.

3. If you want to include a return address on the envelope, select the Return Addresses text box and enter the address. (Note that you can start a new line in the text box by pressing **Enter**.) You can also use the following controls to play around with the return address:

> **Add**   Click on this button to add the address you entered to the drop-down list of return addresses.
>
> **Delete**   Click on this button to delete whatever address is currently displayed in the drop-down list.
>
> **Font**   Click on this button to select the address font from the Return Address Font dialog box.
>
> **Print Return Address**   Activate this check box to have WordPerfect for Windows print the address in the upper left corner of the envelope. If you'd prefer to leave the address off the envelope, deactivate this check box.

4. If you didn't enter a mailing address in the document, use the Mailing Addresses text box to enter it. You can also **A**dd the address to the list, **D**elete one from the list, and change the address **F**ont.

5. If necessary, use the Envelope Definitions drop-down list to select the appropriate envelope size. (The default size is 4.13" × 9.5".)

Printing the Envelope

With your envelope defined, you can either print it out right away or insert it into the current document for later use. If you want to print the envelope, first make sure your printer is up and running. Then load the envelope into the printer. (How you do this varies depending on the type of printer you have; your printer manual should tell you.) When you're ready to go, select the **P**rint Envelope button in the Envelope dialog box.

If you want to print the envelope later, you can insert it into the document by selecting the Append to Doc button in the Envelope dialog box. WordPerfect for Windows adds a new page to the end of the document (by inserting a hard page break) and displays the return and mailing addresses. To print this envelope later, select the mailing address, access the Envelope dialog box, and select Print Envelope.

Changing the Envelope Setup

As usual, WordPerfect for Windows gives you all kinds of bells and whistles to make sure you get exactly the kinds of envelopes you need. The next few sections take you through the various setup options that are available for envelopes.

Adding POSTNET Bar Codes to Envelopes

The U.S. Postal Service (USPS) uses POSTNET bar codes to computerize their mail sorting and speed up mail delivery. If you do bulk mailings, you can save on postal rates by presorting the envelopes and including the official USPS POSTNET bar code as part of the mailing address (as shown in the following figure).

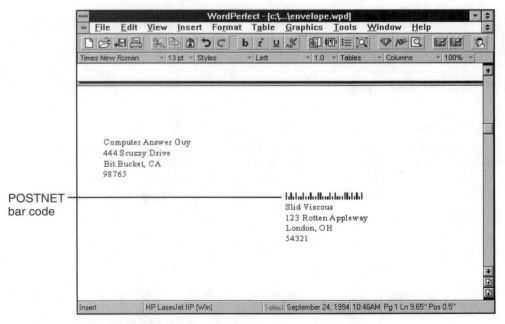

An example POSTNET bar code.

Follow these steps to add a POSTNET bar code to an envelope:

1. Access the Envelope dialog box and define your envelope, as described earlier in this chapter.

2. Click on the Options button. WordPerfect for Windows displays the Envelope Options dialog box, as shown in the following figure.

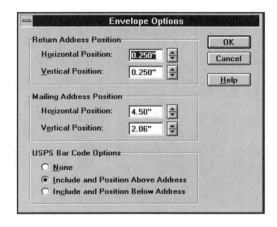

Use the Envelope Options dialog box to monkey around with your envelope.

3. In the USPS Bar Code Options group, select either Include and Position Above Address or Include and Position Below Address.

4. Select **OK** to return to the Envelope dialog box.

5. Print or insert the bar code.

Changing the Address Position

One of the most common problems you'll run into when printing envelopes is that the addresses often don't print where they're supposed to. For example, the mailing address might be too far down, or the return address might be too far to the left. If you don't like where WordPerfect for Windows is printing the return and mailing addresses on the envelope, you can adjust the address positions. Here's how:

1. Pull down the Format menu (or the Layout menu in version 6.0) and select the Envelope command to access the Envelope dialog box.

2. Select the Options button to display the Envelope Options dialog box.

3. Use the Return Address Position and Mailing Address Position groups to adjust the address positions. For the Horizontal Position spinners, enter a value in inches from the left edge of the envelope. For the Vertical Position spinners, enter a value in inches from the top edge of the envelope.

4. Click on **OK** to return to the Envelope dialog box.

5. Print or insert the envelope.

Working with Labels

Instead of printing an address directly on an envelope, you can place the address on a label and then stick the label on the envelope. This is handy if you're using envelopes that are too big to fit in your printer, or if you're using padded envelopes that could cause a printer to choke. Of course, there are many other uses for labels: name tags, floppy disks, file folders, your neighbor's cat. The next couple of sections show you how to define labels and enter text into them.

Defining Your Labels

Labels, of course, come in all shapes and sizes, from the relatively small file folder labels that hold only a line or two, to the much larger "full sheet" labels that can hold a short story. Whatever your needs, WordPerfect for Windows is up to the challenge because it comes equipped to handle literally dozens of different labels.

So the first thing you need to do is tell WordPerfect for Windows what kind of labels you'll be using. Start by pulling down the Format menu (or the Layout menu in version 6.0) and selecting the Labels command to display the Labels dialog box, shown in the following figure.

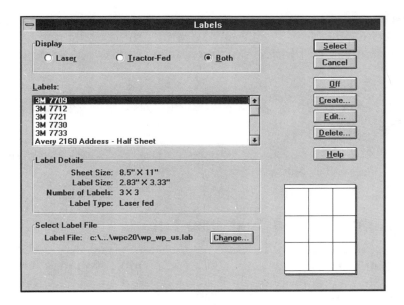

Use the Labels dialog box to let WordPerfect for Windows know what kind of labels you'll be using.

Use the Labels list to select the type of labels you're using. (Handily, WordPerfect for Windows' label names are the same as those used by the label companies.) To make sure you select the right labels, keep an eye on the boxes in the Label Details group; they'll tell you the size of each label and how many you can fit on a single page.

When you're done, choose the Select command. WordPerfect for Windows displays a single label, ready for you to type in your text.

To make the Labels list easier to navigate, you can reduce the number of labels displayed by selecting either Laser (to only display labels designed for laser printers) or Tractor-Fed (to only display labels designed for dot-matrix printers) in the Display group.

Typing Text in Labels

With your first label displayed, you can go ahead and enter your label text. A label is really just a mini-page, so you can enter and format your text as you normally would. When you want to start a new label, press

Ctrl+Enter to insert a hard page break. When you're done, you can print the labels just like a regular document. (See Chapter 9, "Getting It Down on Paper: Printing Documents," to get the poop on printing.)

As with envelopes, you'll likely have to monkey around with your labels to make sure they print properly. One highly useful feature to use with labels is the Center Pages option (discussed in Chapter 15, "Making Your Pages Look Good"). This feature centers your labels between the top and bottom margins.

Converting Existing Text into Labels

Instead of typing your label text from scratch, you may prefer to convert some existing text into labels. For example, you may have a document that contains a bunch of addresses, and you'd like to print each address on its own label. No problem. Here's what you do:

1. Position the insertion point at the beginning of the text you want to convert into labels.

2. Select the type of label you want to use, as described earlier in this section.

3. For each address (or whatever), move the insertion point to the beginning of the address and then press **Ctrl+Enter**. WordPerfect for Windows moves the text to the top of its own label.

The Least You Need to Know

This chapter showed you how to send your documents in style by using WordPerfect for Windows to create your envelopes and labels. Here's a rehash of the main events:

➤ Before defining an envelope, make sure you've selected the printer you'll be using.

➤ You can either enter the mailing address in the document, or wait until you display the Envelope dialog box. If you do put the address in the document, press **Enter** twice after the last line to make sure WordPerfect for Windows will find the address automatically. Alternatively, you can select the address.

➤ To define the envelope, pull down the Format menu and select the Envelope command. In the Envelope dialog box, enter the return address and the mailing address (if necessary), and select an envelope size.

➤ Select the Print Envelope button to print the envelope. To insert the envelope in the current document, select the Append to Doc button instead.

➤ To reduce costs in bulk mailings, include a USPS POSTNET bar code on your envelopes.

➤ To define labels, pull down the Format menu and select Labels. Highlight the labels you're using in the Labels list, and then choose Select.

Chapter 17

Other Ways to Look Good

In This Chapter

➤ Adding and formatting dates and times in a document

➤ Creating footnotes, endnotes, and comments

➤ Using hyphenation for fun and profit

➤ Working with different paper sizes

➤ Miscellaneous ways to fool people into thinking you know what you're doing

This chapter will be your formatting graduate school. Earlier chapters covered the grade school of formatting characters, the high school of formatting lines and paragraphs, and the college of formatting pages. Now you get to do graduate work with things like dates, footnotes, and hyphenation. Believe me, people will be *very* impressed. Will this be as hard as graduate school? No way. You'll still just be learning the basics in the same non-technical fashion that you've come to know and love.

Inserting the Date and Time into a Document

If you need to add a date to a document (if you're just starting a letter, for example), don't bother typing it yourself; let WordPerfect for Windows do it for you.

The first thing you need to do is select the date format you want to use. WordPerfect for Windows has no less than a dozen date and time formats, one of which is sure to satisfy your needs. To select one of these formats, pull down the Insert menu, select the Date command, and then select Date Format from the cascade menu. You'll see the Document Date/Time Format dialog box, shown in the following figure. Select the format you want to use from the Predefined Formats list, and then select **OK**.

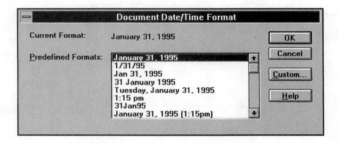

Use the Document Date/Time Format dialog box to select one of WordPerfect for Windows' umpteen date or time formats.

With your format selected, you're ready to insert the date or time. Position the insertion point where you want the date or time to appear, pull down the Insert menu, select **Date**, and then select one of the following commands from the cascade menu:

➤ Date Text   This command inserts the date as though you typed it yourself. (You can also insert the date as text by pressing **Ctrl+D**, or if you have version 6.1, by double-clicking either the date or the time in the status bar.)

➤ Date Code   This command inserts a special code that tells WordPerfect for Windows to always display the *current* date. This means that the date will change if you open the document tomorrow, next week, or next month. (The shortcut key for the date code is **Ctrl+Shift+D**.)

If the date or time that appears is wrong, don't blame WordPerfect for Windows; your computer is the one who's supposed to keep track of these things. If it's fallen down on the job, there's an easy way to fix it. Return to Program Manager, select the **Control Panel** icon from the **Main** group, and then select the **Date/Time** icon. In the Date & Time dialog box, enter the current date in the Date box (use the **mm/dd/yy** format) and the current time in the Time box (use the **hh:mm:ss** format). Select **OK** when you're done, and then exit Control Panel by selecting Exit from the Settings menu.

Adding Footnotes and Endnotes

One of the best ways to make people think you worked *really* hard on a document is to include *footnotes* at the bottom of the page. Footnotes say "Hey, this person took the time and effort to write this little paren-thetical note for my edification or amusement. I think I'll take her out to lunch." To make sure we're on the same page (so to speak), here are some concepts to keep in mind as you work through this section:

➤ A *footnote* is a section of text placed at the bottom of a page. Footnotes are convenient for the reader, but too many on one page can make your text look cluttered.

➤ An *endnote* is a section of text placed at the end of a document. Endnotes are less convenient than footnotes, but they're good for longer entries that would otherwise usurp too much space on a page.

➤ Both footnotes and endnotes usually contain asides or comments that embellish something in the regular document text.

➤ Each footnote is numbered, and each number appears in the document beside the text to which the footnote refers.

If you've ever tried adding footnotes to a page with a typewriter, you know what a nightmare it can be trying to coordinate the size of the note with the regular page text. And if you need to change your footnote numbers? Forget about it.

WordPerfect for Windows changes all that by making footnote creation as easy as typing text. The program arranges things so your pages accommodate any size footnote perfectly, and it'll even manage the footnote numbers for you—automatically!

Creating Footnotes and Endnotes

Since a footnote or endnote always refers to something in the regular text, your first task is to position the insertion point where you want the little footnote/endnote number to appear. Once you've done that, pull down the Insert menu and select either the Footnote or Endnote command. In the cascade menu that appears, select Create. WordPerfect for Windows displays a special typing area that shows you the footnote number. In addition, the Footnote/Endnote feature bar appears. (As a reminder, you work with the feature bar buttons either by clicking on them, or by holding down both **Alt** and **Shift** and pressing the button's underlined letter.)

Now all you do is enter your text (feel free to use any character or line formatting options). When you're done, select Close from the feature bar. WordPerfect for Windows returns you to the document and displays the same number at the insertion point position (see the figure below).

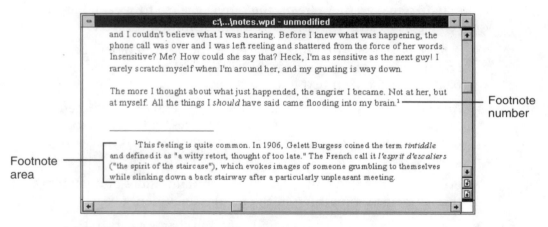

A WordPerfect document with a footnote.

Editing Footnotes and Endnotes

If you need to make changes to a footnote or endnote, select Footnote or Endnote from the Insert menu, and then choose Edit from the cascade menu. In the dialog box that appears, enter the number of the footnote or endnote that you want to edit, and then select **OK**. WordPerfect for Windows displays the appropriate edit screen for you to make your changes. Again, select Close when you're done.

Adding Snide Comments to a Document

When you're writing, you may need to make a quick note to yourself about something related to the text. Or other people may be reading your work on-screen, and they might want to make some snarky remarks for you to see. In either case, you can use WordPerfect for Windows' document comments feature to handle the job. A *comment* is text that appears in a box on-screen, but doesn't print out.

To add a comment, first position the insertion point where you want the comment to appear. Then select Comment from the Insert menu, and choose Create from the cascade menu. WordPerfect for Windows displays the comment editing screen (and of course, another feature bar) in which you can enter your text. You can also format the text and use the following feature bar features:

➤ Initials enters your initials in the comment. (See Chapter 28, "Customizing WordPerfect for Windows," to learn how to store your initials and your name permanently in WordPerfect for Windows.)

➤ Name enters your name in the comment.

➤ Date enters the current date.

➤ Time enters the current time.

When you're done, select Close to return to the document. If you're in Page mode, you'll see a small comment icon on the left of the screen. To see the comment, just click on this icon, and WordPerfect for Windows displays the note in a box, as shown in the following figure. If you're in Draft mode, the comment always appears in a box. If you need to edit a comment, either double-click on the comment icon (if you're in Page mode) or double-click on the comment box (in Draft mode).

One of the keys to productive writing is to build up some momentum. If you're on a roll, but you get stuck on a particular idea or phrase (or if you come across a fact you need to check), don't get bogged down trying to solve it. Ignore it for now and keep going; you can always come back later on and fix things up. Before moving on, though, you should probably make a quick note or two, just to get your ideas down so you don't forget them. Comments, of course, are perfect for this.

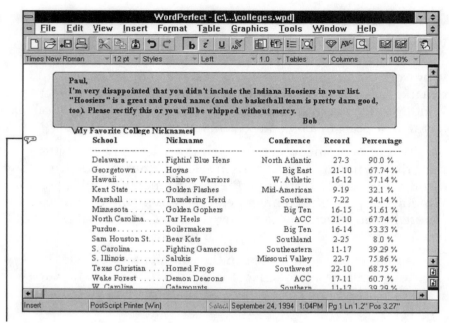

Comment icon

*You can add comments to your WordPerfect for Windows documents.
These comments don't appear when you print the file.*

Using Hyphenation to Clean Up Your Documents

As you've seen by now, WordPerfect for Windows' word wrap feature
really makes typing easier because you don't have to worry about a
looming right margin the way you do on a typewriter. If you're in the
middle of a word when you get to the margin, WordPerfect for Windows just moves the whole word to a new line. While this is convenient, it can make your document look ragged if the word is a large
one. For example, take a look at the first paragraph in the document
shown in the following figure.

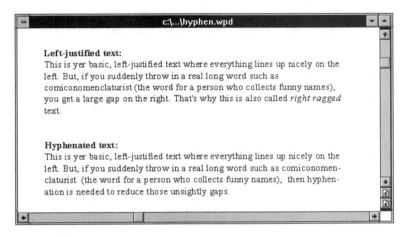

Left-justified text:
This is yer basic, left-justified text where everything lines up nicely on the left. But, if you suddenly throw in a real long word such as comiconomenclaturist (the word for a person who collects funny names), you get a large gap on the right. That's why this is also called *right ragged* text.

Hyphenated text:
This is yer basic, left-justified text where everything lines up nicely on the left. But, if you suddenly throw in a real long word such as comiconomenclaturist (the word for a person who collects funny names), then hyphenation is needed to reduce those unsightly gaps.

Hyphenation can reduce the gaps produced by some longer words.

As you can see, the second line has a large gap on the right because the next word—comiconomenclaturist—was too long to fit. One solution would be to use full justification, where text is aligned with both the left and right margins (see Chapter 14, "Making Your Lines and Paragraphs Look Good"). This often works, but you sometimes end up with lines that look unnatural.

Often, a better solution is to use *hyphenation*, where WordPerfect for Windows takes any long words that won't fit at the end of a line, splits them in two, and adds a hyphen. The second paragraph in the figure above is hyphenated.

Follow these steps to use hyphenation in your document:

1. WordPerfect for Windows adds hyphenation from the current paragraph down to the end of the document. Position the insertion point appropriately, or if you only want to hyphenate the current paragraph, select a block inside the paragraph (a letter or two will do).

2. Pull down the Format menu (or the Layout menu in version 6.0), select

If you just have a word or two you want to hyphenate, forget all this rigmarole. Instead, position the insertion point where you want the word broken, and press **Ctrl+Shift+–** (hyphen). This adds a so-called *soft hyphen*: if you alter the position of the word or margins, the soft hyphen disappears.

183

the Line command, and then select Hyphenation. The Line Hyphenation dialog box appears.

3. Make sure the Hyphenation **On** check box is activated and select **OK**. WordPerfect for Windows examines the text, and if it finds any suitable candidates for hyphenation, it displays the Position Hyphen dialog box that shows you where the hyphen will go.

4. If you don't like where WordPerfect for Windows is going to break the word, click inside the text box at the location you want the hyphen placed, or use the left or right arrow keys to move the hyphen's location.

5. Select Insert Hyphen to, well, insert the hyphen.

6. Repeat steps 4 and 5 for any more words WordPerfect for Windows wants to hyphenate.

Working with Different Paper Sizes

You'll probably do most of your work on good old 8 1/2-by-11-inch paper. However, should the mood strike you, WordPerfect for Windows enables you to set different paper sizes. For example, you could switch to 8 1/2-by-14-inch legal size, or envelopes, or just about anything you want. You can also select a different *orientation*. Normal orientation has the lines of text running parallel to the short side of the page, but if you prefer to have the lines run parallel to the long side of the page, you can.

When you print with the lines of text running parallel to the short side of the page, it is called portrait orientation. When you turn things around so that the lines of text run parallel to the long side of the page, it's called landscape orientation.

To change the paper size or orientation, select **Page** from the Format menu (or the Layout menu in version 6.0), and then select the Paper Size command. The Paper Size dialog box appears. Select a size from the **Paper** Definitions list. The Information area tells you everything you need to know about the highlighted paper. When you've got the one you want, choose the **Select** button. (If you plan to print any document for which you've changed the paper size, don't forget to add the appropriate paper to your printer.)

Blink-of-an-Eye Formatting with QuickFormat

Once you've applied some formatting to a section of text, you may like the results so much that you want to apply the same formatting to other chunks of text in the document. Isn't it a pain, though, to go through an elaborate formatting procedure for each section? Not anymore. WordPerfect for Windows has a QuickFormat feature that lets you copy the formatting from some existing text and apply it to another part of the document with only a couple of mouse clicks. Too good to be true? Nah, just follow these easy steps:

1. If you want to copy paragraph formatting, position the insertion point inside the paragraph you want to use. If you want to copy character formatting, select the text you want to use or just position the insertion point within the text.

2. Pull down the Format menu (or the Layout menu in version 6.0) and select **QuickFormat**. The QuickFormat dialog box appears, as shown in the following figure.

    You can also crank up the QuickFormat feature by clicking on this button in any Toolbar.

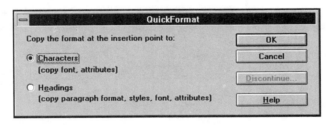

Use the QuickFormat dialog box to tell WordPerfect for Windows what formatting you want to copy.

3. Select either the Characters option (for character formatting) or the Headings option (for paragraph formatting), and then select **OK**. WordPerfect for Windows returns you to the document and adds a paintbrush to the mouse pointer.

4. Using your mouse, select the text to which you want to apply the formatting. You can repeat this for as many sections of text as your heart desires.

5. When you're done, select the Format menu's **QuickFormat** command again to cancel the QuickFormat.

Saving Trees with the Make It Fit Expert

WordPerfect for Windows version 6.1 has a new feature called the Make It Fit Expert, which you can use to cram an existing document into a specified number of pages. For example, suppose your document contains seven full pages, and the eighth page is only about one-third full. You could use the Make It Fit Expert to shrink the document so the whole thing fits onto seven pages. Here's how it works:

1. Pull down the Format menu and select the Make It Fit Expert command. WordPerfect for Windows displays the Make It Fit Expert dialog box, as shown in the following figure.

    You can also display the Make It Fit Expert dialog box by clicking on this button in the 6.1 WordPerfect Toolbar.

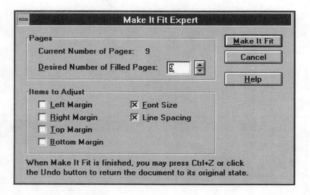

Use the Make It Fit Expert to wedge a document into a specified number of pages.

2. Use the Desired Number of Filled Pages spinner to enter the number of pages you want your document to end up with. (Although you'll usually enter a lower number than the current page count, you're allowed to enter the same number or a higher one.)

3. Use the check boxes in the Item to Adjust group to tell WordPerfect for Windows what kind of things to adjust. By default, the Expert adjusts the Font Size and the Line Spacing, but it can also adjust the margin sizes.

4. When you're done, select **Make It Fit** to begin. WordPerfect for Windows takes a few stabs at it, and then displays the shrunken (or expanded) document.

186

The Least You Need to Know

This chapter took you on a quick graduate course of some other WordPerfect for Windows formatting options. Here's a review before the final exam:

➤ To add either the date or the time to a document, pull down the Insert menu and select the Date command. In the cascade menu, select Date Text to insert a date that won't change, or Date Code to tell WordPerfect for Windows to always show the current date.

➤ Footnotes and endnotes are handy ways to add information to a document without cluttering the text. Select either Footnote or Endnote from the Insert menu, select Create, and then fill in the note. Select Close when you're done.

➤ Comments are an easy way to include notes to yourself or others in a document. Select Comment from the Insert menu, and then select Create from the cascade menu. When the editing screen appears, add your text and then select Close to exit.

➤ Use hyphenation to clean up some of the gaps caused by long words. Select the Format menu's Line command and then select the Hyphenation command.

➤ To work with a different paper size, select the Page command from the Format menu, and then select Paper Size. Pick out the paper you want to use from the dialog box that appears.

➤ To lighten your formatting chores, select the Format menu's QuickFormat command.

➤ To cram a document into a specified number of pages, use the Make It Fit Expert command from version 6.1's Format menu.

Chapter 18

Using Styles to Make Looking Good Look Easy

In This Chapter

➤ The advantages of using styles

➤ Creating your own personal styles

➤ Applying styles to document text

➤ Checking out WordPerfect for Windows' built-in styles

➤ Working with the handy style libraries

➤ Tip-top techniques that'll have you styling in no time

In the last few chapters, we've been looking at the progression of your formatting knowledge as being akin to working through the various levels of school. Since I enjoy beating a metaphor to death as much as the next person, we'll do the same in this chapter. However, you know enough by now that your formal formatting "education" is over; you're in the real world now (or the "RW" as business school types like to call it), where practical concerns outweigh theory. The real world has looming deadlines and meetings in 10 minutes, so you don't want to be fumbling around with lengthy formatting chores.

To that end, this chapter is presented in the spirit of books such as *What They Don't Teach You in Harvard Business School*. In our case, though, it'll be more like *What They Don't Teach You in Beginner WordPerfect for Windows Books*. Specifically, we'll be looking at *styles* and how they can knock even the most complex formatting task down to size. We'll begin by examining styles and learning just what the heck they are. I'll then show you the easy way to create your own styles, how to apply styles to any document text, and more.

What Is a Style and Why Should You Bother?

As you've seen throughout the chapters here in Part III, formatting is essential if you want to produce good-looking documents that get noticed. The problem is that formatting always seems to take up so much time (especially in WordPerfect for Windows).

Suppose you want to add a title to a document. Titles usually appear in a larger, sans-serif font, so you type the text, select it, and then use the Font command to set up the appropriate formatting (as explained back in Chapter 13, "Making Your Characters Look Good"). For good measure, you also center the title. It doesn't look bad, but you decide the text needs to be bold. So, you highlight the text again and make it bold. Things are looking good, but now you decide to use a larger type size. Once again, you highlight the text, and then you make the size adjustment. After fiddling with a few more options (maybe underlining or small caps would look good), you finally get the title exactly right. You've just wasted 10 minutes out of your busy day, but hey, that's the reality of working with WordPerfect for Windows, right?

Wrong. You don't have to stand for this! By learning how to use styles, you can accomplish the same chore in 10 *seconds*, instead of 10 minutes. How is that possible? Well, you see, a *style* is nothing more than a predefined collection of formatting and layout settings. WordPerfect for Windows comes with quite a few styles built-in, but it's also easy to create your own. For example, you could create a "Title" style that consists of, say, an 18-point, bold, underlined Times New Roman font, that's centered between the left and right margins. So to perform the same process that just took you ten minutes, you simply type your document title, select it, and apply the Title style. In the blink of an eye, WordPerfect for Windows formats the text as 18-point, bold, underlined Times New Roman, centered between the left and right margins. That's right: with a single command, WordPerfect for Windows can throw any number of character, line, or paragraph formatting options at the selected text.

Here's a short list of just some of the advantages to using styles:

➤ The most obvious, of course, is the time you'll save. Once you've invested the initial few minutes to create a style, applying any style takes only a few keystrokes or mouse clicks.

➤ You eliminate the trial and error that goes into many formatting chores. When you decide on a look that you like, you capture it in a style for all time.

➤ If you change your mind, however, you can easily edit a style. But if you do, will you have to go back and reapply the style throughout the document? No way. Any text formatted with that style is *automatically* reformatted with the revised style. This feature alone is worth the price of admission.

➤ You can create many different kinds of styles to handle all your needs—whether it's document titles, subtitles, headings, indented paragraphs, special text, whatever. WordPerfect for Windows places no practical restrictions on the number of styles you can create.

➤ Styles make it easy to create documents that have a consistent look and feel. In fact, it's not hard to set up an entire *style library*— a separate file that contains one or more style definitions. You can then access the library styles from any document.

➤ Styles reduce the number of keystrokes and mouse clicks you need to get your job done. In this age where repetitive strain injuries (such as carpal tunnel syndrome) are reaching almost epidemic proportions, anything that reduces the wear-and-tear on our sensitive anatomy is a welcome relief.

If it all sounds too good to be true, well, there is a downside: styles can save you so much time that you may run out of things to do during the day (pause while the laughter dies down).

Creating a Style the Easy Way

Well, since fine words butter no parsnips, as they say (no, they really do), let's get down to business and see how you create a style. The simplest way to go about this is first to format a section of text exactly the way you want it. You then create the style based on this formatting (this is called creating a style by example). Here are the steps you need to follow.

1. Using some existing text, enter the formatting options you want to include in the style. (You can use any of the formatting features we've looked at in the last few chapters.) When you're done, make sure the cursor is inside the formatted text.

2. Pull down the Format menu (or the Layout menu in version 6.0) and select Styles, or press **Alt+F8**. WordPerfect for Windows displays the Style List dialog box.

   You can also access the Style List dialog box by clicking on this button in the Format Toolbar.

3. Select Setup from the Options pop-up list, choose one of the following options from the Style Setup dialog box, and then select **OK**.

   Current Document   If you activate this option, you'll only be able to use this style in the current document.

   Default Template   If you activate this option, the style will be available for all your documents.

4. Select the QuickStyle button (or the QuickCreate button if you're using version 6.0). The QuickStyle dialog box appears, as shown in the following figure.

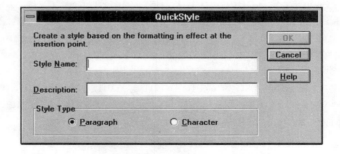

The QuickStyle dialog box appears when you select the QuickStyle button.

5. In the Style Name text box, enter a name for the style (you can enter a maximum of 12 characters).

6. In the Description text box, enter a brief description for the style. (This description appears in the Style List dialog box; it can make it easier to identify the style you want later on.)

To avoid conflicts, don't give your style the name of an existing style.

7. In the Style Type group, select the type of style you want:

Paragraph   When you apply this type of style, the formatting affects the entire paragraph containing the cursor (or the paragraphs containing the currently selected text).

Character   When you apply this type of style, the formatting affects only the selected text or any text typed from the current cursor position.

8. Select **OK**. WordPerfect for Windows returns you to the Style List dialog box and adds the new style to the **Name** list.

9. Select Close to return to the document.

The Easy Part: Applying a Style

Once you've defined a style, you can apply it to any text in the same document (if you chose the Current Document option) or in any other document (if you choose the Default Template option). Here's how you apply a style:

1. If you're applying a paragraph style, position the cursor inside the paragraph you want to format. (If you want to apply the style to multiple paragraphs, select a block that includes some text from each paragraph.) If you're applying a character style, select the text you want to format.

2. Pull down the Format menu (or the Layout menu in version 6.0) and select Styles, or press **Alt+F8** to display the Style List dialog box (see the following figure).

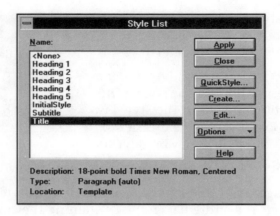

From the Style List dialog box, select the style you want to apply.

3. In the Name list box, highlight the style you want to apply.

4. Select the Apply button. WordPerfect for Windows applies the style.

For added convenience, the Power Bar also includes a Styles list, as shown here.

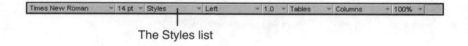

The Styles list

Making Changes to a Style

Hey, nobody's perfect, so occasionally you'll need to edit a style in order to add new formatting, change the existing formatting, or delete a format or two. The following steps show you what to do:

1. Pull down the Format menu (or the Layout menu in version 6.0) and select Styles, or press **Alt+F8** to display the Style List dialog box.

2. Use the Name list box to highlight the style you want to edit, and then select the Edit button. WordPerfect for Windows displays the Styles Editor, as shown in the following figure.

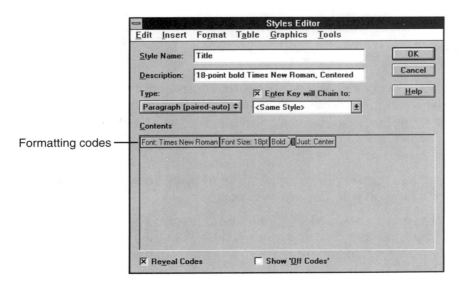

Formatting codes

Use the Styles Editor dialog box to make changes to a style.

3. Use the **Style Name** and **Description** text boxes to modify the name and description of the style, if necessary.

4. Use the **Type** pop-up list to modify the style type, if necessary. (Note: the **Document (open)** style applies the style from the current insertion point position to the end of the document.)

> You can use the Power Bar's Style list to display the QuickStyle dialog box easily. Just pull down the list and select the QuickStyle option.

5. Deactivate the **E**nter Key will Chain to check box if you want to press **Enter** within the style without turning the style off. If you leave this check box active, select one of the following options from the drop-down list:

> ➤ Select <None> to turn the style off when you press Enter.

> ➤ Select <Same Style> to restart the style in the next paragraph when you press Enter. (This is useful for styles where the first line of the paragraph is indented.)

> ➤ Select one of the other styles from the drop-down list if you want to use the style after you press Enter. For example, you

might have a Title style and a Subtitle style. In most cases, you'd probably want the Subtitle style to immediately follow the Title style.

6. The Contents box shows the codes that correspond to the style's formatting options. For example, the code **Font Size: 18pt** represents a type size of 18 points. Similarly, the **Just: Center** code represents Center justification. Use the following techniques to modify these codes:

   ➤ In most cases, you can change an existing code by double-clicking on it to display its dialog box.

   ➤ To insert a new code, use the pull-down menus to select the appropriate formatting options (just as though you were formatting document text). If you want to insert the code before an existing code, click on the existing code first.

   ➤ To delete a code, drag it outside the Contents box.

7. Select **OK** to return to the Style List dialog box.

8. Choose Apply to apply the revised style (remember, though, that WordPerfect for Windows automatically reformats any text that was previously formatted with that style); otherwise, select Close to return to the document.

You can also use the Styles Editor to create a style from scratch. In the Style List dialog box, click on **Create** and then fill in the Styles Editor options as described in this section.

Using System Styles to Avoid Reinventing the Wheel

Before you go off on some kind of style-creating frenzy, you should check out WordPerfect for Windows' *system styles*. The system styles (as opposed to *user styles* that you create yourself) are built-in styles that come with WordPerfect for Windows. They cover everything from headers and footers to headings and footnotes.

To see these styles for yourself, access the Style List dialog box, and then select **Setup** from the Options pop-up list. In the Style Setup dialog box that appears (see the following figure), activate the System Styles check box, and then select **OK**. WordPerfect for Windows returns you to the Style List dialog box and displays a seemingly endless list of new styles.

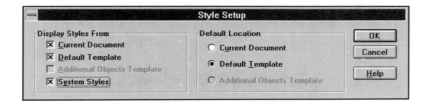

WordPerfect for Windows displays the Style Setup dialog box when you select Setup from the Options list.

You're free to use these system styles just like any other style (by applying them to your documents, or even by editing them to suit your taste). If you want to examine a system style before you use it, highlight it and select the Edit command. When you've seen what havoc the style will wreak upon your text, select **Cancel** to return to the Style List dialog box.

Working with Style Libraries

When you create your own styles, WordPerfect for Windows gives you an all or nothing choice. If you create the style for the current document only, you can't use it for any other document; if you create the style in the default template, the style is available for every document.

But you may want to create different sets of styles for different types of documents. You could create certain styles for memos and letters, and then create completely different styles for, say, newsletters or flyers. Instead of fumbling through millions of different styles trying to find the one you want, you should create a *style library*. A style library is a special file that exists on this earth only to store styles. Once you've created a library, you can then *assign* it to a document, and like magic, all the stored styles become instantly available. So, for example, you could create a library of newsletter styles, and only open this library when you're working on a newsletter. The next couple of sections show you how to save your styles in a library and how to access library styles.

Depositing Styles in a Library

To save the styles you've created in a library, access the Style List dialog box and then, in the Options pop-up list, select the Save As command. In the Save Styles To... dialog box that appears (see the following figure), use the Filename text box to enter a name for the file. Make sure the User Styles option is activated, and then select OK.

Use the Save Styles To... dialog box to enter a name for your style library.

Check Out Time: Accessing Library Styles

The whole purpose of creating style libraries, of course, is so you can access your carefully defined styles from other documents. To do this, display the Style List dialog box, and then follow these steps:

To make it easier to work with your style libraries, make sure you give them an extension different from what you normally use for your documents. Most people use the extension .STY (for example, STYLES.STY).

1. In the Options pop-up list, select the Retrieve command. The Retrieve Styles From dialog box appears.

2. Use the Filename text box to enter the name of the style library file you want to use. If you're not sure about the name, click on the list button to the right of the Filename text box, and then use the Select File dialog box to pick out the file. (WordPerfect for Windows stores style library files in the WPWIN directory, by default.)

198

3. Select **OK**. If the style library contains a style with the same name as an existing style, a dialog box appears asking if you want to overwrite the current styles.

4. Select **Yes**. WordPerfect for Windows returns you to the Style List dialog box and displays the library styles in the Name list box.

The Least You Need to Know

This chapter showed you how to use styles to make formatting a breeze. Here's a quick review of your newfound know-how:

➤ A style is a predefined collection of formatting and layout options.

➤ Styles save time by reducing formatting chores to a few keystrokes or mouse clicks. They also enable you to produce consistently formatted documents, and they make it easy to modify a document's formatting.

➤ To display the Style List dialog box, pull down the Format menu and select the **Styles** command, or press **Alt+F8**.

➤ To create a new style, add the appropriate formatting to the document, and then select **QuickStyle** in the Style List dialog box.

➤ To apply a style, position the cursor or select a text block, highlight the style you want in the Style List, and then choose Apply.

➤ To save styles in a style library, choose Save As from the Options pop-up list in the Style List dialog box, and then enter a name for the library file (be sure to include an extension such as .STY).

Part IV
Fiddling with Your Files

The topics in this part look at the "forest" of your files as a whole, rather than the "trees" of the individual characters, words, and pages. In this bird's-eye view, you'll learn how to work with multiple files and document windows (Chapter 19), how to manage files directly from WordPerfect for Windows (Chapter 20), and how to wield the ever-so-handy QuickList and QuickFinder features (Chapter 21).

MOMENTS IN COMPUTER HELL #607:

MISSING THE SAVE

WINICK

Working with Multiple Documents

In This Chapter

➤ The fastest ways to switch between open documents

➤ All about windows

➤ Moving, sizing, closing, and arranging windows

➤ Fascinating juggling lore to think about while playing with all those documents

Remember the minor juggling craze that bounced around the country a few years ago? Well, your faithful scribe was one of many who jumped on that strange bandwagon. No, I didn't become any kind of expert (or run off and join the circus), but I did learn the basic three-ball pattern. I've kept it up to this day—and will, on a dare, attempt to juggle three of just about anything (which, believe me, has scared the heck out of many a party hostess).

If you missed that particular craze, WordPerfect for Windows lets you do some juggling of your own because you can open as many as *nine* documents at the same time. (Nine is a lot of documents, but it's still short of the official world's record for juggling, which is a mind-boggling *eleven* rings at once.) This not only lets you work with several documents simultaneously, but it's great for quickly comparing two or more documents, or pasting info between files. Best of all, everything's blindingly simple, as you'll soon see.

Switching Among Multiple Documents

Opening several documents is easy. Select the File menu's Open command to display the Open File dialog box, and then select the files you need from the Filename list. Here's a recap of the techniques you can use to make multiple selections in a list:

➤ If the files you need are listed consecutively, click on the first file, hold down **Shift**, and then click on the last file.

➤ For random files, hold down the **Ctrl** key and click on each file.

➤ If you prefer the keyboard, highlight the first file, press **Shift+F8**, and then for the other files you need, highlight each one and press the **Spacebar**. When you're done, press **Shift+F8** again.

Once you have your files open, you need some way of switching among them. WordPerfect for Windows gives you three methods:

➤ If you can see any part of the document's window, click on it. (I'll explain what a "document window" is in the next section.)

➤ Pull down the **Window** menu and select the document from the list that appears at the bottom of the menu.

➤ Hold down **Ctrl** and tap **F6** to cycle backward through the documents. To cycle through the documents in the order that you opened them, hold down **Ctrl** and **Shift** and tap **F6**.

Multi-Document Possibilities

One of the benefits of multiple open documents is that you can share text among them. There are endless uses for this capability, but here's a sampler:

➤ You could take sections of a report and use them in a memo or letter.

➤ If you have one or more files organized as a project, you could take chunks out and use them to create a summary document.

➤ You could create a document to hold boilerplate (bits of often used text), and keep it open all the time. You could then copy stuff from the file (or add more things to it) at will.

The good news is that this is all extremely simple to do. Here are the basic steps:

1. Open the appropriate files, and display the document that has whatever text you need.

2. Block the text. (If you need some blocking basics, refer to Chapter 11, "Block Partying: Working with Blocks of Text.")

3. Use the appropriate Edit menu command to cut or copy the text. (This was also covered in Chapter 11.)

4. Switch to the document into which you want to place the text.

5. Position the insertion point where you want the text to appear, and then paste it.

WordPerfect for Windows' Adjustable Windows

As I've said, every time you open a document, WordPerfect for Windows sets up and displays the file in a new work area. In WordPerfect for Windows, these work areas are called *windows*. This makes some sense, I suppose. After all, at any one time, the screen can only show you a part of a document, so it's like looking through a window at your text.

The window in which you're currently working is called the **active window**.

You can think of your computer as a room with nine different windows. As you've just seen, you can display a document in any of these windows, and you can switch among them.

Framing a Window

The problem with windows is that normally you can look through only one at a time on your screen. It would be nice, on occasion, to be able to see maybe a couple of documents at the same time. Sound impossible? Hah! With WordPerfect for Windows' *window frames*, it's easier than you think. What does framing do? Well, it puts a border around a window and lets you do all kinds of crazy things. For instance, you can:

➤ Change the size of the window.

➤ Move the window to a different location.

➤ Make the window really small so it's out of the way.

➤ Make the window really big so you can't see anything else.

To access this voodoo, you can either pull down the document's Control menu (by pressing **Alt+-** (hyphen) or by clicking on the document's Control-menu box, as pointed out in the figure below) and then select **Restore**, or you can click on the **Restore** button (also shown in the following figure). (Why are we *restoring* the window? You'll find out later in this chapter.)

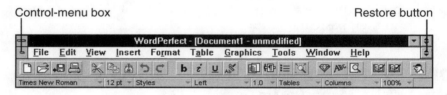

The Control-menu box and Restore button for a document.

As you can see in the following figure, your window becomes smaller, and it suddenly sprouts a border with various funny symbols on it.

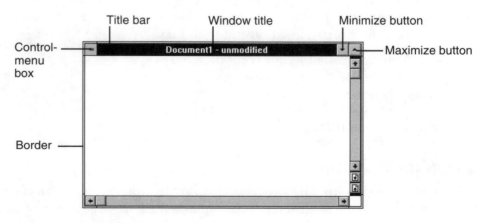

A document window.

Anatomy of a Window

Here's a summary of the new features you get when you frame a window. (I'll talk about things like moving and sizing windows later in the chapter.)

Window title   This tells you the name of the document.

Title bar   You can use this area to move the window with a mouse.

Border   This is the window's frame. You use it to change the size of the window with a mouse.

Maximize arrow   You use this arrow to increase the window to its largest extent (the normal window view you've been using until now).

Minimize arrow   This arrow shrinks the window to an icon.

Control-menu box   You can use this object to move and size a window with your keyboard.

Adjusting Your Windows

Okay, so now you know how to frame a window. I know what you're thinking: How does this affect *me*? Well, it's quite simple, really: a framed window is an *adjustable* window, which means you can move it around, make it different sizes, and more. In other words, you have *control* over what you see on your screen. The next few sections show you how to take advantage of that control.

Once you start playing around with windows, you'll often end up with a bunch of them scattered willy-nilly about the screen. And when that happens, you may forget which one is the active window. Here are two active window indicators you can look for:

➤ The blinking insertion point

➤ The title bar with the darker color

Sizing Up Your Windows

If you'd like to see a couple of windows on-screen at the same time, one way to do it is to change the size of each window so they both fit.

This is (by far) easiest with a mouse, but the keyboard will do in a pinch. The secret to sizing a window with the mouse is to use the *borders* that appear when you frame the window. Here's what you do:

1. Position the mouse pointer over one of the window borders according to the following guidelines:

If you decide you don't want the window resized after all, just press **Esc.**

   ➤ If you want to change the width of the window, move the pointer over the left or right border.

   ➤ If you want to change the height of the window, move the pointer over the top or bottom border.

   ➤ If you want to change the width and height at the same time, move the pointer over one of the window corners.

   In each case, you'll know the mouse pointer is positioned correctly when it changes to a two-headed arrow (see the following figure).

2. Hold down the left mouse button and then move the mouse to drag the border. As you drag, WordPerfect for Windows displays a gray outline to show you the new size, as shown in the following figure.

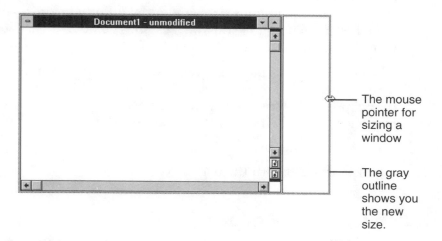

The mouse pointer for sizing a window

The gray outline shows you the new size.

To size a framed window with a mouse, drag one of the window's borders.

3. When things look about right, release the mouse button. WordPerfect for Windows dutifully redraws the window in the new size.

   If you prefer to use the keyboard, you need to follow these steps:

1. Switch to the window you want to size.

2. Press **Alt+-** (hyphen) to open the document's Control menu and then select the **S**ize command. A gray outline appears around the window.

3. Use the arrow keys to size the window outline.

4. Once the outline is the size you want, press **Enter**. WordPerfect for Windows redisplays the window in the new size.

Windows on the Move

One of the problems with having several windows open at once is that they have a nasty habit of overlapping each other. Instead of cursing WordPerfect for Windows' ancestry, you can try moving your windows around so they don't overlap (or so they overlap less).

Things are, once again, *way* easier with a mouse:

1. Position the mouse pointer over the window's title bar. The pointer changes to an arrow this time.

2. Hold down the left mouse button and drag the window's title bar. As you do, WordPerfect displays a gray outline of the window.

3. When you have the outline where you want it, just release the mouse button. WordPerfect redisplays the window in the new location.

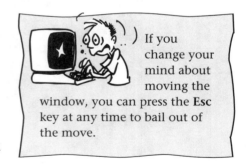

If you change your mind about moving the window, you can press the **Esc** key at any time to bail out of the move.

Here's the drill if you prefer to use a keyboard:

1. Switch to the window you want to move.

2. Press **Alt+-** (hyphen) to open the document's Control menu and then select the **M**ove command. A gray outline appears around the window.

3. Use the arrow keys to move the window outline.

4. Once the outline is in the location you want, press **Enter**. WordPerfect for Windows redisplays the window in the new location.

Letting WordPerfect for Windows Do the Work: Cascading and Tiling

All this moving and sizing stuff is fine for people with time to kill. But the rest of us just want to get the job done and move on. To that end, WordPerfect for Windows includes a Cascade command and a couple of Tile commands that'll arrange your windows for you automatically. (Speaking of having time to kill, did you know that the world's record for the longest time juggling three objects without a drop is a mind-numbing 8 hours, 57 minutes?)

The Cascade command arranges your open windows in a spiffy diagonal pattern that puts the active window on top and shows only the title bars of the other open windows (see the figure below). This is good for those times when you want things nice and neat, but you don't need to see what's in the other windows. To cascade your windows, pull down the **Window** menu and select the Cascade command.

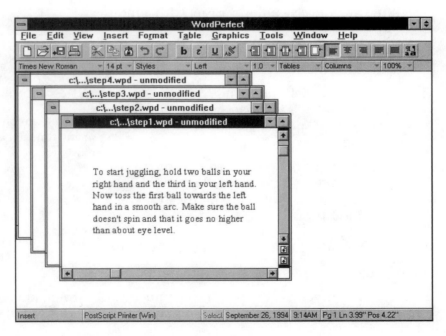

Some windows arranged in a cascade pattern.

Tiling divides up your screen and gives equal real estate to each window. The **Window** menu's Tile Horizontal command stacks the open windows one on top of the other with the active window at the top (see the following figure). The Tile Vertical command lines up the windows side by side with the active window on the left. (If you're using version 6.0, the **Window** menu has only one Tile command.)

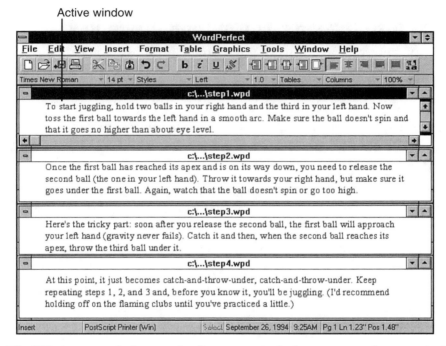

Active window

The Tile command gives each of your open windows an equal amount of screen space.

This pattern lets you work in one window and still keep an eye on what's happening in the other windows (you never know what those pesky little devils might be up to).

The Minimalist Approach: How to Minimize a Window

You'll often find you have some windows you know you won't need for awhile. You could move them out of the way or make them smaller. However, that takes time, and our goal is always to make things as easy as possible. Fortunately, there's an alternative: you can *minimize* the window down to a mere icon of its former self.

If you use a mouse, you can minimize a window in no time at all, simply by clicking on the window's **Minimize** button (the one pointing down).

It takes a bit more effort if you're using the keyboard. In this case, press **Alt+-** (hyphen) and then select the Minimize command from the Control menu.

Taking It to the Max: Maximizing a Window

If you get tired of all this frame monkey business, you can *maximize* a window to its normal size.

If you use a mouse, all you have to do is click on the window's **Maximize** button (the one pointing up). From the keyboard, press **Alt+-** (hyphen) and then select the Maximize command.

Restoring a Window

When you maximize or minimize a window, Windows is smart enough to remember what the window used to look like. It does this so you can easily restore the window to its previous size and position.

With a mouse, you have two ways to restore a window:

➤ If you maximized the window, the Maximize button now appears with double arrows. This is called the Restore button (makes sense, doesn't it?). Simply click on this button to revert the window to its previous state.

➤ If you minimized the window, you restore it by double-clicking on its icon.

From the keyboard, you need to use one of these methods:

➤ To restore a maximized window, pull down its Control menu and select the **Restore** command.

➤ To restore a minimized window, pull down the **Window** menu and select the document from the list.

Closing a Window

You can use the Control menu to close a window quickly with your mouse. (This is the same as selecting the File menu's Close command.) All you do is double-click on the Control-menu box. If you've made changes to the document, WordPerfect for Windows will, of course, ask you to save them as it normally does.

You can also close a window by pressing **Ctrl+F4**.

The Least You Need to Know

This chapter gave you the lowdown on using multiple documents in WordPerfect for Windows. You learned some basic techniques for switching among open documents, and for using WordPerfect for Windows' window frames. Here's the highlight film:

➤ To switch between documents, either select the one you want from the list at the bottom of the **Window** menu, or press **Ctrl+F6** to cycle through the documents.

➤ To display a frame around a document window, click on the **Restore** button, or press **Alt+-** (hyphen) and select Restore from the Control menu.

➤ To size a framed window, drag its borders. You can also select Size from the Control menu and then use the arrow keys.

➤ To move a framed window, drag the title bar to the location you want. From the keyboard, select the Control menu's Move command and then move it with the arrow keys.

➤ If you'd prefer WordPerfect for Windows to arrange your windows for you, open the **Window** menu and choose from the Cascade, **Tile** Horizontal, and Tile Vertical commands.

➤ To reduce a window to its smallest size, click on the **Minimize** button or select Minimize from the Control menu. To increase a window to its largest size, click on the **Maximize** button or select the Control menu's Maximize command.

Chapter 20

Managing Files in WordPerfect for Windows

In This Chapter

➤ A quick briefing on files and directories

➤ Setting up WordPerfect for Windows to work with files

➤ Copying, moving, renaming, and deleting files

➤ Creating and deleting directories

➤ A snappy analogy designed to knock some sense into all this DOS mumbo-jumbo

Most people run Windows programs not only because the fancy-shmancy graphics look good on the screen, but because they don't want to have to deal with DOS. For some, the very *idea* of the DOS prompt is enough to induce big-time fear and loathing.

But the truth is, sooner or later (hopefully later), you're going to have to deal with DOS in some way. You're going to need to copy or rename a file, create a directory, or delete the hard disk detritus that has accumulated over the years.

But friends, I'm here today to tell you there's good news. I'm here to tell you that, yes, you have to deal with DOS—but, no, you don't have to deal with DOS *directly*. WordPerfect for Windows has built-in features that tame the DOS beast, and while they may not make this stuff any more pleasant, they do make it easier. This chapter tells you everything you need to know.

Files and Directories: A Brief Primer

When people ask me to explain files and directories to them (well, no, it doesn't happen all *that* often), I always tell them to think of their computer as a house. Not just any old house, mind you, but one with all kinds of servants waiting to do their bidding. (People usually start warming up to the analogy at this point.) The inside of the house—you can think of this as your computer's hard disk—has maids, valets, cooks, and so on; these are the programs (such as WordPerfect for Windows) installed on the hard disk. Outside the house there are gardeners, landscapers, and chauffeurs; these are the devices attached to the computer (such as the keyboard, printer, or modem).

In the simplest possible terms, your computer's *files* are equivalent to the various elements inside the house. As I've said, the people (the servants) are the files that run your programs. The inanimate objects in the house—the furniture, appliances, utensils, and so on—are the data files (such as WordPerfect for Windows documents) that you or your software use.

Imagine, for a moment, that this house had no rooms, and that all the stuff inside was just scattered randomly throughout. Clearly, trying to *find* anything in such a place would be, if not impossible, at least frustrating. The problem, of course, is that there's no organization. A normal house has many different rooms, and usually everything in one room is related in one way or another. So, if you were looking for either cooking utensils or food, you'd probably look in the kitchen instead of the bedroom. (I said *probably*.)

Your computer's hard disk also contains a number of "rooms," and these are called *directories*. In a properly organized hard disk, each directory normally contains a number of related files. For example, your WordPerfect for Windows directory contains all the files (and, possibly, some of your documents) that WordPerfect for Windows uses. You may also have separate directories for other programs installed on your computer.

Let's extend the analogy a little further. Some rooms in a house have a smaller room attached to them (such as a walk-in closet in a bedroom, or a dining room in a living room). Even storage spaces like pantries and cupboards are "room-like" because they store objects. These are examples of what we could call "subrooms." Directories can also have "subrooms," and these are called—you guessed it—*subdirectories*. Your main WordPerfect for Windows directory has a number of subdirectories. In particular, it probably has a WPDOCS subdirectory that you've been using to store all your documents.

The "Directory Dialog" Approach to Managing Files

Windows comes with a program called File Manager that's designed to handle your file and directory maintenance chores. However, if all you need to do is rename a file or create a directory, it's a pain to have to switch back to Program Manager, start File Manager, perform the operation, and then return to WordPerfect for Windows.

To avoid this drudgery for basic DOS operations, WordPerfect for Windows uses the "directory dialog" approach. This just means that any dialog box that lets you select a file (such as Open File or Save As) already shows much of the same information that File Manager does. So why not let people manage their files right from these dialog boxes? It's more convenient, and by adding a few customization options, you can set up these dialog boxes to make file management a breeze.

In the examples that follow, I'll be using the Open File dialog box. This one's a safe choice because the worst that can happen is that you open a file. If you use, say, the Save As dialog box, you might accidentally save your current document under a new name or in a new location.

Customizing the Directory Dialog Boxes

You can make your file drudgery easier by altering the directory dialog boxes with a few simple customization options. To check these out, select the File menu's Open command (or press **Ctrl+O**) and then select the Setup button. You'll see the Open/Save As Setup dialog box, shown in the following figure.

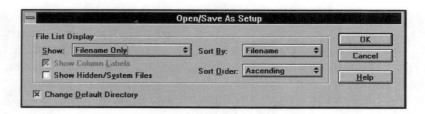

Use the Open/Save As Setup dialog box to customize the Open File and Save As dialog boxes for file management.

The various options in the File List Display group let you customize the appearance of the Filename list in the Open File and Save As dialog boxes. Here's a summary of the available controls:

➤ **Show** This pop-up defines what stuff you see in the file list. You normally see only the file names, but you can also choose to display the file's size and the date and time it was last modified, or you can display "descriptive" names. I'll be showing you how to add descriptive names to your documents in Chapter 27, "A WordPerfect for Windows Miscellany."

➤ **Sort By** This pop-up determines how WordPerfect for Windows sorts the file list. Filename is the default option, but you can also sort by Extension, Size, Date/Time, Descriptive Name, or Descriptive Type.

➤ **Sort Order** Select either an Ascending sort (from A to Z) or a Descending sort (from Z to A).

The Open/Save As Setup dialog box also has a Change Default Directory check box. In a directory dialog box, the "default" directory is the one that WordPerfect displays when you first open the dialog box. For example, when you display the Open File dialog box, the default directory is usually OFFICE\WPWIN\WPDOCS. If you've activated the Change Default Directory check box and you change directories, WordPerfect for Windows assumes that you want the new directory to become the default for the dialog box. If this isn't what you want, be sure to deactivate the Change Default Directory dialog box.

Managing Your Files

Okay, let's see how you actually do some of this file managing that I've been going on and on about. The following sections take you through some of the more common tasks that'll crop up from time to time. I'm going to assume you're already in the Open File dialog box, that you've taken the requisite deep breaths, and so on.

Sneaking a Peek at a Document

I *hate* opening the wrong document. It means that not only have I wasted the time it took to open the file, but now I have to close it and go hunting around for the correct one. What a bother. Happily, you can avoid this fate by actually taking a peek at the file before you open it. Just highlight the file in the Filename list and select the View button. WordPerfect for Windows opens the Viewer window and displays the file (see the following figure). If you want to view other files, you can leave the Viewer window open and pick out the new file from the Open File dialog box.

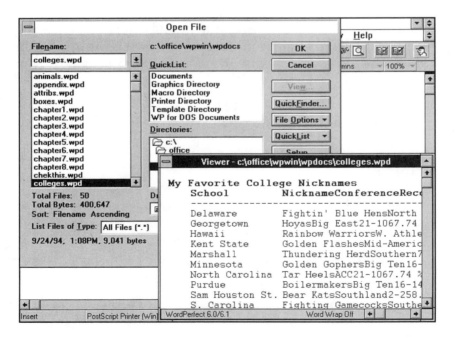

You can use the Viewer window to eyeball a file before opening it.

If you want to see more of a file displayed in the Viewer window, activate the window and then use the usual WordPerfect for Windows navigation keys, or if you have a mouse, the scroll bar. (This is all covered in Chapter 8, "Day-to-Day Drudgery II: Navigating Documents.")

The Viewer has a few options you can use to make your life a bit easier. Right-clicking inside the Viewer window displays a QuickMenu of commands. Here's a summary of the more useful ones:

Find   This command displays the Find dialog box so you can look for a word or phrase in the document. You can also display the Find dialog box by pressing **F2**. (To learn more about the inner workings of the Find feature, double back to Chapter 12, "Search and Ye Shall Replace.")

Font   This command displays a stripped-down version of the Font dialog box (which we looked at back in Chapter 13, "Making Your Characters Look Good"). You can use this to change the font displayed in the Viewer window. Pressing **F9** will also bring up the Font dialog box.

Print   This command displays a modified version of the Print dialog box (see Chapter 9, "Getting It Down on Paper: Printing Documents"). You can also display the Print dialog box by pressing **F5**.

Word Wrap   This command toggles the Viewer window's word wrap feature on and off. When Word Wrap is off, each line can extend beyond the Viewer window's right border. If Word Wrap is on, the Viewer displays each line in full within the window's confines.

When you're done with the Viewer, press **Alt+F4** to return to the directory dialog box you're using.

Coping with File Copying

Copying is one of the most common file tasks. For example, you might want to copy some files to a floppy disk to give to a colleague. If you need to copy some files to a floppy disk or to another directory, just follow these steps:

1. Highlight the files you want to copy.

2. In the File Options pop-up list, select the Copy command. You'll see either the Copy File dialog box (if you're copying a single file) or the Copy Files dialog box (if you're copying multiple files; see the following figure).

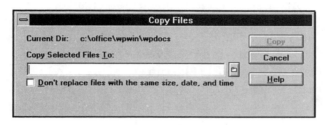

Copy Files

Current Dir: c:\office\wpwin\wpdocs

Copy Selected Files <u>T</u>o:

☐ <u>D</u>on't replace files with the same size, date, and time

Copy
Cancel
<u>H</u>elp

Use the Copy Files dialog box to copy a bunch of files to a new location.

3. In the Copy File dialog box, enter the destination for the file in the **To** text box. For the Copy Files dialog box, use the Copy Selected Files **To** text box. To be safe, always include the drive and directory. For example, to copy to a floppy disk in drive A, you'd enter A:\.

4. If you're copying to a floppy disk, place the disk in the appropriate drive.

5. To save some time, you can activate the **Don't** replace files with same size, date, and time check box. This tells WordPerfect for Windows not to bother replacing one file with another that's exactly the same.

6. Select the Copy button to start the copy process.

7. If a file with the same name already exists in the destination directory, WordPerfect for Windows displays the Confirm File Replace dialog box to ask if you want to replace the file. If you're sure you don't need the other file, select Yes. If you're copying multiple files, you can select the Yes to All button to avoid being pestered again.

Before you select Yes when you're asked if you want to replace a file, make sure you're sure. Once you overwrite a file, it's gone for all time.

Mucking About with File Moving

When you copy a file, the original remains as is, and WordPerfect for Windows makes a clone of the file in the drive and directory you specify. When you move a file, however, WordPerfect for Windows first copies the file to the destination, and then it *deletes* the original file. Why is this useful? Well, suppose you create a new directory (which I'll tell you how to do in a sec) called LETTERS to hold only those WordPerfect for Windows documents that are letters. If you already have some letters in your WPDOCS directory, you'll want to move them to the new LETTERS directory. By moving them instead of copying them, you avoid cluttering your hard disk with redundant files.

To move a file, highlight it in the Filename list, and then select the Move command from the File Options pop-up. From here, you follow the same steps that I outlined in the last section for copying. There is one caveat, however: Don't try to move a file that's already open, or WordPerfect for Windows will display an error message.

Giving a File a Better Name

Those arcane file naming rules that DOS imposes on us (which we slogged though back in Chapter 7, "Day-to-Day Drudgery I: Saving, Opening, and Closing") make it hard to give your documents meaningful names. (Although, as I've mentioned, WordPerfect for Windows lets you add "descriptive names" to your documents; see Chapter 27, "A WordPerfect for Windows Miscellany.") The good news is that if you don't like a document's current name, you're free to change it to something else anytime you like. Here's how to rename a file:

Don't move or rename any files in your main WordPerfect for Windows directories (unless it's a document you created yourself). WordPerfect for Windows expects things to be named a certain way, and if something is off by even a letter, the program will complain something fierce (or it may refuse to run altogether).

1. If the file you want to rename is already open in WordPerfect for Windows, close it, and if necessary, save your changes.

2. Open the File menu and select Open to display the Open File dialog box.

3. In the Filename list, highlight the file you want to rename.

4. Select the Rename command from the File Options pop-up list. WordPerfect for Windows displays the Rename File dialog box.

5. In the To text box, enter the new name for the file. (If you don't include a drive and directory with the file name, WordPerfect for Windows renames the file in whatever directory is listed as the **Current Dir** at the top of the dialog box.)

6. Select the **Rename** button. WordPerfect for Windows renames the file.

Deleting Files

As you're learning WordPerfect for Windows, you'll probably create all kinds of garbage files while you practice the program's features. This is fine, but after awhile these files can really clutter up your hard disk, which makes finding stuff in the directory dialog boxes a real needle-in-a-haystack exercise. You can use the Delete option to do periodic housecleanings. Just highlight the file or files you want to scrap, and then select Delete from the File Options pop-up (you can also just press the **Delete** key). When WordPerfect for Windows asks you to confirm the deletion, select the Delete button.

Unless you have special undelete software (or at least version 5 of DOS), deleted files are gone for good, so you should be absolutely sure you can live without a file before you expunge it. If you have any doubts whatsoever, use the Viewer window to take a gander at the file's contents. (If you have DOS 5 or later and you do happen to delete a file accidentally, you may be able to recover it. To learn how, I'd suggest picking up a copy of *The Complete Idiot's Guide to DOS* by the most excellent Jennifer Fulton.)

Creating Directories

You can add new rooms to your computer house by creating new directories. First select the directory under which you want the new directory to appear. For example, to add a directory called C:\OFFICE\WPWIN\MARGE, you'd first select the C:\OFFICE\WPWIN directory. Then you select Create Directory from the File Options pop-up list. In the Create Directory dialog box that appears, use the New Directory text box to enter the name for the new directory. Then select Create to get things going.

The Least You Need to Know

This chapter gave you a quick tour of WordPerfect for Windows' file management fun. Here's a brief rundown of what was important:

➤ WordPerfect for Windows lets you use directory dialog boxes such as Open File or Save As to manage your files.

➤ Select the Setup button to customize the dialog box for easier file management.

➤ To work with a file, highlight it and then select a command (Copy, Move, Rename, and so on) from the File Options pop-up.

Chapter 21

Finding Files Quickly with QuickLists and QuickFinder

In This Chapter

➤ A brief primer on wild-card characters

➤ How to create a QuickList

➤ Using a QuickList to display a subset of your documents

➤ How to create a QuickFinder index

➤ Using QuickFinder to find a file

➤ Gaining the upper hand on your documents (before they gain the upper hand on you)

If you use WordPerfect for Windows regularly, you probably create at least a few documents a week, if not a few documents a day. While this doesn't sound like much, over time you can easily end up with dozens or even hundreds of WordPerfect for Windows files littering your computer's hard disk. Before things get completely out of hand, you need to start thinking about how you're going to handle all that verbiage.

The directory dialog boxes can help separate the wheat from the chaff (by deleting old files, or moving files to different locations; see Chapter 20, "Managing Files in WordPerfect for Windows," for details), but it's not a total solution. This chapter examines two features that can make it easier to keep a handle on your files: QuickList and QuickFinder.

File Name Flexibility: Understanding Wild-Card Characters

Before we check out what QuickLists and QuickFinder can do, it'll help immensely if you know what *wild-card characters* are. If you've ever played poker, you know you can designate one or more cards to be "wild," and they can then assume any value during the game. WordPerfect for Windows' wild-card characters operate in a similar fashion, only they're designed to give you more flexibility when dealing with file names.

Why do we need such flexibility? Well, as you'll see later on in this chapter, both QuickLists and QuickFinder deal with subsets of the files on your hard disk. With wild-card characters, it's easy to specify exactly the file names you want to work with. (Don't sweat it if this isn't all that clear to you now; things should come nicely into focus as we go along.)

WordPerfect for Windows has two wild-card characters—the question mark (?) and the asterisk (*). The question mark matches a single character. When you insert a question mark in a file name, you're saying "I wanna deal only with certain files that have any character at this position." For example, *letter?.wpd* would cover any file name where the first six characters are *letter*, the seventh character is anything at all, and the extension is *.wpd* (such as LETTER1.WPD, LETTER2.WPD, LETTERS.WPD, and so on).

Remember, though, that the ? can match only a single character. So *letter?.wpd* wouldn't include a file name such as LETTER57.WPD (because there are two characters between *letter* and *.wpd*). One way to handle these kinds of situations is to just add more question marks. For example, *letter??.wpd* would cover all file names that begin with *letter*, end with *.wpd*, and have anything for *both* the seventh and eight characters.

The asterisk matches multiple characters. For example, **.wpd* covers all files that have any primary name (the part to the left of the dot), and the extension *.wpd* (such as CHAPTER.WPD, WORF.WPD, or WHATS_UP.WPD).

To help this stuff sink in, here are a few examples that show wild cards in action:

File specification	What you get
?o?ato.wpd	All file names where the first and third characters are anything, the second character is *o*, the fourth through sixth characters are *ato*, and the extension is *.wpd* (such as TOMATO.WPD and POTATO.WPD, but not POTATOE.WPD).
letter?.*	All file names that begin with *letter*, have anything for the seventh character, and have any extension (such as LETTER5.WPD or LETTERS.WP). This example shows that it's perfectly okay to combine the two wild-card characters.
c*.txt	All file names that begin with *c* and have the extension *.txt* (such as CHAP_1.TXT and CRIMINY.TXT).
memo.*	All file names where the primary name is *memo* and any extension (such as MEMO.WPD and MEMO.DOC).
.	Files with any primary name and any extension (every file).

When you combine names such as **.wp*, *letter?.wpd*, and **.** with the drive and directory of the files, you end up with something called a **file specification**, because it specifies exactly which files you want to work with. (The cognoscenti, however, almost always abbreviate this to "file spec"—and pronounce it *file speck*.) For example, consider the following file specification:

c:\office\wpwin\wpdocs*.wpd

This refers to all files with the .WPD extension in the OFFICE\WPWIN\ WPDOCS directory on the C drive. (If you're a little leery of directories, I'd suggest taking a look at Chapter 20, "Managing Files in WordPerfect for Windows," to learn the basics.)

Working with QuickLists

A QuickList is a file listing narrowed down to only those files with certain names. If you recall our computer house analogy (you know, the one we looked at in Chapter 20, "Managing Files in WordPerfect for Windows," where your computer is like a house, and the objects inside the house are like the files are your hard drive; yeah, *that* computer house analogy), a normal directory list would be like looking at a complete inventory of, say, the kitchen's contents. A QuickList for the kitchen, however, might include only the appliances or utensils.

For example, suppose you write a quarterly report for your company, and you always name the report something like 3RDQTR94.WPD, 1STQTR95.WPD, and so on. You could create a QuickList of, say, only those reports from 1994 (???QTR94.WPD). Then, instead of wading through all your other documents to find the report you want, you could narrow things down by displaying the QuickList.

Displaying the QuickList Files

WordPerfect for Windows comes with several predefined QuickLists that you can use to display a subset of files. Here's a summary:

QuickList	Displays files in:
Documents	C:\OFFICE\WPWIN\WPDOCS subdirectory
Graphics Directory	C:\OFFICE\WPWIN\GRAPHICS subdirectory
Macro Directory	C:\OFFICE\WPWIN\MACROS subdirectory

QuickList	Displays files in:
Printer Directory	C:\OFFICE\SHARED\WPC20 subdirectory
Template Directory	C:\OFFICE\WPWIN\TEMPLATE subdirectory

To display the files in a QuickList, first open a directory dialog box. (For example, select the File menu's Open command to display the Open File dialog box.) In the **QuickList** box (see the following figure), double-click on the QuickList you want to use. (If you're using version 6.0 and you don't see a QuickList box, select the Show **B**oth command from the QuickList pop-up.)

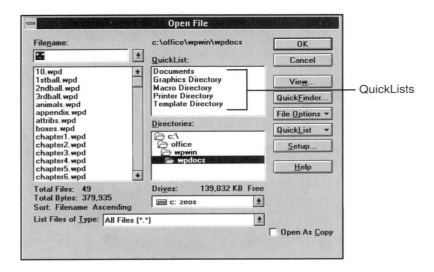

QuickLists

The QuickList box displays all your QuickLists.

Adding a QuickList Item

If WordPerfect for Windows' QuickLists don't cut the mustard, you can easily add your own. Here are the steps required:

1. In the QuickList pop-up, select the Add Item command. WordPerfect for Windows displays the Add QuickList Item dialog box, as shown in the following figure.

*Use the Add QuickList Item dialog box to enter a description and file specifi-
cation for your QuickList.*

2. Use the Directory/Filename text box to enter the file specification
   for the files you want to appear in the QuickList. Here are some
   guidelines to follow:

   ➤ Always begin the file specification with the letter of the disk
      drive that contains the files (this will almost always be the
      drive you used to install WordPerfect for Windows—usually
      C) followed by a colon (:).

   ➤ After the colon, enter the name of the directory in which the
      files can be found. Be sure to include backslashes (\) between
      the directory names.

   ➤ (Optional) Finish the specification with the file name/wild
      card combination that defines the files you want to see. If
      you want to see all the files in the directory, however, just
      leave off the file name part; WordPerfect for Windows will
      assume you want to see every file in the directory.

3. Use the Description text box to enter a brief description of the
   files that will appear in the QuickList (for example, **My 1994
   Quarterly Reports**). You can enter up to 40 characters, so there's
   lots of room to be creative (which will also make it easier to find
   your QuickLists).

4. When you're done, select **OK** to return to the QuickList dialog
   box.

There's no problem if you need to make changes to a QuickList.
Just display the Open File dialog box, highlight the QuickList
you want to modify, and then select the Edit Item command
from the QuickList pop-up menu. The Edit QuickList Item

dialog box that appears is identical to the Add QuickList Item dialog box you saw earlier.

If you're sick and tired of a particular QuickList entry and you want to get rid of it, all you need to do is highlight it in the QuickList box, and then select Delete Item from the QuickList pop-up menu. When WordPerfect for Windows asks if you're sure you want to delete it, select Yes.

Trying QuickFinder On for Size

Way back in Chapter 12, "Search and Ye Shall Replace," I showed you how to hunt down text in the current document using WordPerfect for Windows' Find feature. A slightly different scenario occurs when you want to find (and usually open) a document the name of which you can't remember, but you're sure it contains some specific words or a particular phrase. For example, you may be trying to find your Christmas list from last year, and you know it contains the word "Super Soaker." You can't use Find, of course, because the document isn't open yet; you could use the Viewer in a directory dialog box to take a sneak peek at each of your documents, but I assume you've got better things to do over the next week or so. So what's a body to do?

I'm glad you asked. WordPerfect for Windows' QuickFinder feature can create an alphabetical index of every word contained in your documents. It's then an easy matter to search this index for, say, "Super Soaker," and WordPerfect for Windows will display a list of every file containing this phrase. Pretty slick, huh? The next few sections show you how to work with QuickFinder.

Creating a QuickFinder Index

The first step is to create the alphabetical index of words from your documents. As you'll see, QuickFinder is quite flexible about the whole thing, enabling you to create different indexes for different subsets of files.

To define your QuickFinder index, follow these steps:

1. In any directory dialog box, select the QuickFinder button. The QuickFinder dialog box appears.

2. Select the Indexer button. WordPerfect for Windows displays the QuickFinder File Indexer dialog box.

231

3. Select the Create button. Now the Create Index Name dialog box appears (see the following figure).

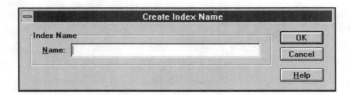

Use the Create Index Name dialog box to create a QuickFinder index.

4. Use the Name text box to enter a brief description for the index. For example, if you'll be including all your documents in the index, enter **All My Documents**. When you're done, select **OK** to return to the Create Index dialog box.

5. In the Add Directory (and File Pattern) text box, enter a file specification that defines which files you want to include in the index. For example, to include every file in WordPerfect for Windows' WPDOCS subdirectory, type **C:\OFFICE\WPWIN\WPDOCS**.

6. Select the Add button. WordPerfect for Windows adds the file specification to the Directories to Index list.

7. If you want to add other directories and files to the index, repeat steps 5 and 6.

8. Select the Generate button. WordPerfect for Windows then creates the indexes by marching through each of your documents and alphabetizing each word it finds. (Depending on the number of files you're using and the speed of your computer, this may take as little as a few seconds, or as much as a few minutes.) When it's done, WordPerfect for Windows displays a dialog box telling you how many files were indexed and some other useless info.

9. Select **OK** to return to the QuickFinder File Indexer dialog box.

10. Select Close to return to the QuickFinder dialog box.

11. If you want to perform a search, skip to the next section. Otherwise, select Close to return to the document.

Using a QuickFinder Index to Find a File

Once you've created a QuickFinder index, you can use it to search for documents that contain specific words or phrases. Here are the steps to follow:

1. If necessary, display the QuickFinder dialog box, as described in the last section.

2. Make sure the Search In pop-up list displays QuickFinder Index.

3. If you've defined multiple QuickFinder indexes, use the Search In drop-down list to select the one you want to use.

4. In the Search For text box, enter the text you want to find.

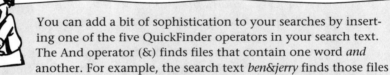

You can add a bit of sophistication to your searches by inserting one of the five QuickFinder operators in your search text. The And operator (&) finds files that contain one word *and* another. For example, the search text *ben&jerry* finds those files that contain the word *ben* and the word *jerry*. The Or operator (|) finds files that contain one word *or* another. For example, the search text *ben|jerry* finds those files that contain either the word *ben* or the word *jerry*. The Not operator (!), like the by now overused expression from *Wayne's World*, finds files that do not contain a specific word. For example, if you enter *!ben* as the search text, QuickFinder finds those files that don't contain the word *ben*. The other two operators are already familiar to you: the question mark (?), which matches a single character, and the asterisk (*), which matches multiple characters.

5. Select Find. WordPerfect for Windows scours the index and then displays the Search Results List showing all the files that contain the text you specified (see the following figure). If the search text was not found, a different dialog box appears to let you know. In this case, select **OK** to return to the QuickFinder dialog box.

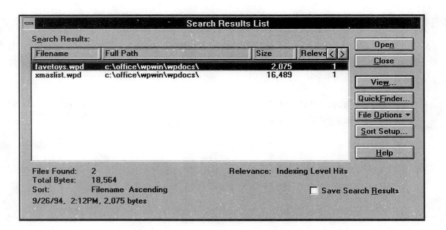

If WordPerfect for Windows finds any files that contain your search text, it displays them in the Search Results List.

6. If you want to open one of the files, highlight it and then select the Open button. (You can also select View to check out the file, or you can use the commands in the File Options pop-up list to work with the selected file; see Chapter 20, "Managing Files in WordPerfect for Windows," for details on these commands.) Otherwise, select Close to return to the Open File dialog box.

Updating a QuickFinder Index

Life goes on, of course, after you create a QuickFinder index. In particular, you'll still be creating new documents and editing existing ones. This is fine, but it means that your QuickFinder indexes will no longer accurately reflect the words in your documents. To fix this problem, you need to update the index, as described in the following steps:

1. In a directory dialog box, select the QuickFinder button to display the QuickFinder dialog box.

2. Select the Indexer button. WordPerfect for Windows displays the QuickFinder File Indexer dialog box.

3. In the Index Names list, highlight the index you want to update.

4. Select the Generate button. The Index Method dialog box appears.

5. Select one of the following index methods and select **OK**:

Update Index With New or Modified Files   This option makes the update go faster, but it slows down your QuickFinder searches.

Index All Files   This option takes longer to update, but it keeps your QuickFinder searches operating at top speed.

6. Select Close to return to the QuickFinder dialog box.

The Least You Need to Know

This chapter showed you the basics of two of WordPerfect for Windows' handiest tools: QuickLists and QuickFinder. Let's take a fond look back at some of the chapter's more memorable moments:

➤ Understanding wild-card characters is crucial for getting the most out of QuickLists and QuickFinder. The question mark (?) matches individual characters, and the asterisk (*) matches multiple characters.

➤ A QuickList is a listing of files that has been narrowed down so it includes only files with names that match a particular file specification.

➤ To display a QuickList's files, double-click on the QuickList item in the QuickList box.

➤ To add a new QuickList item, select Add Item from the QuickList pop-up list.

➤ To create an index, select the QuickFinder button, select the Indexer button, and then select Create.

➤ To use a QuickFinder index to find a file, select the QuickFinder button, enter your search text in the Search For text box, and then select Find.

Part V
Wielding WordPerfect for Windows' Tools

At this stage of your WordPerfect for Windows wanderings, you know enough to create and print reasonably polished documents that will look good in just about any setting. But if that was all there was to WordPerfect for Windows, it wouldn't be as popular as it is (and nowhere near as expensive, either!). No, this baby is brimming with fancy-shmancy features, most of which are for hard-core word jockeys (and so have little to do with the likes of you and me). However, there are a few of these features that not only can add an extra level of sophistication to your documents, but that can even make it easier to work with WordPerfect for Windows. Too good to be true? Nah. Just try on the nine chapters in this section for size, and you'll see!

Chapter 22

Using the Spell Checker and Thesaurus

In This Chapter

➤ Checking your spelling with Spell Check

➤ Handling unusual capitalizations and duplicate words

➤ Using WordPerfect for Windows' Thesaurus

➤ A downright fascinating collection of word words

Words. Whether you're a logophile (a lover of words) or a logophobe (one who has an aversion to words), you can't leave home without 'em. Whether you suffer from logomania (the excessive use of words) or logographia (the inability to express ideas in writing), you can't escape 'em. So far, you've seen ways to edit words, ways to organize them, and ways to get them all dressed up for the prom, but when it comes down to using them, well, you've been on your own. Now that changes, because in this chapter you'll learn about a couple of tractable tools—Spell Check and Thesaurus—that'll help you become word-wise (or perhaps even word-perfect). Who knows? With these tools in hand, you may become a full-fledged logolept (a word maniac).

Check

Nothing can ruin the image of your finely crafted documents more than a few spelling mistakes. In the old days, we could just shrug our shoulders and mumble something about never being good at spelling. With WordPerfect for Windows, though, you have no excuses because the darn program comes with a utility called Spell Check—a built-in spelling checker. Spell Check's electronic brain is stuffed with a 100,000-word strong dictionary that it uses to verify your spelling attempts. If it finds something that isn't right, it lets you know and gives you a chance to correct it. You can even make Spell Check smarter by adding your own words to its dictionary.

Cranking Up Spell Check

Here are the steps you need to follow to perform a spell check on your text:

 You should save your document before running Spell Check. Not only might you be making a lot of changes to the document, but it takes time—and if a power failure should hit, you'd lose all your changes.

1. Select the text you want spell checked:

    ➤ If you want to check the entire document, you can skip to step 2 because Spell Check scours the whole document by default.

    ➤ If you'd prefer to restrict Spell Check to a small chunk of text, make sure you select the text before starting Spell Check. For example, if you only want to check the spelling of a single word, select the word. (Remember that the quick way to select a word is to double-click on it. For more handy block selection shortcuts, see Chapter 11, "Block Partying: Working with Blocks of Text.")

    ➤ The Spell Check in version 6.1 can also check text box text in a dialog box. In this case, make sure the insertion point is inside the text box you want to check.

2. Start Spell Check using one of the following methods:

    ➤ Pull down the Tools menu and select the Spell Check command.

    ➤ Press **Ctrl+F1**. (If you're checking the text in a text box, you can only start Spell Check by pressing **Ctrl+F1**.)

➤ Right-click inside the typing area and select Spell Check from the QuickMenu.

➤ 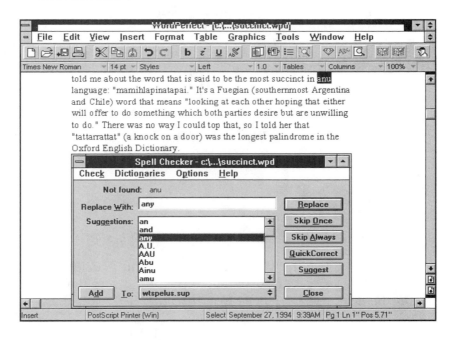 Click on this button in the 6.1 WordPerfect Toolbar.

3. If the Spell Checker dialog box appears and the Replace With text box is blank, it means Spell Check hasn't started doing its thing yet. You need to prod it by selecting the Start button.

4. If Spell Check finds something amiss in your document, it highlights the word in the text and displays the word in the Spell Checker dialog box, along with some suggested alternatives, as shown below.

The Spell Checker dialog box appears when Spell Check finds a word that's not in its vocabulary.

At this point you have the following options:

➤ If you want to use one of Spell Check's suggestions, highlight the word in the Suggestions list and select the Replace button.

➤ If you don't see the word you want among Spell Check's alternatives, you can type your own in the Replace With text box and then select Replace.

➤ If you want WordPerfect for Windows to correct the misspelling automatically in the future, highlight the appropriate correction in the Suggestions list and then select the QuickCorrect button. (I'll explain what QuickCorrect is all about later in this chapter.)

➤ If the word Spell Check doesn't recognize is perfectly legitimate (such as your name, your company's name, or too-hip words such as *cowabunga*), you can select Skip Once to skip this instance of the word, Skip Always to skip all instances of the word in the document, or Add to include the word in Spell Check's vocabulary.

5. You'll need to repeat step 4 each time Spell Check finds an aberrant spelling. When it's gone through the entire document (block, text box, or whatever), you'll see the Spell Checker dialog box shown in the following figure.

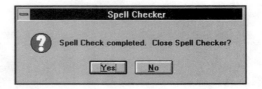

Spell Check displays this dialog box when its checking chores are done.

6. Select Yes to return to the document. If you'd prefer to stay with Spell Checker (say, to set some of the options we'll be looking at in the next section), select No, instead.

When using Spell Check, keep in mind that Spell Check is good, but it's not *that* good. In particular, it won't flag words that are merely *misused* (as opposed to misspelled). For example, Spell Check is perfectly happy with either "we're going wrong" or "were going wrong," since everything is spelled correctly. For this grammatical stuff, see Chapter 23, "Painless Grammar Checking."

Setting Spell Check's Options

Spell Check comes with a few options that control how it performs its duties. Here's a quick rundown of some of the more useful commands on the Options menu:

Words with Numbers If your document contains words with numbers in them (such as *Fireball XL-5*), turn off this command to tell Spell Check not to flag these sorts of words.

Duplicate Words When you activate this option, Spell Check looks out for the same word twice in in a row (like that). In this case, Spell Check highlights the second word and displays the Spell Checker dialog box. Select **R**eplace to fix the problem. If the duplication is okay (for example, Pago Pago or "Tora, Tora, Tora!"), select Skip **O**nce.

Irregular Capitalization If you leave the Shift key down a split second too long, you'll end up with words like "SHift" and "TIerra del FUego." When this command is activated, Spell Check flags these unusual capitalizations and displays some suggestions. Again, choose the correct capitalization from the Suggestions list, and then select **R**eplace.

Auto Replace When this command is active and you replace one word with another, Spell Check automatically replaces every other occurrence of the misspelled word with the correct one.

Auto Start When this command is active, Spell Check dives right into its checking routine when you start it up.

Recheck All Text Spell Check is smart enough to know how much of a document it has already checked. So, in subsequent spell checks, it only goes through those parts of the document that it hasn't looked at. Activating this command forces Spell Check to go back and check the entire document.

You can also use the commands in the Check menu to tell Spell Check how much of the document you want it to go through. Most of these commands are straightforward (**W**ord, **S**entence, and so on), but three deserve a bit of explanation:

While Spell Check is a handy tool, its big problem, of course, is that it won't tell you the meaning of a word. For that, you're going to have to rely on a good old-fashioned dictionary, and since Spell Check isn't infallible, don't treat it as a substitute for a thorough proofreading.

Page This command checks only the page where the insertion point is currently located. For this command to function properly you need to do two things: position the insertion point inside the page you want to check, and turn off the Auto Start command in the Options menu (this gives you a chance to activate the **Page** command before the spell check begins).

To End of Document This command checks the text from the current insertion point position to the end of the document. Again, you need to place the insertion point accordingly, and you need to deactivate the Auto Start command.

Number of Pages This command lets you restrict the spell check to a certain number of pages, beginning with the current page. When you select this option, the Number of Pages dialog box appears. Enter the number of pages to check in the spinner provided, and then select **OK**.

The Magic of QuickCorrect

Few of us are expert typists, so we all have a word or two that we constantly fumble. For me, it's *accommodate*; I can never seem to remember the correct number of c's and m's. Another common typing malady is transposing two letters in the heat of battle: typing *teh* instead of *the*, for example. In the past, I used to go back and correct the obvious errors, and then I'd just leave the rest, assuming Spell Check would bail me out later on.

This is not the most efficient way to work. Going back to correct mistakes just slows you down and can ruin a perfectly good train of thought. And having Spell Check constantly correct the same words over and over gets old very quickly.

These are common enough problems that the WordPerfect for Windows programmers, bless their nerdy hearts, decided to do something about them. They reasoned that if many people repeatedly botch the same words, why not have WordPerfect for Windows keep an eye out for these misspellings and fix them automatically? The result (which was first introduced in version 6.0a) was QuickCorrect—a utility that can actually correct your spelling on the fly! No guff. Go ahead and type *teh* and then press the **Spacebar**. See? QuickCorrect automatically corrected your typing to *the*. Is that wild or what? Here are some other misspellings to try out: *adn, don;t, occurence, sieze*. In fact, QuickCorrect is programmed with well over a hundred common spelling gaffes. (I was tempted to say that QuickCorrect was like having one of your high school English teachers constantly looking over your shoulder, but the very idea of such a thing gave me the willies.)

Of course, not everybody makes the same mistakes. We all have our personal spelling pet peeves, and there are bound to be some that aren't in QuickCorrect's list. The good news is that you can easily add your own. Here's how it's done:

1. Pull down the Tools menu and select the **QuickCorrect** command (or press **Ctrl+Shift+F1**). WordPerfect for Windows displays the QuickCorrect dialog box, as shown in the following figure.

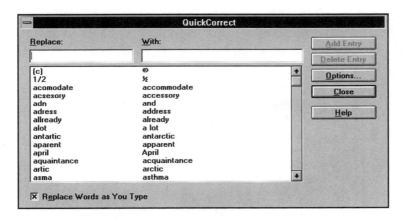

Use the QuickCorrect dialog box to add your own entries to QuickCorrect's list.

2. In the **Replace** text box, enter the incorrect spelling of the word you want to add to the list.

3. In the **With** text box, enter the correct spelling of the word.

4. Select the Add Entry button. QuickCorrect adds the word to its list.

5. Repeat steps 2–4 to add other words to the list.

6. When you're done, select Close.

Using the Splendiferous Thesaurus

Did you know that the English language boasts about 616,500 words (plus about another 400,000-or-so technical terms)? So why use a boring word like *boring* when gems such as *prosaic* and *insipid* are available? What's that? Vocabulary was never your best subject? No problemo. WordPerfect for Windows' built-in Thesaurus can supply you with enough synonyms (words with the same meaning) and even antonyms (words with the opposite meaning) to keep even the biggest word hound happy.

Starting the Thesaurus

To see what the Thesaurus can do, place the insertion point inside a word, pull down the Tools menu, and then select Thesaurus (or press **Alt+F1**). WordPerfect for Windows highlights the word and then displays the Thesaurus dialog box, shown in the next figure.

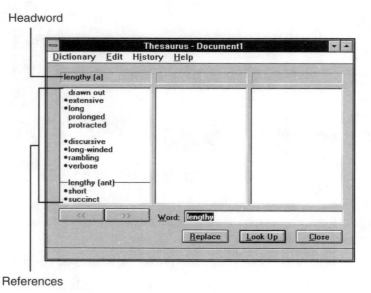

The Thesaurus dialog box.

The Thesaurus displays your word at the top of the first column and displays a list of words beneath it. Depending on the word you used, the list will be divided in up to four different sections: adjectives (a), verbs (v), nouns (n), and antonyms (ant). You can use the up or down arrow keys or the scroll bar to navigate the list. If you see a word you'd like to use instead of the original, highlight it and select the Replace button.

Displaying More Words

Not all of the reference words will have exactly the same meaning as the headword. You can often get more ideas by asking the Thesaurus to display the synonyms for one of the reference words. To do this, just highlight the reference word and press **Enter**, or double-click on it. The Thesaurus displays a new list of words in the next column.

The word at the top of the column is called the **headword**. The words in the list are called **references**.

If you like, you can keep repeating this process to get new lists of words in other columns as well. To navigate between the columns of words, use the left and right arrow keys, or click on the left and right arrows in the Thesaurus dialog box. If you get lost among the columns, pull down the History menu and select the headword you want to switch to.

The Least You Need to Know

This chapter showed you how to get control of your words with WordPerfect for Windows' Spell Check and Thesaurus utilities. Here's a quick review for the logofascinated:

➤ To start Spell Check, select **S**pell Check from the Tools menu, or press **Ctrl+F1**.

➤ To correct a spelling mistake found by Spell Check, either edit the word in the Replace **W**ith box or highlight one of Spell Check's suggestions, and then select **R**eplace.

➤ If Spell Check flags a word that is actually spelled correctly, you can select the A**d**d button to include the word in Spell Check's vocabulary.

➤ The QuickCorrect feature fixes spelling errors on the fly. To add your own frequently misspelled words to QuickCorrect's list, pull down the Tools menu and select QuickCorrect, or press **Ctrl+Shift+F1**.

➤ WordPerfect for Windows' Thesaurus can give you a list of synonyms and antonyms for a word. Just place the insertion point inside the word and select the Tools menu's Thesaurus command, or press **Alt+F1**.

Chapter 23

THIS WON'T HURT A BIT...

Painless Grammar Checking

In This Chapter

➤ About Grammatik, WordPerfect for Windows' grammar checker

➤ Using Grammatik to check your documents interactively

➤ Fixing (or ignoring) grammatical errors

➤ Allowing for different writing styles

➤ Idiot-proof grammar checking that absolutely doesn't require you to know a thing about predicates or prepositions

---

Grammar ranks right up there with *root canal* and *tax audit* on most people's Top Ten Most Unpleasant Things list. And it's no wonder: all those dangling participles, passive voices, and split infinitives. One look at that stuff and the usual reaction is "Yeah, well split this!"

If you're like me, and couldn't tell a copulative verb from a correlative conjunction if your life depended on it, help is just around the corner. WordPerfect for Windows comes with a tool that will *check your grammar for you.* That's right, this utility—it's called Grammatik—will actually analyze your document phrase by phrase, sentence by sentence, and tell you if things aren't right. It'll even tell you how to fix the problem, and often will be able to do it for you at the press of a key. It's about as painless as grammar gets, and it's the subject of this chapter.

Using Grammatik: The Basic Steps

Without further ado, here are the basic steps to follow to use this Grammatik thing:

1. Open or switch to the document you want to check.

2. Position the cursor appropriately:

   ➤ If you're checking a sentence or paragraph, place the insertion point inside the sentence or paragraph.

   ➤ If you're checking a block, select the block.

   ➤ If you want Grammatik to check everything from the insertion point to the end of the document, make sure the insertion point is where you want it to be.

3. Pull down the Tools menu and select the Grammatik command, or press **Alt+Shift+F1**.

    You can also start Grammatik by clicking this button in the 6.1 WordPerfect Toolbar.

4. Tell Grammatik how much of the document to check by pulling down Grammatik's Check menu and activating one of the following commands: Sentence, Paragraph, Document (this is the default command), To End of Document, or Selected Text.

 If Grammatik starts checking before you get a chance to activate a command in the Check menu, you need to tell it to hold its horses. You do this by pulling down the Preferences menu, selecting Environment, and then deactivating the Start checking immediately check box. You don't have to bother with this if you always want Grammatik to check the entire document.

5. If the Grammatik dialog box appears, but nothing's happening, select the Start button to get things under way.

6. If Grammatik finds a problem, it displays the Grammatik dialog box shown in the following figure.

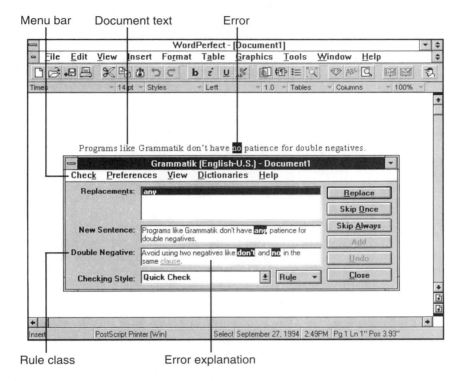

The Grammatik dialog box shows you the grammar gaffe you've made.

7. Handle the error (as described later in this chapter), and continue checking the document.

8. When the grammar check is complete, a dialog box appears to ask if you want to close Grammatik (see the following figure). Select Yes to return to the document. If you'd rather hang around in Grammatik (if, for example, you'd like to play around with some of the program options we'll be discussing later on), select No to return to the Grammatik dialog box.

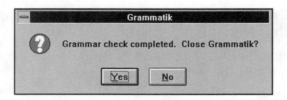

Grammatik displays this dialog box when it's finished carping about your grammar.

The Lay of the Grammatik Land

The Grammatik dialog box gives you lots of info, so it helps to know what the heck you're looking at. Here's a summary of the various sections:

Menu bar   These menus enable you to control Grammatik's settings.

Rule class   Grammatik divides grammar problems into more than 60 different types or *classes*. This line tells you which class the current problem falls under (for example, **Double Negative**).

Error explanation   This shows you the grammar faux pas that caused Grammatik to go "tsk, tsk." It also tells you what Grammatik thinks you ought to do about it.

Some of Grammatik's explanations can get pretty technical. If you feel brave enough, you can look up some of the more arcane terms. If the error explanation has a word or phrase in green, underlined text, you can display a definition of the term by clicking on it. You can also pull down Grammatik's Help menu and select the Grammar and Writing command.

New Sentence   This box sometimes shows you Grammatik's corrected version of the sentence containing the error.

Replacements   This is where Grammatik suggests replacements for the errant prose. You'll see this only on certain types of problems.

Handling Grammatik's Errors

Once Grammatik displays an error, you need to decide what to do with it. In some cases, the problems Grammatik finds are the result of a typing mistake. In this case, you can edit the document text directly by clicking inside the typing area and then making your changes. When you're done, click on the **Resume** button in the Grammatik dialog box.

In other cases, Grammatik may flag problems in a rule class that you don't care about. For example, Grammatik usually scolds you for using clichés in your writing. If you happen to *like* using clichés, you can tell Grammatik to shut up about them. You do this by selecting the Turn Off command from the Rule pop-up list (or, if you're using version 6.0, by deactivating the Rule Class check box) the next time a cliché error appears.

The rest of your choices are handled by the buttons in the Grammatik dialog box:

Replace   This button tells Grammatik to fix the problem using its suggested replacement. If the problem is a spelling error, you'll see a list of possible words in the Replacements box. In this case, highlight the word you want and press **Enter**.

Resume   If you pause Grammatik (say, to edit some text in the document), this button cranks Grammatik back up again.

Skip Once   This button tells Grammatik to bypass this instance of the error and move on.

Skip Always   This button (one of my favorites) tells Grammatik to just ignore the error altogether.

Add   If Grammatik has incorrectly flagged a word as misspelled, select this button to add the word to Grammatik's vocabulary.

Undo   Select this button to reverse Grammatik's most recent replacement.

Close   When you've had enough of independent clauses and indefinite pronouns, this button shuts down the Grammatik window and returns you to the friendly confines of your document.

Grammatik is probably one of the most sophisticated software programs on the market today. As you've seen, it can do some pretty amazing things—but in the end, it's no match for the English language. There are just too many strange rules, and too many ways to throw sentences together. As a result, Grammatik often either misses some obvious problems or flags things that are okay. The screen below shows an example in which Grammatik missed a glaring error, but flagged something that was fine.

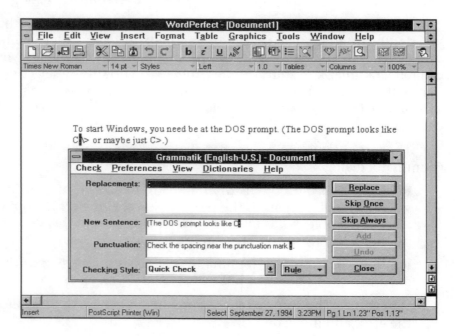

Grammatik is good, but it's no match for the complexity of English.

The phrase "you need be" is bad English in anyone's books (except, possibly, for the bogus Indians in Grade-B westerns), but Grammatik missed it completely. On the other hand, it thinks there's something wrong with "the spacing near the punctuation mark :." (It was probably thrown off by the prompt symbol C:\>. It seems DOS messes with *everyone's* head!)

The lesson here is not that Grammatik is a lousy program, because it's not. It's just that you shouldn't lean on it too heavily. Take Grammatik's advice with a grain of salt, and always proofread your work yourself.

Working with Checking Styles

Obviously, not all documents are created equal. Some are stiff and formal, while others are relaxed and jaunty (and others, like portions of this book, are just downright silly). Each of these styles requires different standards of grammar. For example, in more relaxed writing, jargon and clichés are okay, and in technical writing, longer and more complex sentences will be the norm.

For these different kettles of fish, Grammatik lets you choose from several different checking styles and levels of formality. And, if you're feeling spunky enough, you can even create your own custom styles. The next few sections tell you everything you need to know.

Selecting a Different Style

Grammatik has quite a few different checking styles, including Formal Memo or Letter, Technical or Scientific, and Fiction. To select a style that suits the kind of writing you do, display the Grammatik dialog box and select the style you want from the Checking Style drop-down list. (In version 6.0, pull down the Options menu, select the Writing Style command and select the style you want from the Writing Style dialog box.)

Editing a Checking Style

Grammatik's built-in styles are designed to handle general situations, but they may not suit the way you work. For example, you may like the Informal Memo or Letter checking style, but you'd prefer if it checked for passive voice. Grammatik is happy to let you remake the existing styles in your own image. Here are the steps to follow:

1. In the Grammatik dialog box, pull down the Preferences menu and select the Checking Styles command. The Checking Styles dialog box appears.

2. Highlight the style you want to edit and select the Edit button. Grammatik displays the Edit Rules dialog box (see below). This dialog box is divided into three areas:

    Rule Classes   This list shows all of Grammatik's rule classes. An activated check box means the rule class is turned on for this style. The area below the list gives you an explanation of each rule class. For a more detailed explanation, click on the ? button (or press **Alt+?**).

Maximum Allowed   The text boxes in this group show the limits the style places on various grammar options.

Formality Level   The level of formality is a measure of how exacting Grammatik is when it checks your documents. The Informal level is the most easygoing (it'll accept contractions, such as *it'll*, for example), while the Formal level won't let you get away with too much.

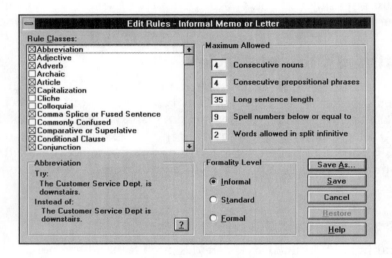

Use the Edit Rules dialog box to edit a built-in checking style.

3. To turn on a rule class for this checking style, activate the appropriate check box in the Rule Classes list. To turn off a rule class, deactivate its check box.

4. Use the Maximum Allowed text boxes to set your own limits for things like consecutive nouns and sentence length.

5. Select a formality level for the style.

6. Select the Save button. Grammatik saves the new settings and returns you to the Checking Styles dialog box. (An asterisk appears beside the checking style to remind you that you've made changes to the style.)

7. If you want to use the new style, make sure it's highlighted and then choose the Select button.

If you change your mind about the changes you've made to a built-in style, you can reset the style to its original state. First, highlight it in the Checking Styles dialog box and select Edit. In the Edit Rules dialog box, select the Restore button and then select Save.

Creating a Custom Style

Once you've used Grammatik for a while, you may notice that certain types of ignorable errors keep cropping up. For example, Grammatik may complain about sentences being too long, or numbers that should be spelled out (using "two" instead of "2"). Believe me, it doesn't take long before these things get awfully annoying. The remedy isn't to chuck Grammatik out the window, but to create your own styles that don't check for these errors.

Here are the steps to follow to create your own custom style:

1. In the Grammatik dialog box, pull down the **Preferences** menu and select the Checking Styles command. The Checking Styles dialog box appears.

2. Highlight the style that most closely resembles the one you want to create. For example, if you want to create an informal style, choose Quick Check or Informal Memo or Letter.

3. Select the Edit button to display the Edit Rules dialog box.

4. Use the Rule Classes list, the Maximum Allowed text boxes, and the Formality Level options to define your style (as explained in the previous section).

WordPerfect for Windows' Spell Check checks spelling, doubled words, and unusual capitalizations anyway (see Chapter 22, "Using the Spell Checker and Thesaurus"), so you can speed up Grammatik by creating a custom style that doesn't use these checks. In the Rule Classes list, deactivate **Capitalization**, **Doubled Word or Punctuation**, and **Spelling**.

5. Select the Save As button. Grammatik displays the Save As Checking Style dialog box.

6. Enter a name for the new style in the Custom Style Name text box and select **OK**. Grammatik returns you to the Checking Styles dialog box and adds your new style to the list.

7. If you want to use your style, make sure it's highlighted and then choose the **Select** button.

Checking Out Some Grammatik Options

Grammatik has a few bells and whistles you can try to make your grammar-checking chores a little easier. For starters, you can use the Check menu to select how much of the document you want Grammatik to check. You can check the current Sentence, the current Paragraph, the entire Document, or from the insertion point To End of Document.

If you pull down the Preferences menu and select the Environment command, Grammatik displays the Environment dialog box, shown in the following figure. Here's a summary of some of these options:

Provide spelling suggestions   Deactivate this check box if you don't want Grammatik to offer spelling suggestions when it finds a misspelled word. (This can speed up the grammar check.)

Show help prompts   When you highlight a command in the Grammatik menu bar, a brief explanation of the command normally appears in Grammatik's title bar. If you don't want to see these prompts, deactivate this check box.

Start checking immediately   When this check box is activated, Grammatik gets to work immediately when you start it up. If you normally like to change a Grammatik setting or two for different documents (for example, you might want to choose a different checking style), deactivate this check box to prevent Grammatik from starting without your say-so.

Check headers, footers, and footnotes in WordPerfect   When this check box is activated, Grammatik extends its grammar checking chores to include your document's headers, footers, footnotes, and endnotes.

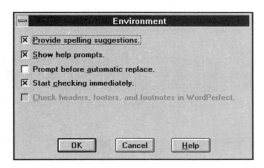

Use the Environment dialog box to set up the Grammatik environment.

If you're dying to know details such as how many words, sentences, and even syllables are in the document, or if you'd like to compare your document's readability with that of a Hemingway short story, pull down Grammatik's View menu and select the Statistics command. The first dialog box you see is called Basic Counts, and it provides a few vital statistics for the document. This dialog box also contains the following buttons:

Flagged   This button displays the Flagged dialog box, which shows you a list of the rule classes your prose violated (and how many times Grammatik invoked each rule class). This is a good way to find out your grammatical weak points.

Readability   This button displays the Readability dialog box. Use the Comparison document drop-down list to select the document to which you want to compare your work. You can choose a Hemingway short story, the Gettysburg Address, or the instructions for a 1040EZ tax form. Grammatik then runs a comparison between the two documents using four readability measures: grade level, passive voice, sentence complexity, and vocabulary complexity.

Close   Select this button when you're done and you want to return to the Grammatik window.

The grammar hounds in the audience (or just those who are gluttons for punishment) might want to check out the **View** menu's **P**arts of Speech and **P**arse Tree commands. These commands show the various parts of speech (nouns, verbs, conjunctions, and so on) that Grammatik assigns to the words in the problem sentence.

The Least You Need to Know

This chapter showed you the ins and outs of using Grammatik, WordPerfect for Windows grammar checking program. Here's a recap:

➤ To start Grammatik, select **G**rammatik from the **T**ools menu, or press **Alt+Shift+F1**.

➤ When Grammatik flags a possible error, you can edit the document text directly, turn off the rule class (by selecting **T**urn Off from the **R**ule pop-up list), or use the buttons in the Grammatik window to tell the program what to do next.

➤ Grammatik can allow for different writing styles. To work with a different style, select it from the Checking Style drop-down list.

➤ To edit an existing checking style, or create your own style, pull down the **P**references menu and select the Checking Styles command. In the dialog box that appears, highlight the style and select **E**dit.

Chapter 24

Image Is Everything: Working with Graphics

In This Chapter

➤ Sprucing up your documents with clip art

➤ Creating fancy boxes for your text

➤ Drawing lines

➤ Playing with the TextArt feature

➤ More fun, time-wasting tools to guarantee you never get any work done

Television commercials assure us that "Image is everything." And since they wouldn't put it on TV if it wasn't true (!), you need to think about the image your documents present to the outside world. You've seen in earlier chapters how a few fonts and other formatting options can do wonders for drab, lifeless text. But *anybody* can do that kind of stuff. To make your documents really stand out from the crowd, you need to go graphical with clip art figures, lines, and boxes. Happily, WordPerfect for Windows has the tools that not only get the job done, but make the whole thing a snap. This chapter gives you the graphics nitty-gritty.

Working with Graphics Boxes

Most WordPerfect for Windows graphics appear inside *graphics boxes*. These boxes are like islands floating in the sea of your document because the regular text flows around them. But unlike real islands, graphics boxes can be moved and sized, and you can apply a fistful of formatting options to them.

What can you put inside a graphics box? Well, all kinds of things, really, but the most common are clip-art images and text (which I'll look at in this chapter), and drawings (which I'll cover in the next chapter).

Adding a Clip Art Figure to a Document

Chapter 25, "Drawing with WordPerfect Draw," shows you how to create your own drawings and add them to a document. If you don't have the time, inclination, or talent for these artistic endeavors, don't worry. WordPerfect for Windows comes with its own *clip art* collection. Clip art is professional-quality artwork you can incorporate into your documents free of charge. You get over one hundred images of everything from a centerpiece to a zipper. But the real fun begins after you've added the graphic—because you can then move it around, change its size, rotate it, add a caption, you name it.

Adding a clip art figure is as easy as opening a file. Here's what you do:

1. Position the insertion point where you want the image to appear in the document.

2. Pull down the **Graphics** menu and select **Im**age (if you're using version 6.0, select the **F**igure command instead). WordPerfect for Windows displays the Insert Image dialog box, which is similar to the other directory dialogs you've seen (such as Open File and Save As). In this case, WordPerfect for Windows displays the Graphics subdirectory that contains the clip art files.

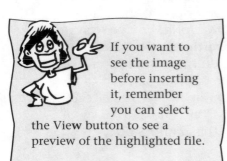 If you want to see the image before inserting it, remember you can select the View button to see a preview of the highlighted file.

Clicking this button in either the 6.1 WordPerfect Toolbar or the Graphics Toolbar will also display the Insert Image dialog box.

3. Highlight the file you want to open from the Filename list and
select **OK**. WordPerfect for Windows creates a graphics box (or,
more specifically in this case, a *figure box*), inserts the image inside
the box, and displays the Graphics box feature bar (see the following figure).

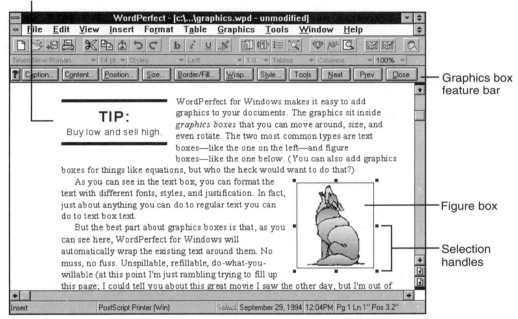

*A WordPerfect for Windows document with graphics boxes containing
text and clip art.*

Once you have your image in the document, you can move it
around, change its size, add a caption, and more. I'll show you how to
do these things later in this section. For now, you can return to the
document by clicking outside of the graphics box or by selecting Close
in the feature bar.

Many of the clip art files (for example, APPROVED.WPG and ASAP.WPG) contain only a couple of words and no real artwork at all. What gives? These files are for creating *watermarks*— translucent images or bits of text that print "underneath" the existing text on a page. If you'd like to try this out, select the **Watermark** command from the Format menu, and then select **Create** from the Watermark dialog box. In the Watermark feature bar that appears, select **Image** and insert one of the graphics files.

Adding a Text Box

Throughout this book I've placed various notes, tips, and cautions in separate sections like this:

Placing text in its own box like this is a great way to highlight important material and get the reader's attention.

You can do the same thing in your WordPerfect for Windows documents by creating a text box. Here are the steps:

1. Position the insertion point where you want the box to appear.

2. Pull down the **Graphics** menu and select the **Text Box** command. WordPerfect displays a box with its own insertion point as well as the Graphics box feature bar.

   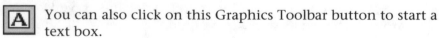 You can also click on this Graphics Toolbar button to start a text box.

3. Enter and format your text just as you would in the typing area.

4. When you're done, you can return to the document by clicking outside of the text box or by selecting **Close** in the feature bar.

Selecting a Graphics Box

If you need to make changes to a graphics box, you have to select it first. You can do this in four ways:

➤ Click on the graphics box.

➤ Select Next or Prev in the feature bar to cycle through the graphic boxes in order.

➤ If your document has only one graphics box, select the Edit Box command from the Graphics menu, or press **Shift+F11**.

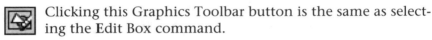 Clicking this Graphics Toolbar button is the same as selecting the Edit Box command.

➤ If your document has multiple graphics boxes and you don't feel like cycling through them, things get a little stickier. First select Edit Box from the Graphics menu to display the Edit Box dialog box. Now you have two choices: select Document Box Number and enter the number of the graphics box (WordPerfect for Windows numbers the boxes according to their position in the document); or select the type of box from the Counters list, activate the Counter Number option, and then enter the number of the type of box you selected. Select **OK** to get the heck out of there.

Every graphics box has a border that defines its boundaries. When you select a box, WordPerfect for Windows displays black *selection handles* around the frame. (Take a look at the figure box in the picture shown earlier to see an example of these selection handles.)

Adding a Caption to a Graphics Box

Captions are an easy way to add explanatory text to a figure box or other graphic. Here are the steps to follow to add a caption:

1. Select the graphics box with which you want to work.

2. Select the feature bar's Caption button. WordPerfect for Windows displays the Box Caption dialog box.

The commands discussed in this section and many of the following sections are also available in the Quick-Menu for each graphics box. Just right-click on the box to see the QuickMenu list.

3. Use the controls in the Caption Position group to change the position of the caption, if necessary.

4. Select the Edit button. WordPerfect for Windows returns you to the document, displays the default caption, and starts the Caption Editor.

5. Enter the caption text you want.

6. When you're done, click outside the graphics box or select the feature bar's Close button.

Editing the Contents of a Graphics Box

If you want to change the text inside a text box or the figure inside a figure box, select the Content button from the feature bar. This displays the Box Content dialog box. You have two options:

➤ For a figure box, use the Filename text box to enter the name of a different clip art file. (If you're not sure of the name, click on the list button to the right of the text box and select the file you want from the Select File dialog box.)

You can also edit text box text by simply double-clicking inside the box.

➤ For a text box, select the Edit button. WordPerfect for Windows returns you to the document and activates the Text Box Editor. Make your changes and either click outside the box or select Close on the feature bar.

Moving a Graphics Box

When you add a graphics box to a document, its position isn't set in stone, which means you can move it anywhere you like. There are two methods you can use:

➤ With your mouse, position the mouse pointer inside the box you want to move and then drag the box to its new location. (As you're dragging, the mouse pointer changes to a four-sided arrow and you'll see a dotted outline around the box. This is perfectly normal behavior.)

➤ Click on **P**osition in the feature bar to display the Box Position dialog box. Use the controls in the Position Box group to set the new position for the box. When you're done, select **OK**.

Sizing a Graphics Box

If a graphics box doesn't have the dimensions you want, it's no problem changing the size. Again, you can use either of two methods:

➤ With your mouse, select the box you want to size, and then drag one of the selection handles until the box is the size and shape you want. Which selection handle should you use? Well, if you want to change the size horizontally or vertically, use the appropriate handle on the middle of a side. To change the size in two directions at once, use the appropriate corner handle.

➤ Click on **S**ize in the feature bar to open the Box Size dialog box. Use Box Size group controls to set the width and height, and then select **OK**.

Setting the Border and Fill Styles for a Graphics Box

As I mentioned earlier, every graphics box has a border surrounding it. A figure box displays its entire border, but text boxes only show the top and bottom. If you'd like something with a little more pizzazz, Word-Perfect for Windows comes with over two dozen different border styles.

But wait, there's more. You can also change something called the *fill style*. The fill style is the background on which the contents of the box are displayed. The default is plain white, but you can choose from all kinds of weird and wonderful patterns. The following figure shows some example boxes with various borders and fill styles.

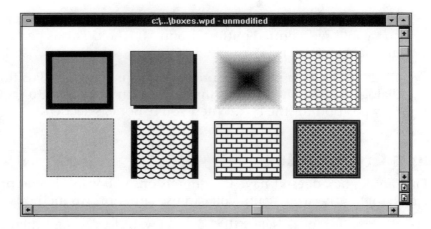

A few of WordPerfect for Windows' border and fill styles.

To change the border and fill styles, select the box you want to work with and then select **Border/Fill** in the feature bar. In the Box Border/Fill Styles dialog box that appears, use the **Border Style** and **Fill Style** options to select the styles you want. Select **OK** when you're done.

Wrapping Text Around a Graphics Box

One of the things that makes graphics boxes so easy to use is that WordPerfect for Windows automatically wraps the regular document text around the box. And moving or sizing the box is no problem because the text adjusts along with the box.

By default, WordPerfect for Windows wraps text around the box border and wraps on the side of the object that has the largest amount of white space. To change these defaults, select the feature bar's **Wrap** button and select your options from the Wrap Text dialog box.

Working with the Image Tools Palette

WordPerfect for Windows also includes a set of tools for working with the images inside figure boxes. The Image Tools Palette is a set of icons that control image attributes such as rotation, scaling, colors, and more. To display the palette, select the Tools button in the feature bar. The palette appears next to the image, as you can see in the following figure.

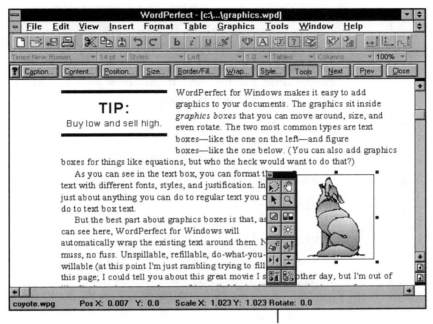

Image Tools palette

The Image Tools palette.

Here's a summary of the available tools:

 Rotate rotates the image. When you select this tool, rotation handles appear around the image, and you drag a handle to perform the rotation. The **Rotate** info in the status bar tells you the degree of rotation.

 Move moves the image within the box (not to be confused with moving the *entire* box, which we discussed earlier). When you select this tool, the mouse pointer changes to a hand when you place it over the image. Drag the image to move it. The **Pos X** and **Y** info on the status bar tells you the current position.

 Pointer resets the mouse pointer to its default behavior.

Scale scales the image. Selecting this tool displays three more tools: use the magnifying glass to scale a selected area by dragging; use the double arrows to scale the entire image using scroll bars; use the **1:1** tool to reset the image. The **Scale** X and Y status bar info tracks the current scale.

Complement changes the image colors to their complementary values (red changes to green, blue changes to yellow, and so on).

Black & White displays the image in black and white.

Contrast sets the contrast between the light and dark areas of the image. Select this tool, then choose a contrast level from the examples provided.

Brightness sets the brightness (or the *saturation*) of the colors in the image. Select this tool and then choose a brightness level from the example box.

Reset resets the image attributes to their original values.

Fill Attributes controls the colors inside the image. You can choose the normal colors, no colors, or white only.

Mirror Vertical flips the image along its vertical axis.

Mirror Horizontal flips the image along its horizontal axis.

Image Edit starts WordPerfect Draw to let you edit the image (see Chapter 25, "Drawing with Word-Perfect Draw," to learn how to use WordPerfect Draw).

Image Settings displays the Image Settings dialog box to let you set values for most of the preceding tools.

To close the Image Tools palette, double-click on the box in the upper left corner of the palette.

Working with Lines

A simple line across a document is a great way to separate different sections of your text. WordPerfect for Windows lets you add either horizontal or vertical lines, and you can customize each line by setting different styles, colors, and lengths.

Adding a Line

To add a line to a document, position the insertion point where you want the line to appear, pull down the Graphics menu, and then select either **Horizontal Line** (or press **Ctrl+F11**) or **Vertical Line** (or press **Ctrl+Shift+F11**). WordPerfect for Windows inserts the new line at the insertion point.

 Click this Graphics Toolbar button to insert a horizontal line.

 Click this Graphics Toolbar button to insert a vertical line.

Selecting a Line

To select a line, simply click on it with your mouse. (Unfortunately, WordPerfect for Windows has no way of selecting a line from the keyboard.) When you select a line, you'll see the usual selection handles surrounding it.

Moving a Line

To move a line, you can use either of the following methods:

➤ Drag the line to its new location.

➤ Select the line, and then select the Edit Line command from the Graphics menu. In the Edit Graphics Line dialog box, use the Horizontal and Vertical controls to set the new position for the line. When you're done, select **OK**.

271

Sizing a Line

You can size a line either lengthwise (to make it longer or shorter) or widthwise (to make it thicker or thinner). You can use either of the following techniques:

➤ Select the line you want to size and then drag one of the selection handles until the line is the size and shape you want.

➤ Select the line and then select the Graphics menu's Edit Line command. In the Edit Graphics Line dialog box, use the Length and Thickness controls to change the size, then select **OK**.

Setting the Line Style and Color

As it does with graphics boxes, WordPerfect for Windows offers a number of styles and colors for your graphics lines. To check them out, select Edit Line from the Graphics menu to display the Edit Graphics Line dialog box. The Line Style controls give you more than 30 different styles to choose from. Some of the styles come with a preset color. If you'd like to use a different color, select one from the Line Color control.

Playing with TextArt

One of the most addictive of WordPerfect for Windows' features has to be TextArt. This little utility enables you to take plain old text and bend it in all sorts of bizarre ways. You can also rotate the text, add shadows, place borders around each letter, and change the text colors and patterns. It's a lot of fun and, hey, it sure beats workin'.

Starting TextArt

To crank up TextArt, just select the TextArt command from the Graphics menu. In a few seconds you'll see the TextArt screen, as shown in the following figure.

 Clicking on this button in the 6.1 WordPerfect Toolbar also fires up TextArt.

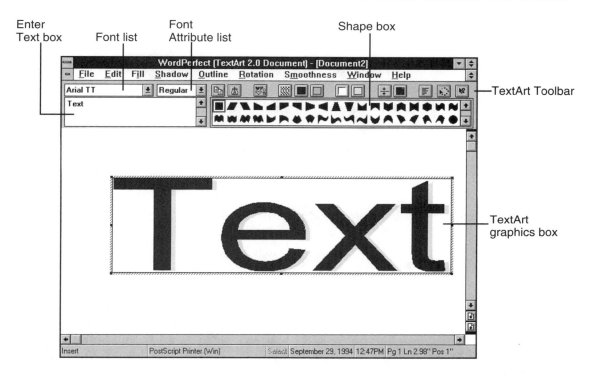

The TextArt screen is chock full of fun font effects.

Using TextArt

As you can see in the preceding figure, when TextArt loads, it actually replaces both the WordPerfect for Windows' menu bar and Toolbar with its own. (The File and Window menus remain unchanged, however.) When you work with TextArt, you'll usually follow these general steps:

1. Type the text you want to work with in the Enter Text box. You can enter as many characters as you like on as many lines as you like (press **Enter** to create a new line).

2. Use the Font and Font Attribute lists to select a font for the text.

3. If you want to bend the text into a shape, click on the shape you want from the Shape box.

4. Use the TextArt menus to play around with the text. Here's a summary:

> The **Fill** commands control the color and pattern that fills the text.
>
> The **Shadow** commands control the appearance of the text's shadow.
>
> The **Outline** commands control the width and color of the text outline.
>
> The **Rotation** commands rotate the text.
>
> The **Smoothness** commands determine how smooth the text looks.

5. When you're done, click outside the TextArt graphics box to return to the normal WordPerfect for Windows screen.

When TextArt adds the graphic to your document, it places it in a graphics box just like the ones you saw earlier for figures and text. This means that you can use the same feature bar options to add a caption or move and size the text. If you want to use TextArt to make changes to the graphic, just double-click on the box, and TextArt loads automatically. (Alternatively, you can select the graphics box, pull down the Edit menu, select TextArt 2.0 Document Object, and then select Edit.)

Many menu bar commands are also available in the TextArt Toolbar.

The Least You Need to Know

This chapter took you through some of WordPerfect for Windows fun graphics tools. Here's what happened:

➤ You can insert graphics boxes anywhere in your document, and WordPerfect for Windows automatically wraps the existing text around the box.

➤ To include clip art images in a document, select the Graphics menu's Image command and then select a clip art file from the Insert Image dialog box.

➤ To include a text box, select Text Box from the Graphics menu.

➤ Use the Graphics box feature bar to change box attributes such as captions, contents, position, and size.

➤ To add a line to your document, pull down the Graphics menu and select either Horizontal Line or Vertical Line.

➤ For a good graphics time, run the TextArt command from the Graphics menu and go crazy with the TextArt program's special effects.

Chapter 25

Drawing with WordPerfect Draw

In This Chapter

➤ Navigating the WordPerfect Draw window

➤ Drawing lines, boxes, circles, and other shapes

➤ Drawing freehand lines

➤ Editing your drawings

➤ Using Draw to create fancy-schmancy charts

If you enjoyed finger painting when you were a kid, you'll get a kick out of WordPerfect Draw, the drawing program that comes free with WordPerfect for Windows. Oh sure, you can use it for practical stuff like logos, charts, and whatnot, but to my mind, WordPerfect Draw's real reason for being is sheer fun. Think about it: all you do is select a "tool" to work with and then just wiggle your mouse around the screen. Magically, you get all kinds of cool shapes and patterns. Throw in a few colors and you have a recipe for hours of entertainment.

Starting WordPerfect Draw

Before you begin, position the insertion point where you want the graphics box to appear. To start WordPerfect Draw, pull down the Graphics menu and select the Draw command. As you can see in the following figure, WordPerfect Draw inserts a graphics box into the document and replaces the WordPerfect for Windows menu bar and Toolbar with its own. (The File and Window menus remain the same, however.)

 Clicking this Graphics Toolbar button also starts WordPerfect Draw.

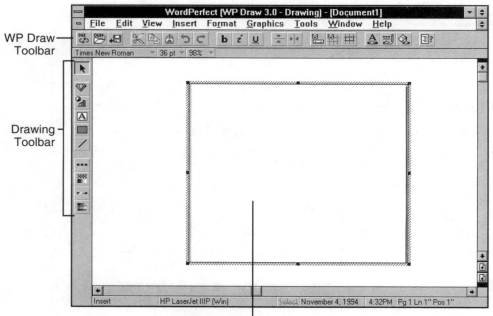

The WP Draw window.

Drawing with WordPerfect Draw

The best way to approach WordPerfect Draw is simply to have fun fooling around with the various drawing implements and colors. However, there *is* a basic method for using each tool.

1. Select a drawing tool using either the Drawing Toolbar or the Insert menu's Drawing Tools command. (I'll talk about the available drawing tools as we go along.)

2. Select one or more attributes (line style, color, and so on) for the object you're drawing, using either the Drawing Toolbar or the Format menu. (I'll talk about how you select the attributes later in this chapter).

3. Move the pointer into the drawing area and draw the shape you want (as explained in the next few sections).

Drawing Rectangles and Circles

You can use rectangles and circles to create most of the basic building blocks for your drawing. Here's how they work:

1. Pull down the Insert menu, select Drawing Tools, and then select either **Rectangle**, **Rounded Rectangle** (a rectangle with rounded corners), **Circle**, or **Ellipse**.

    You can also select one of these tools by clicking on this button in the Drawing Toolbar and then selecting the shape you want.

2. Move the mouse pointer into the drawing area and position it where you want the shape to start. The pointer, you'll notice, changes to a cross.

3. Drag the pointer until the object is the size and shape you want, and then release the mouse button.

> If you make a mess during the drawing, you can start again by simply pressing the **Esc** key *before* you finish drawing the shape. If you've already finished the shape, you can still get rid of it by selecting Undo from the Edit menu.

> To draw a perfect square using the Rectangle tool, hold down **Shift** while dragging the mouse.

WordPerfect Draw's rectangles are perfect for creating company organization charts. You can use the Line tool (described in the next section) to join the boxes and the Text tool (described later on) to add people's names and job titles.

Drawing Lines and Curves

The following steps show you how to draw lines and curves with WordPerfect Draw:

1. Pull down the Insert menu, select Drawing Tools, and then select either Line, Polygon, Curve, or Closed Curve.

   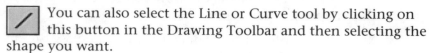 You can also select the Line or Curve tool by clicking on this button in the Drawing Toolbar and then selecting the shape you want.

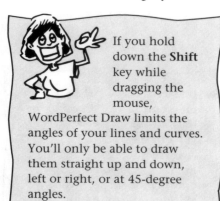 If you hold down the **Shift** key while dragging the mouse, WordPerfect Draw limits the angles of your lines and curves. You'll only be able to draw them straight up and down, left or right, or at 45-degree angles.

2. Move the mouse pointer into the drawing area and position it where you want the line or curve to start. The pointer changes to a cross.

3. Drag the mouse until the first line is the length you want and then release the button.

4. Drag the mouse again either to draw a second line (in the case of the Polygon and Line tools) or to curve the line (for the Closed Curve and Curve tools). Release the button when you're done.

5. If you want to add more lines or curves, repeat step 4.

6. When you're done, double-click to finish the object.

Drawing Freehand Lines

As you've seen, WordPerfect Draw makes it easy to draw lines, circles, and polygons. Too easy, some would say. For a real challenge, try using the Freehand tool to draw lines that follow the mouse pointer. Here's what you do:

1. Pull down the Insert menu, select Drawing Tools, and then select Freehand.

2. Move the mouse pointer into the drawing area and position it where you want the shape to start. The pointer changes to a cross.

3. Hold down the left mouse button and drag the mouse to and fro. As you drag, a line follows your every move.

4. When you're done, release the mouse button.

Adding Text to a Drawing

WordPerfect Draw is mostly for your right brain, but if your left brain wants to get in on the act, you can use one of the Text tools to add text to a drawing. Here's how it works:

1. Pull down the Insert menu and select either Text Area (to draw a box to use for multiple lines of text) or Text Line (for a single line of text).

     You can also work with text by clicking on this button in the Drawing Toolbar and then selecting the tool you want.

2. Move the mouse pointer into the drawing area and position it where you want the text to appear.

3. If you're using the Text Area tool, drag the mouse to create the box for the text. If you're using the Text Line tool, click the left mouse button.

4. Pull down the Format menu and select the Font command (or press **F9**). Use the Font dialog box to select a font for your text, and then select **OK**.

5. Enter your text in the box. When you're done, click outside the box to add the text to the drawing.

Adding an Image to a Drawing

One of the easiest ways to get the drawing you want is to start with one of WordPerfect for Windows clip art files and modify it to suit your needs. To try this out, follow these steps:

1. Select the Insert menu's QuickArt command.

    You can also click on this Drawing Toolbar button to select the QuickArt tool.

2. Move the mouse pointer into the drawing area and drag the mouse to create a box for the image. WordPerfect Draw displays the Insert Figure dialog box.

3. Highlight the image file you want to use, and then select Insert. WordPerfect Draw inserts the image into the box.

Working with Objects

Once you've added an object or two to your drawing, you may need to make adjustments to the size, position, or attributes of an object. This section shows you how to do all this and more.

Selecting an Object

You need to select an object before you can work with it. WordPerfect Draw gives you four different methods for selecting:

➤ To select a single object, click on the **Select** tool and then click on the object you want. WordPerfect Draw surrounds the object with *selection handles*, as shown in the following figure.

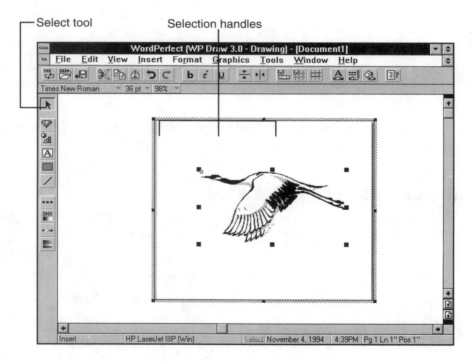

When you select an object, WordPerfect Draw surrounds it with selection handles.

➤ To select multiple objects, click on the **Select** tool and then hold down **Shift** as you click on each object.

➤ To select all the objects in a specific area of the drawing, click on the **Select** tool, move the pointer into the drawing area, and then drag the mouse to create a box. WordPerfect Draw selects every object that's completely inside the box.

➤ To select every object in the drawing, pull down the Edit menu, choose Select, and then choose All from the cascade menu.

Moving an Object

To get your drawing just right, you may need to move some of the objects around. No sweat: click on the **Select** tool and position the pointer inside the object. Then hold down the left mouse button and drag the mouse to move the object to its new home. To help out, WordPerfect Draw displays an outline of the object as you move it. When the object is where you want it to be, release the mouse button.

To make a copy of an object, hold down **Ctrl** while dragging the mouse.

Sizing an Object

Until you get used to the WordPerfect Draw tools, one of the hardest things to do is get the right size for your objects. Fortunately, changing the size of a shape is easy. Just select the object you want to size and then drag one of the selection handles. Here are some things to keep in mind when sizing:

➤ To change the width, drag one of the left or right side handles away from the object (to make it fatter) or inside the object (to make it skinnier).

➤ To change the height of an object, drag one of the top or bottom handles away from the object (to make it taller) or inside the object (to make it shorter).

➤ To change both the width and height at the same time, drag one of the corner handles.

➤ To change two sides (either the left and right or the top and bottom) at once, hold down **Alt** while dragging a handle.

➤ If you hold down **Ctrl** while dragging a handle, Draw leaves the original object intact and creates a copy of the object in the new size.

Deleting an Object

While you're getting a grip on WordPerfect Draw, you'll likely end up with a few failed experiments that you don't want in your finished drawing. To remove these rogue elements, select them, and then either select Cut from the Edit menu or press **Delete**. If the drawing is a complete disaster and you want to start with a fresh slate, select the Edit menu's Clear command (or press **Ctrl+Shift+F4**).

Playing with an Object's Attributes

Every WordPerfect Draw object has a number of attributes that determine what the thing looks like. For our purposes, these attributes generally fall into three categories:

➤ Line attributes control the look of the object's lines. This applies not only to line, polygon, and curve objects, but also to the outlines of objects such as rectangles and circles. To change the line attributes, select the object, pull down the Format menu, and select the Line Attributes command. In the Line Attributes dialog box, use the Line **W**idth, **S**tyle, and **A**rrowhead controls to define your line. Then select **OK**.

Click on this Drawing Toolbar button to see a box of line attributes, and then click on the one you want.

➤ Fill attributes determine what the inside of closed objects (such as rectangles and circles) looks like. To try out different fill attributes, select the object, and then select the Format menu's Fill Attributes command to display the Fill Attributes dialog box. Use the Fill **T**ype, **P**attern, **F**oreground Color, and **B**ackground Color controls to create a fill. Then select **OK**.

Click on this Drawing Toolbar button to see a box of fill styles, and then click on the one you want.

➤ Color attributes, of course, control the colors of your object's lines and fills. Pull down the Format menu and select Color Attributes to display the Color Attributes dialog box. Select the appropriate option (Fill Foreground, Fill Background, Line Color, or Text Color), and then select a color square from the Current Palette box. Select **OK** when you're done.

 Click on this Drawing Toolbar button to see a palette of line colors, and then click on the one you want.

 Click on this Drawing Toolbar button to see a palette of fill colors. Left-click for the foreground color, and right-click for the background color.

Adding a Chart to a Drawing

If you plan to include numbers in your document (such as last year's sales figures or next year's budget), you can spice things up by displaying the numbers in a chart. WordPerfect Draw comes with a Data Chart tool that lets you enter your numbers in a spreadsheet-like table. The Data Chart tool then creates the chart automatically.

If you feel like giving it a go, here are the steps to follow:

1. Pull down the Insert menu and select the Data Chart command.

 Clicking on this Drawing Toolbar button also selects the Data Chart tool.

 You can add a basic bar chart directly from a WordPerfect for Windows document. Just pull down the Graphics menu, select the Chart command, and then skip to step 5. If you'd prefer a different style of chart, pull down the Chart menu, select Gallery, and then select the type you want from the Data Chart dialog box (see steps 3 and 4).

 Clicking this Graphics Toolbar button also starts the Data Chart tool.

2. Move the pointer into the drawing area, and then drag the mouse to create a box for the chart. When you release the button, WordPerfect Draw displays the Data Chart dialog box.

3. Use the Chart Type list to highlight the kind of chart you'd like to use. WordPerfect Draw displays several examples of the chart type you selected.

4. Highlight one of the chart examples, and then select **OK**. WordPerfect Draw adds a chart to the drawing and displays a Datasheet with some sample data (see the following figure).

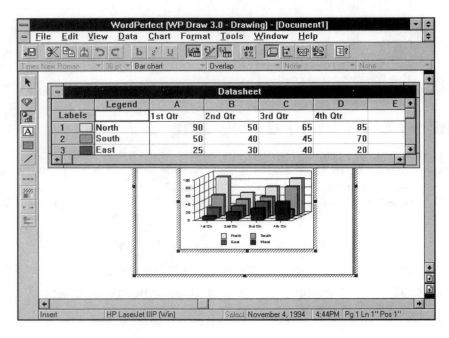

Use the Datasheet to fill in the data for your chart.

5. Use the Datasheet to enter your own data for the chart. As you edit or add numbers, the chart changes to reflect the new entries. (The Datasheet works much like a WordPerfect for Windows table. See Chapter 26, "Techniques for Terrific Tables," to learn some table basics.)

6. When you've finished your data entry chores, pull down the **View** menu and select the **Datasheet** command to get rid of the Datasheet.

The Least You Need to Know

This chapter showed you how to have all sorts of fun with WordPerfect Draw, WordPerfect for Windows' cool drawing program. Here's a summary of the important stuff:

➤ To load WordPerfect Draw, select Draw from the Graphics menu.

➤ To start drawing, first select a tool from the Insert menu or from the Drawing Toolbar. Then move the pointer into the drawing area and drag the mouse to create an object.

➤ Use the Select tool to select pieces of your drawing that you want to move, size, or delete.

➤ Use the commands on the Format menu to jazz up the attributes of your WordPerfect Draw objects.

➤ To create a chart, select the Insert menu's Data Chart command, and then draw a box in your drawing to hold the chart.

Chapter 26

Techniques for Terrific Tables

In This Chapter

➤ What is a table and why are tables useful?

➤ Creating tables both from scratch and by converting existing text

➤ Populating a table with data

➤ Miscellaneous table-editing techniques

➤ Using formulas to turn mild-mannered tables into powerful spreadsheets, able to leap tall calculations in a single bound

In this chapter, you'll learn a bit of computer carpentry as I show you how to build and work with tables. Don't worry, though, if you can't tell a hammer from a hacksaw; the kinds of tables we'll be dealing with are purely electronic because in WordPerfect for Windows, a *table* is a rectangular grid of rows and columns in a document. You can enter all kinds of info into a table, including text, numbers, and graphics. And if you're feeling really ambitious, you can even create formulas that turn the table into a reasonably powerful spreadsheet. No guff. This chapter takes you ever-so-gently through everything you need to know.

What Is a Table?

Despite their name, WordPerfect for Windows tables aren't really analogous to those big wooden things you eat on every night. Instead, as I've said, a WordPerfect for Windows table is a rectangular arrangement of rows and columns on your screen. The figure below shows an example table.

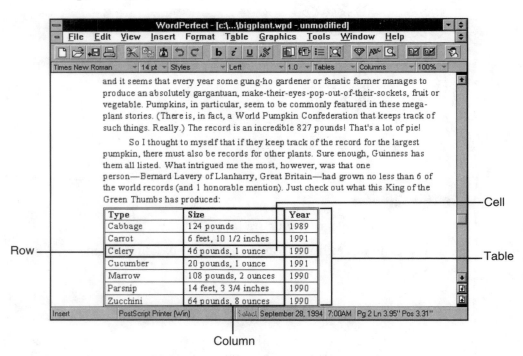

A table in a WordPerfect for Windows document.

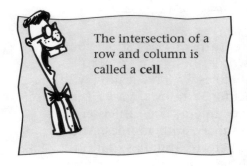

The intersection of a row and column is called a **cell**.

Way back in Chapter 14, "Making Your Lines and Paragraphs Look Good," you learned how to use tabs to make your text line up all nice and pretty. So why use a table when tabs can do a similar job? Good question. Here are just a few advantages that tables bring to the table (sorry about that):

➤ Each table cell is self-contained. You can edit and format the contents of a cell without disturbing the arrangements of the other cells.

➤ The text wraps inside each cell, making it a snap to create multiple-line entries.

➤ You can format a table as a whole, including the font, justification, and the style and color of the lines that separate each cell.

➤ You can create formulas that perform calculations on one or more table cells. You can add 'em up, multiply 'em together, or divide 'em by the square root of the price of tea in China. Whatever you need.

WordPerfect for Windows Woodworking: How to Build a Table

WordPerfect for Windows gives you two ways to create a table: you can either build it from scratch by creating the table and then entering the info, or you can convert existing text into a table. The next couple of sections take you through both methods.

Building a Table from Scratch

If you don't have the table data already in your document, it's usually easiest to create the table first and then enter the data later. Follow these steps to create a table:

1. Position the cursor where you want the table to appear in the document.

2. Pull down the Table menu and select the Create command, or press **F12**. WordPerfect for Windows displays the Create Table dialog box, shown in the following figure.

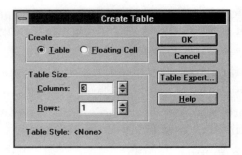

Use the Create Table dialog box to specify the size of the table.

3. Use the Columns spinner to enter the number of columns for the table. (Don't sweat it if you're not sure how many columns you need; you can always add more columns—or delete extra ones— later on.)

4. Use the Rows spinner to enter the number of rows for the table. (Again, you can just guess at the number of rows you need, and then make any adjustments later.)

5. Select **OK**. WordPerfect for Windows returns you to the document and inserts the table.

Using the Table QuickCreate Feature in Version 6.1

The Power Bar in WordPerfect for Windows version 6.1 has a Table QuickCreate button that lets mouse devotees create a table in no time flat. Here's how it works:

1. Move the insertion point to where you want the table to appear.

2. Move the mouse pointer over the Table QuickCreate button (see the following figure), and then press and hold down the left mouse button. A grid drops down from the Power Bar.

The Table QuickCreate button

3. With the mouse button still held down, move the pointer down into the grid and highlight the number of rows and columns you want in your table.

4. Release the mouse button. WordPerfect for Windows creates the table. (If you decide you don't want a table after all, move the mouse pointer off the grid, and then release the mouse button.)

Miraculously Converting Existing Text into a Table

If you already have some text formatted with tabs, you can still get into the table act because WordPerfect for Windows makes it easy to convert existing text into a table. You begin by selecting the text you want to convert. Then pull down the Table menu and select Create. In the Convert Table dialog box that appears, make sure the Tabular Column option button is active, and then select **OK**. WordPerfect for Windows returns you to the document and fits the text into a table with the appropriate number of rows and columns.

Entering Table Values

Once you've created your table, your next task is to enter the table values (or you may need to make changes to the existing values, if you converted some text into the table). As I mentioned earlier, the intersection between each row and column in a table is called a *cell*, and it's in these cells that you enter your text.

To try this out, click on the cell you want to work with, or use the up and down arrow keys to move the cursor into the table. Then use the following keyboard techniques to get around:

Press	To move
Tab	Right one column
Shift+Tab	Left one column
Up arrow	Up one row
Down arrow	Down one row

Now just enter the value you want to appear in the cell. Here are some guidelines to keep in mind:

➤ If your text is longer than the width of the cell, WordPerfect for Windows wraps the text and adjusts the height of the cell to accommodate the entry.

➤ To start a new line, press **Enter**.

➤ To enter a tab, press **Ctrl+Tab**.

If you have cells with multiple lines, pressing up arrow or down arrow will only move you between lines. To hop over a cell with multiple lines, press **Alt+up arrow** or **Alt+down arrow**.

Table Refinishing: Formatting a Table

Okay, now that you've built your table and filled it with data, it's time to step back a little and cast a critical eye on your creation. Do you need to format the table text? Would you prefer it if a particular column was wider or narrower? How about trying a different border?

For some table chores, you can simply use the formatting commands you suffered through earlier in this book. For example, to change the font of the text in a cell, just highlight the text and then choose your font options (as described in the Chapter 13, "Making Your Characters Look Good"). If you want to work with multiple cells at once, you can either select the ones you need (using the same blocking techniques we looked at back in Chapter 11, "Block Partying: Working with Blocks of Text"), or you can use the following table-specific methods:

➤ To select an entire column, move the mouse pointer to the top of any cell in the column (the mouse pointer will change to an upward-pointing arrow), and then double-click.

➤ To select an entire row, move the mouse pointer to the left edge of any cell in the row (the mouse pointer will change to a left-pointing arrow), and then double-click.

➤ To select the entire table, move the mouse pointer to the top of any cell or to the left edge of any cell, and then triple-click.

Changing the Width of a Column

When you create a table, WordPerfect for Windows doesn't know how wide you'll need the columns, so it just assigns a default width. As you can imagine, this default value will be too narrow for some columns and too wide for others. To get a better fit for your data, you can adjust the column widths using the following technique:

1. With your mouse, move the pointer over the right edge of any cell in the column you want to adjust. The mouse pointer changes to a vertical bar with arrows pointing left and right (see the following figure).

Mouse pointer for adjusting column widths

Drag the right edge of a column to change its width.

2. Press and hold down the left mouse button.

3. Drag the mouse either to the left (to make the column narrower) or to the right (to make it wider). As you drag, WordPerfect for Windows displays a dashed line to show the new column width.

4. When the column is the width you want, release the mouse button.

Instead of messing about with different column widths, you can save some time by having WordPerfect for Windows size your columns automatically. Specifically, the program can adjust a column's width to accommodate the widest data in the column. Just position the insertion point in any cell of the column you want to adjust, and then try either one of the following methods:

You can also adjust a column's width by placing the insertion point inside any cell in the column and then pressing either **Ctrl+<** (to make the column narrower) or **Ctrl+>** (to make the column wider).

➤ Right-click anywhere inside the table and select the Size Column to Fit command from the QuickMenu.

➤ ⊞ Click on this button in the Tables Toolbar.

Inserting a New Row or Column into the Table

Unlike real carpentry, building a WordPerfect for Windows table doesn't require all kinds of advance planning. (Which is good news for those of us who wouldn't know a blueprint from a blue moon.) This is fortunate because you won't know in advance how many rows or columns you're going to need in many of the tables you create. That's not a problem, though, because it's easy enough to just create a basic table and then toss in a new row or column whenever you need it. The following steps show you how it's done:

1. Decide where you want the new row or column to appear and then position the insertion point as follows:

   ➤ If you're inserting a new row, position the insertion point in any cell in a row that will be adjacent to the new row. If you're adding a new row to the bottom of the table, use a cell in the last row of the table.

   ➤ If you're inserting a new column, position the insertion point in any cell in a column that will be adjacent to the new column. If you're adding a new column to the right of the table, use a cell in the rightmost column of the table.

2. Pull down the Table menu and select the Insert command. (Or, right-click anywhere inside the table and select the Insert command from the QuickMenu.) WordPerfect for Windows displays the Insert Columns/Rows dialog box, as shown in the following figure.

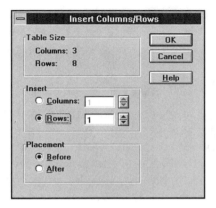

Use the Insert Columns/Rows dialog box to specify the number of columns or rows to insert.

3. Use either the Columns or Rows spinner to specify how many columns or rows you want to insert.

4. In the Placement group, select the option that specifies where you want the new row or column to appear:

   Before Select this option if you want the new column to appear to the left of the current column, or if you want the new row to appear above the current row.

   After Select this option if you want the new column to appear to the right of the current column, or if you want the new row to appear below the current row.

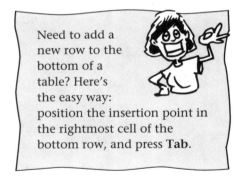

Need to add a new row to the bottom of a table? Here's the easy way: position the insertion point in the rightmost cell of the bottom row, and press **Tab**.

5. Select **OK**. WordPerfect for Windows returns you to the document and inserts the new row or column.

Deleting a Row or Column

If you end up with an extraneous column or row in your table, you should remove it to keep things neat and tidy. Just position the insertion point inside the row or column you want to blow away, pull down the Table menu, and then select the Delete command. (Or you can right-click on the table and select **Delete** from the QuickMenu.) In the Delete dialog box that appears, select **Columns** if you're deleting a column, or **Rows** if you're deleting a row. Select **OK**, and you're done.

Formatting Table Numbers

Most tables include numbers of one kind or another. They could be dollar amounts, percentages, dates, or even numbers that require scientific notation. Whatever the value, your numbers will usually look better (and be more readable) if they're properly formatted (with, say, dollar signs for monetary values). To keep you from having to fumble with the appropriate formatting, WordPerfect for Windows is happy to do it for you, as the following steps show:

1. Position the insertion point appropriately:

   ➤ If you're formatting a single cell, place the insertion point inside the cell.

   ➤ If you're formatting an entire column, place the insertion point inside any cell in the column.

   ➤ If you're formatting the entire table, place the insertion point inside any cell.

2. Pull down the **Table** menu and select **Number Type**, or press **Alt+F12**. (Alternatively, right-click on the table and select **Number Type** from the QuickMenu.) WordPerfect for Windows displays the Number Type dialog box.

   You can also display the Number Type dialog box by clicking on this button in the Tables Toolbar.

3. Select either **Cell**, **Column**, or **Table**.

4. In the Available Types group, select the number format you need. Watch the Preview box to get an idea of what the formatting will look like.

5. Select **OK** to return to the table with the new formatting in effect.

Formatting with the Handy Table Expert

WordPerfect for Windows has all kinds of other table formatting commands that can change things like the borders, colors, and fill patterns for a table. However, instead of slogging through all that stuff, let's just look at a handy new feature in version 6.1: the Table Expert. The Table Expert contains dozens of predefined table styles that automatically apply specific font, border, and color combinations to your entire table. It's about as easy as table formatting gets, as you'll see in the following steps:

1. Place the insertion point inside any cell in the table.

2. Pull down the Table menu and select the Expert command. (Or you can right-click on the table and select Expert from the QuickMenu.) WordPerfect for Windows displays the Table Expert dialog box, as shown below.

 Clicking this button in the Tables Toolbar also accesses the Table Expert dialog box.

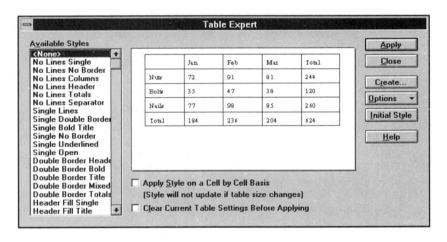

Use the Table Expert for one-click table formatting.

3. Highlight a predefined format from the Available Styles list. The fake table in the middle of the dialog box shows you what the highlighted style will look like.

4. When you've chosen a style that suits your fancy, select Apply.

Number Crunching: Working with Formulas

Although many tables simply display information, you can also use *formulas* to turn the table into a spreadsheet that performs calculations. A formula is an expression that calculates a result. Most formulas consist of one or more values (called *operands*) combined with one or more *operators*. In WordPerfect for Windows, an operand can be any one of the following:

➤ A number

➤ A function (a predefined formula that comes with WordPerfect for Windows)

➤ The value of another cell in the table

To reference other cells, you use the cell's table *address*. The address of a cell is a combination of the column and row that form the cell. For example, the cell in the top left corner of a table is formed by the intersection of column A and row 1, so this cell's address is A1. To reference a cell from another table, precede the cell's address with the name of the table (the first table you created is Table A, the second is Table B, and so on) followed by a dot (for example, Table A.A1).

To make table addresses a little easier to follow, you can tell WordPerfect for Windows to display its *row and column indicators*. These indicators show the column letters across the top of the document and the row numbers down the left side of the document (see the following figure). To turn on these indicators, right-click on the table and activate the Row/Column Indicators from the QuickMenu.

 Clicking on this button in the Tables Toolbar also toggles the row and column indicators.

Operators combine the operands mathematically. The following table lists the operators you can use in your table formulas.

Operator	Example	What it does
+	A1+A2	Adds A1 and A2 together
–	A1–A2	Subtracts A2 from A1
*	A1*A2	Multiplies A1 and A2
/	A1/A2	Divides A1 by A2
^	A1^A2	Raises A1 to the power of A2

For example, suppose your document is an invoice of items purchased. The invoice includes a table that shows the quantity ordered, the item ordered, and the price of the item. The invoice also needs to show the *extended price* for each item (the quantity ordered multiplied by the unit price of the item). Suppose the first item has the quantity ordered in cell A2 and the unit price in cell C2. To calculate the extended price, you'd use the following formula:

A2*C2

The following figure shows an example of an invoice that uses calculation in a table.

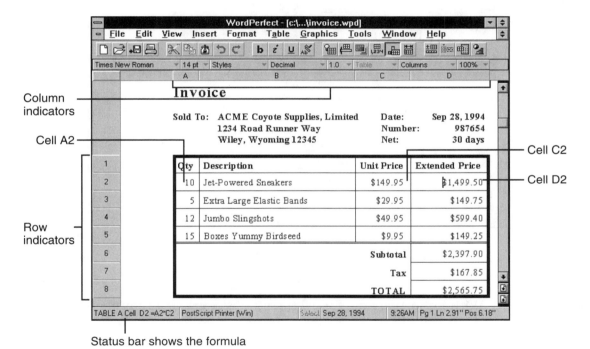

A table that uses formulas for calculations.

Creating a Formula

To make your formula creation chores a little easier, you should use WordPerfect for Windows' *formula bar*. To display it, pull down the Table menu and select Formula Bar. (You can also right-click on the

301

table and select the QuickMenu's Formula Bar command.) The following figure shows the formula bar in action.

Clicking the Tables Toolbar button also displays the formula bar.

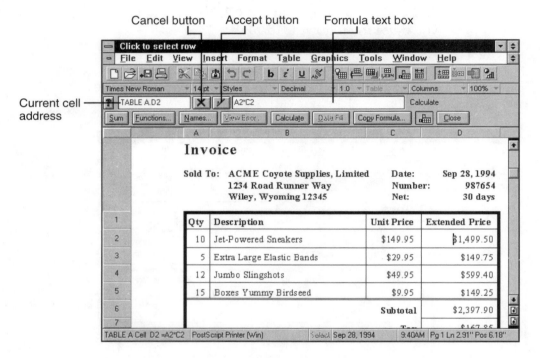

WordPerfect for Windows' formula bar makes it easy to add formulas to your tables.

Without further ado, follow these steps to create a formula and display its result in a table cell:

1. Place the insertion point inside the cell where you want the formula result to appear.

2. Click inside the formula bar's formula text box.

3. Enter an operand.

4. Enter an operator.

5. Repeat steps 3 and 4 until the formula is complete.

6. Click on the Accept button. WordPerfect for Windows displays the formula result in the cell.

Fun with Functions

A *function* is a predefined formula that calculates a special result. WordPerfect for Windows comes with dozens of functions that can calculate everything from the maximum value in a list of numbers to the monthly payment for a loan. Most functions take the following form:

> *NAME(argument1, argument2,...)*

NAME is the name of the function, and *argument1* and *argument2* are the values the function uses to calculate its result (these values are called *arguments*). These values can be numbers, text, other functions, or table cells. For example, suppose you want to calculate the average of the numbers in cells A1, A2, and A3. WordPerfect for Windows' AVE function can do the job, as shown in this formula:

> **AVE(A1,A2,A3)**

Follow these steps to insert functions in your formulas:

1. Select the cell. In the formula text box, position the insertion point where you want the function to appear.

2. Select the Functions button. WordPerfect for Windows displays the Table Functions dialog box.

3. In the Functions list, highlight the function you want to use.

4. Select the Insert button. WordPerfect for Windows returns you to the Formula text box and inserts the function. If the formula has arguments, you'll see placeholders where the arguments should go. For example, the AVE function appears as AVE(List).

> By the way, if you're using consecutive cells, you can use the colon operator (:) to reference the cells in a short form notation. For example, instead of saying *A1,A2,A3*, you could say *A1:A3*.

5. Replace the function placeholders with the actual arguments you want to use in the function.

6. Select the Accept button to enter the formula.

The Least You Need to Know

This chapter showed you the ins and outs of WordPerfect for Windows tables. This is a rather large topic, and there's no way a single chapter can do it justice. However, we did manage to cover all the basics, which is enough to get you started. Just to help things sink in, here's a quick review:

➤ A table is a rectangular grid of rows and columns.

➤ To create a table, pull down the Table menu and select Create (or press **F12**). If you're creating a table from scratch, tell WordPerfect for Windows the number of rows and columns you need.

➤ To enter table text or numbers, select a cell and then type in the value.

➤ You can use WordPerfect for Windows' formatting commands (fonts, justifications, and so on) to jazz up the table, or you can use the table-specific commands found in the Table menu.

➤ A formula is an expression that performs calculations and returns a result. It consists of one or more operands (such as numbers, text, or cell addresses) combined with one or more operators (such as +, –, and *). To display the result of an expression in a cell, display the formula bar, select the cell, and then enter the expression in the formula text box.

Chapter 27

A WordPerfect for Windows Miscellany

> **In This Chapter**
>
> ➤ Working with abbreviations
>
> ➤ Adding bullets and numbers to your text
>
> ➤ Getting the big (or small) picture with Zoom
>
> ➤ Creating a document summary
>
> ➤ Arranging document text in columns

This chapter presents five handy WordPerfect for Windows features for your fun and pleasure: abbreviations, bullets and numbers, Zoom, document summary, and columns. No, they're not related in any way, but I wanted to fit them in somewhere because they can be quite useful. Happy reading!

The Long and Short of Abbreviations

My sources tell me that a place in New Zealand has the record for the longest name: a finger-deadening 85 letters! Imagine having to type *that* all day long. Actually, with WordPerfect for Windows, you wouldn't have to. Why? Because the handy Abbreviation feature lets you designate a short abbreviation for long or frequently used terms (such as your company name or, in my case, the phrase "WordPerfect

for Windows" that I've had to use *ad nauseum* throughout this book).
All you do is type the abbreviation and then tell WordPerfect for
Windows to expand it to its full form. This is useful with a capital U.

For the curious, here's that New Zealand place name in all its
glory:

Taumatawhakatangihangakoauauotamateaturipukakapikimaun-
gahoronukupokaiwhenuakitanatahu.

It means, in case you're wondering, "The place where Tamatea, the man with
the big knees, who slid, climbed, and swallowed mountains, known as
landeater, played his flute to his loved one."

Creating and Expanding an Abbreviation

Abbreviations are extremely simple both to define and to expand. As
proof, here's how you create an abbreviation:

1. Select the word or phrase you want to abbreviate.

2. Pull down the Insert menu and select the Abbreviations command. WordPerfect for Windows displays the Abbreviations dialog
   box.

3. Select Create to display the Create Abbreviation dialog box.

4. Using the Abbreviation Name text box, enter a short abbreviation
   for the word or phrase (a letter or two is all you need).

5. Select **OK** to return to the Abbreviations dialog box, and then
   select Close.

Once you've defined an abbreviation, just type it, place the insertion point anywhere inside or immediately to the left or right of the
abbreviation, and press **Ctrl+A**. (You can also select Abbreviations from
the Insert menu, select the abbreviation from the Abbreviations list
box, and choose the Expand button.)

Renaming an Abbreviation

If you need to rename an existing abbreviation (say, to make the abbreviation shorter or to avoid a conflict with another abbreviation), follow these steps:

1. Pull down the Insert menu and select Abbreviations to display the Abbreviations dialog box.

2. In the Abbreviations list, highlight the abbreviation you want to rename and click the Rename button. WordPerfect for Windows displays the Rename Abbreviation dialog box.

3. Enter the new name in the Rename Abbreviation text box and select OK to return to the Abbreviations dialog box.

4. Select Close to return to the document.

Deleting an Abbreviation

If you have any abbreviations you no longer need, deleting them is no problem. Here are the steps to follow:

1. Pull down the Insert menu and select Abbreviations to display the Abbreviations dialog box.

2. In the Abbreviations list, highlight the abbreviation you want to delete.

3. Select the Delete button. WordPerfect for Windows asks you to confirm the deletion.

4. Select Yes.

5. Select Close to return to the document.

Inserting Bullets and Numbers

If your document includes lists of items, you can make your lists more readable by using bullets or numbers to identify each item (see the following figure). WordPerfect for Windows offers bullets in a number of different styles, and it lets you include several different kinds of numbers that can increment automatically with each item.

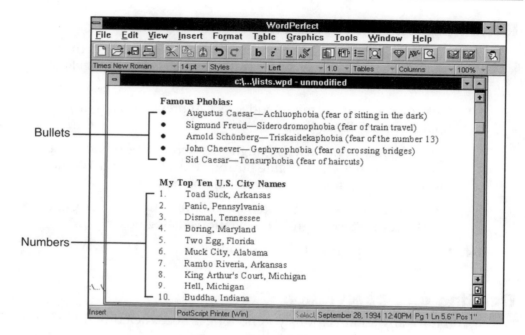

An example of a bulleted list and a numbered list.

Follow these steps to insert bullets or numbers in a document:

1. If you're inserting bullets or numbers in existing text, select the paragraphs you want to use.

2. Pull down the Insert menu and select Bullets & Numbers. (You can also right-click inside the typing area and select Bullets from the QuickMenu.) WordPerfect for Windows displays the Bullets & Numbers dialog box, shown in the following figure.

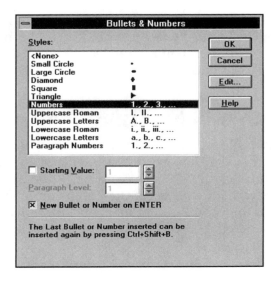

Use the Bullets & Numbers dialog box to select the type of bullets or numbers you want to use.

3. In the **Styles** list, click on the bullet or number style you want to use.

4. If you selected a number and you want to start with a number other than 1, activate the Starting Value check box and enter a number in the spinner.

5. If you selected the Paragraph Numbers style, use the **Paragraph** Level spinner to enter the paragraph level.

6. If you'll be entering multiple items in the list, activate the New Bullet or Number on ENTER check box. WordPerfect for Windows automatically inserts a new bullet or an incremented number each time you press **Enter**.

7. Click on **OK** to return to the document.

8. Enter your list (if necessary). If you elected not to have WordPerfect for Windows insert new bullets or numbers automatically, you can do it manually by pressing **Ctrl+Shift+B**.

Clicking on this button in the 6.1 WordPerfect Toolbar also inserts a bullet.

309

9. If WordPerfect for Windows is adding new bullets automatically and you've finished entering your list, select the Insert menu's Bullets & Numbers command, deactivate the New Bullet or Number on ENTER check box, and then select **OK**.

A Zoom with a View: Using the Zoom Feature

Normally, WordPerfect for Windows displays your document pages at more or less life size. However, you can enlarge or reduce the size of each page with WordPerfect for Windows' Zoom feature. Just pull down the View menu and select the Zoom command. The following table outlines the various Zoom dialog box options. (Note that these options have no effect on what your documents look like when you print them out.)

Select	To
50% or 75%	Reduce the size of the page to 50% or 75% of its normal size.
100%	See the page at normal size.
150% or 200%	Increase the size of the page to 150% or 200% of its normal size.
Margin Width	Increase the size of the page so the area between the margins takes up the full width of the screen.
Page Width	Increase the size of the page so the area between the left and right edges (including the margins) takes up the full width of the screen.
Full Page	Reduce the size of the page so you can see the entire page on-screen.
Other	View the page at whatever magnification makes you happy (the maximum is 400% and the minimum is 25%).

When you've chosen the magnification you want, select **OK** to return to the document. If you prefer, you can also select a Zoom option from the Power Bar. Press and hold down the left mouse button over the Zoom button (see below), and then select the percentage you want from the list that appears.

| Times New Roman ▼ | 14 pt ▼ | Styles ▼ | Left ▼ | 1.0 ▼ | Tables ▼ | Columns ▼ | 100% ▼ |

The Zoom button

 Click this button in the 6.1 WordPerfect Toolbar to toggle the document between normal size and Full Page size.

Working with Document Summaries

A *document summary* is about what you'd expect: a summary of a document's vital statistics: when it was created, who created it, the subject matter, and so on. You can also include a descriptive name for the file and then use this name in the Open File or Save As dialog boxes in place of (or in addition to) the cryptic 8-character name required by DOS. (See Chapter 20, "Managing Files in WordPerfect for Windows," for details.)

Creating a Document Summary

To create a summary for the current document, pull down the File menu and select the Document Summary command. The Document Summary dialog box appears. This is a fairly simple affair, as dialog boxes go; it's mostly text boxes, so you just fill in the blanks. (Note, however, that WordPerfect for Windows fills in the **Revision Date** and **Creation Date** text boxes automatically. If you'd like to enter a different date in the **Creation Date** text box, click on the icon beside it to display a calendar from which you can select the appropriate date.) In particular, if you'd like to get out from under the yoke of those impossible-to-decipher DOS file names, be sure to fill in the **Descriptive Name** box (you can enter up to 255 characters, so there's lots of room to be *very* descriptive). You can also use the scroll bar to display more fields. That's about it, really.

Customizing the Document Summary Dialog Box

The fields you see in the Document Summary dialog box aren't set in stone. WordPerfect for Windows actually has dozens of fields you can include in the summary to record things like a department name, editor's name, or project name. Just select the Configure button, and WordPerfect for Windows displays the Document Summary Configuration dialog box. Here's how it works:

➤ The Selected Fields list shows, in order, the fields currently displayed in the Document Summary dialog box. To change the order, just use your mouse to drag a field to a different location.

➤ The Available Fields list shows all the fields that you can use in the Document Summary dialog box. Fields that are checked are currently selected. You can toggle fields on and off by clicking on them.

➤ When you've got your new configuration, you can use it as the default configuration in all your document summaries by activating the Use as Default button.

When you're done, select **OK** to return to the Document Summary dialog box.

Working with Columns, Just Like the Pros

WordPerfect for Windows, of course, is good for more than just the odd letter or memo. All kinds of people are using the program to self-publish things like newsletters, booklets, pamphlets, fanzines, and more. To give these kinds of documents a more professional look, WordPerfect for Windows enables you to arrange text into columns, just like you see in newspapers and magazines (see the following figure). The next few sections show you how to define columns and enter text into them.

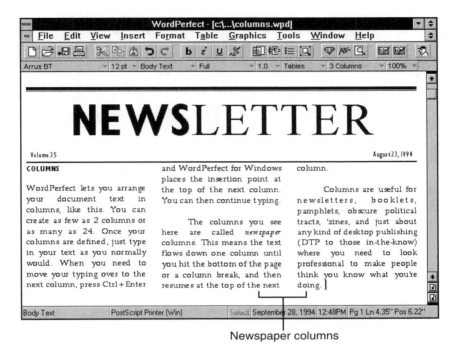

WordPerfect for Windows makes it a breeze to arrange your document text in columns.

Defining Your Columns

Columns have always been one of those features that many people avoid like the plague because, well, they just seem too complicated (and aren't worth the bother). WordPerfect for Windows has changed all that, however, and it's now easier than ever to set up and use columns. To prove it for yourself, just follow these steps to define columns for your document:

1. Position the cursor in the paragraph where you want to start the columns. (If you haven't entered the document text yet, that's okay; it's perfectly acceptable to set up your columns first and then type in the text later.)

2. Pull down the Format menu (or the Layout menu in version 6.0), select the Columns command, and then select Define. WordPerfect for Windows displays the Columns dialog box, shown in the following figure.

313

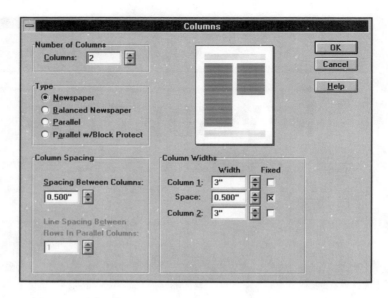

Use the Columns dialog box to define your columns.

3. Use the Columns spinner to enter the number of columns you want.

4. In the Type group, select the type of columns you want from the following options:

Newspaper   The text flows down the page until it hits either the bottom of the page or a *column break* (see "Typing Text in Columns" to learn about column breaks). The text then resumes at the top of the next column.

Balanced Newspaper   The same as Newspaper, except the columns are of equal length.

Parallel   The document text is grouped in rows across the page (much like a spreadsheet). In most cases, it's easier to create a table than use parallel columns (see Chapter 26, "Techniques for Terrific Tables," for details).

Parallel w/Block Protect   The same as Parallel, except that WordPerfect for Windows makes sure that each row is kept together. If part of one row extends onto the next page, WordPerfect for Windows shoves the entire row onto the next page.

5. Use the Column Spacing group to set the following options:

> **S**pacing Between Columns   This spinner determines the default amount of space WordPerfect for Windows places between columns.

> Line Spacing **B**etween Rows in Parallel Columns   This spinner determines the line spacing (single-spaced, double-spaced, and so on) used between the rows in parallel columns.

6. Use the controls in the Column Widths group to adjust the width of each column and the amount of space between individual columns.

7. Select **OK**. WordPerfect for Windows returns you to the document and converts the existing text (if any) into columns.

Instead of monkeying around with the Columns dialog box, you can use the Power Bar's Columns button to set up your columns quickly. Press and hold down the left mouse button over the Columns button (see the following figure), and then select the number of columns you want from the list that appears.

The Columns button

Typing Text in Columns

Once you have defined your columns, your next step is to fill in the columns by typing some text (unless, of course, you converted existing text into columns). Here are some guidelines to follow when typing text columns:

➤ Typing text in a column isn't all that different from typing text in a normal document. Just place the cursor in the column you want to use and start pecking away. If the columns are empty, you have to begin at the top of the first column.

➤ If you want to move the cursor to the next column before you reach the end of the page (this is called *inserting a column break*), press **Ctrl+Enter**.

➤ Entering text in parallel columns is slightly different from entering text in newspaper columns because you generally work across the rows instead of down the columns. In this case, position the cursor in the first column, type your text, and insert a column break (again, by pressing **Ctrl+Enter**) to move to the next column in the same row. When you insert a column break in the last column, WordPerfect for Windows starts a new row and moves the cursor back to the first column.

➤ To navigate your columns, use the keys listed in the following table:

Press	To Move To
Alt+left arrow	The same line in the column to the left
Alt+right arrow	The same line in the column to the right
Alt+Home	The top of the current column
Alt+End	The bottom of the current column

The Least You Need to Know

This chapter presented a hodgepodge of five unrelated—but decidedly useful—features. Here's a retrospective look at what the heck happened:

➤ Abbreviations are one- or two-letter short forms for long words or phrases. To create an abbreviation, select the Insert menu's Abbreviations command, and then select Create. To expand an abbreviation, place the insertion point in or beside the abbreviation and press **Ctrl+A**.

➤ To add bullets or numbers to your text, pull down the Insert menu and select the Bullets & Numbers command.

➤ Use the View menu's Zoom command to change the magnification at which you display your documents.

➤ To create a document summary, pull down the File menu and select the Document Summary command.

➤ To display your text in columns, position the cursor, pull down the Format menu, select Columns, and then select Define.

Chapter 28

Customizing WordPerfect for Windows

In This Chapter

➤ Customizing WordPerfect for Windows' display

➤ Redoing the WordPerfect for Windows environment

➤ Setting some file options

➤ Customizing the Toolbar and Power Bar

➤ Customizing the status bar

➤ Numerous techniques that'll help you put your best WordPerfect for Windows foot forward

WordPerfect for Windows is one of those programs you can accessorize. Oh, sure, it looks fine in its basic outfit—but add a bauble here or a trinket there, and you get a whole new look. The good news is that this new look also makes WordPerfect for Windows both easier to use and more powerful. A fairy tale? No way. Just read this chapter to find out how easy it all is.

As you're reading, note that WordPerfect for Windows has dozens of customization options, so there's no way I can hope to cover all of them in a single chapter. Instead, I'll just show you how to get to the various dialog boxes and I'll point out some of the more useful controls as we go along. If I pass over something that catches your eye, press **F1** and the WordPerfect for Windows' Help system will give you more info.

First Things First: Displaying the Preferences Dialog Box

All of WordPerfect for Windows' customization options are available from the Preferences dialog box shown in the following figure. (Although you'll see as we go through this chapter that there are also a few sneaky shortcuts you can use.) To display this dialog box, pull down the Edit menu and select the Preferences command. (If you're using version 6.0, select the Preferences command from the File menu.)

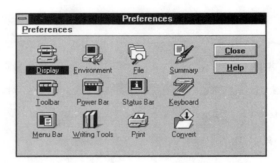

Use the Preferences dialog box to access all of WordPerfect for Windows' customization options.

Dealing with the Display Preferences

The Display Preferences govern the look and feel of the WordPerfect for Windows screen. For example, you can turn the scroll bars off and on, and you can set the default view mode. Follow these steps to set the Display Preferences:

1. In the Preferences dialog box, select the **Display** icon, or pull down the **Preferences** menu and select the **D**isplay command. The Display Preferences dialog box appears, as shown in the following figure.

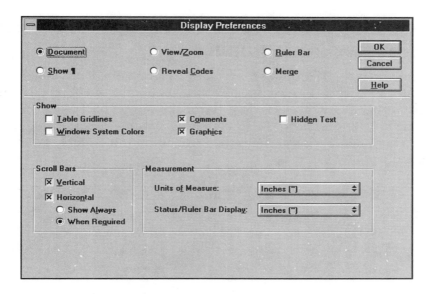

The controls in the Display Preferences dialog box affect the look and feel of the WordPerfect for Windows' screen.

2. Make sure the **Document** option is activated, and then choose the document display options you want. For example, use the **Vertical** and **Horizontal** check boxes to toggle the scroll bars on and off.

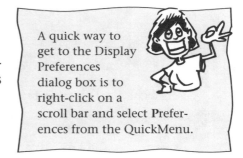

A quick way to get to the Display Preferences dialog box is to right-click on a scroll bar and select **Preferences** from the QuickMenu.

3. Activate the **View/Zoom** option, and then select an option in the Default View and Default Zoom groups.

4. To change the Ruler Bar's behavior, select **Ruler** Bar and select your options from the controls that appear. In particular, if you'd like the Ruler Bar to appear with all new documents, activate the Show Ruler Bar on New and Current Document check box.

5. When you're done, select **OK** to return to the Preferences dialog box.

Customizing the WordPerfect for Windows Environment

WordPerfect for Windows' *environment* is a miscellaneous collection of items that covers various aspects of the program's operation. To take a look at them, either select the **Environment** icon in the Preferences dialog box, or pull down the Preferences menu and select the Environment command. This displays the Environment Preferences dialog box, shown below.

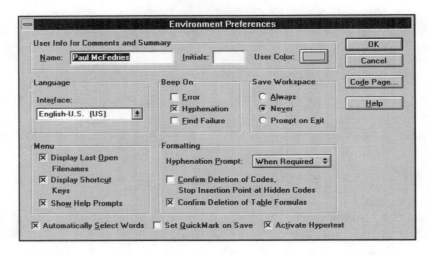

Use the Environment Preferences dialog box to set up WordPerfect for Windows to suit your taste.

There are all kinds of little goodies in this dialog box, but I'll just discuss the highlights:

➤ If you use the Comments feature, fill in your Name and Initials. This lets you insert them with the click of a button from the Comments feature bar (see Chapter 17, "Other Ways to Look Good").

➤ The WordPerfect for Windows *workspace* is a collection of open documents and their window positions. (See Chapter 19, "Working with Multiple Documents," to learn how to work with document windows.) If you use the same documents each day, activate the Always option in the Save Workspace group. This tells WordPerfect for Windows to remember which documents were open whenever you exit the program. Then, the next time you start the program, it reloads those same files automatically. If you'd prefer to be prompted about saving the workspace, activate the Prompt on Exit option, instead.

➤ If you find yourself constantly opening and closing the same documents, make sure the Menu group's Display Last Open Filenames check box is activated. This gives you a list at the bottom of the File menu of the last four documents you used. You can open any of these documents simply by selecting it from the list.

➤ If you like to hyphenate your documents (as described in Chapter 17, "Other Ways to Look Good") but you hate being constantly prompted, select Never from the Hyphenation Prompt pop-up list.

➤ The QuickMark feature (see Chapter 8, "Day-to-Day Drudgery II: Navigating Documents") provides a handy way to navigate a document. If you like to use it, activate the Set QuickMark on Save check box. This sets a QuickMark at the current insertion point position whenever you save your document.

➤ As explained in Chapter 11, "Block Partying: Working with Blocks of Text," WordPerfect for Windows version 6.1 selects text word-by-word if you use a mouse. If you'd prefer to select text character-by-character, deactivate the Automatically Select Words check box.

When you're done, select **OK** to put the new settings into effect.

Fooling Around with the File Preferences

WordPerfect for Windows has a collection of file preferences that govern things like the default directory for your documents, graphics files, templates, and which extension the program uses when you save a document. To check these out, follow these steps:

1. In the Preferences dialog box, select the **File** icon, or pull down the **Preferences** menu and select File. The File Preferences dialog box appears.

2. Make sure the Documents/Backup option is activated.

3. If you want to store your documents in a directory other than WordPerfect for Windows' WPDOCS subdirectory, use the Default Directory text box to enter the new directory.

4. If you'd prefer to use a file extension other than .WPD (such as .DOC), enter the alternate extension in the Use Default Extension on Open and Save text box.

5. To have WordPerfect for Windows perform timed backups of your documents, activate the Timed Document Backup every check box and enter the number of minutes between backups in the spinner.

6. To save the original document every time you edit and save a document, activate the Original Document Backup check box. This tells WordPerfect for Windows to save the original document with the extension BK!.

7. If you're up to it, check out the other options in the File Preferences dialog box (Templates, and so on).

8. When you've had enough, select **OK** to return to the Preferences dialog box.

Customizing the Toolbars

As you've seen throughout this book, WordPerfect for Windows' Toolbars give you push-button access to many of the program's features. WordPerfect also gives you a few customization options to make the Toolbars even more convenient (if you can stand it). In the Preferences dialog box, select the **Toolbar** icon, or pull down the **Preferences** menu and select Toolbar. The Toolbar Preferences dialog box appears.

Setting Some Toolbar Options

The appearance of each Toolbar is controlled by a dialog box of options. To display this dialog box, select the Options button. Here's a summary of the controls you get in the Toolbar Options dialog box:

You can also display the Toolbar Preferences dialog box by right-clicking the Toolbar and selecting Preferences from the QuickMenu.

➤ The option buttons in the Appearance group control the look of the Toolbar buttons. The normal style is Picture, but you can also select Text (to show the buttons with text only), or Picture and Text (to show the buttons with both text and pictures).

➤ If you chose either Text or Picture and Text, use the Font Face and Font Size lists to format the button text.

➤ The option buttons in the Location group determine where the Toolbars reside. You can choose Top (the normal position), Bottom, Left, Right, or Palette (this gives you a "floating" Toolbar that you can move around).

There's an easier way to display a Toolbar in a different location. Exit all the dialog boxes and move the mouse pointer over any blank space in the Toolbar. The mouse pointer turns into a hand. Now press and hold down the left mouse button, and then drag the Toolbar around the screen. As you drag, a gray outline shows you where the Toolbar will appear. When you release the mouse button, WordPerfect for Windows deposits the Toolbar in the new location.

➤ I'll show you in the next section how to customize a Toolbar by adding new buttons. If you add more buttons than can fit in the width of the screen, WordPerfect for Windows displays the extra buttons on a second row. Use the Maximum Number of Row/Columns to Show spinner to specify the number of Toolbar rows to display.

When you're done, select OK to return to the Toolbar Preferences dialog box.

Remaking Toolbars in Your Own Image

You can customize the buttons on each Toolbar to suit your needs and the way you work. Specifically, you can remove buttons you wouldn't use in a million years, and you can add new buttons for features you use regularly. Here's how it's done:

1. In the Toolbar Preferences dialog box, use the Available Toolbars list to highlight the Toolbar you want to customize.

2. Select the Edit button. WordPerfect for Windows displays the Toolbar at the top of the screen, and the Toolbar Editor appears, as shown in the following figure.

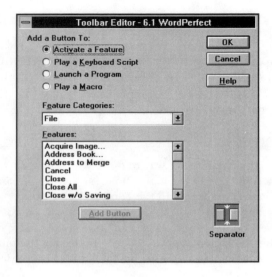

Use the Toolbar Editor to add and remove Toolbar buttons.

3. Use the following techniques to customize the Toolbar:

➤ To add a button, use the Feature Categories list to select a category, and then drag the feature you want from the **Fea**-tures list to the Toolbar. (If you just want to add the button to the end of the Toolbar, click on **Add Button**.)

➤ To add a space, drag the Separator to the Toolbar.

➤ To move a button, drag it along the Toolbar.

➤ To remove a button, drag it off the Toolbar.

4. When you've finished playing, select **OK** to return to the Toolbar Preferences dialog box.

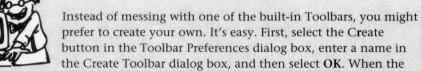

Instead of messing with one of the built-in Toolbars, you might prefer to create your own. It's easy. First, select the **C**reate button in the Toolbar Preferences dialog box, enter a name in the Create Toolbar dialog box, and then select **OK**. When the Toolbar Editor appears, just follow the techniques from steps 3 and 4 above to add buttons and separators to the Toolbar. To use your new Toolbar, highlight it in the Toolbar Preferences dialog box and choose the **S**elect button.

Customizing the Power Bar

The Power Bar contains lots of useful lists, but they may not be the tools *you* use every day. You can remedy this by customizing the Power Bar to suit the way you work. Follow these steps:

1. In the Preferences dialog box, select the **Power Bar** icon, or pull down the **Preferences** menu and select the Power Bar command. The Power Bar Options dialog box appears, as shown in the following figure.

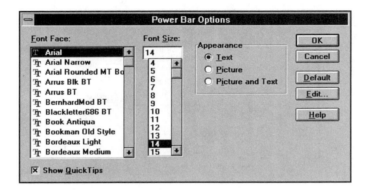

Use the Power Bar Options dialog box to customize the Power Bar.

2. In the Appearance group, select either Text, **Picture**, or Picture and Text.

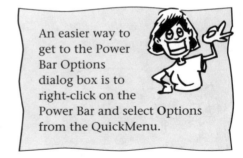

An easier way to get to the Power Bar Options dialog box is to right-click on the Power Bar and select Options from the QuickMenu.

3. If you chose either Text or Picture and Text in step 2, use the **F**ont Face and Font **S**ize lists to set the font for the Power Bar text.

4. Select the Edit button. WordPerfect for Windows displays the Power Bar version of the Toolbar Editor.

5. Use the same techniques that I outlined in the last section for customizing a Toolbar. When you're done, select **OK** to return to the Power Bar Options dialog box.

6. Select **OK** to return to the Preferences dialog box.

Customizing the Status Bar

The default Status Bar shows you things like the current printer, whether or not text is selected, the date and time, and the insertion point position. This is a good start, but there's more info you might want to see. You can add new items to the Status Bar and remove existing items by following these steps:

1. In the Preferences dialog box, select the **Status Bar** icon, or pull down the **P**references menu and select St**a**tus Bar. The Status Bar Preferences dialog box appears, as shown in the following figure.

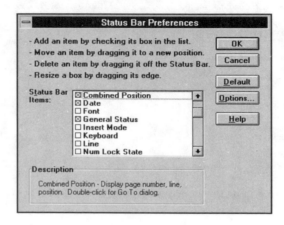

Use the Status Bar Preferences dialog box to redo the Status Bar to suit your fancy.

You can bypass the Preferences dialog box and go directly to the Status Bar Preferences dialog box by right-clicking on the Status Bar and selecting **P**references from the QuickMenu.

2. The check boxes in the Status Bar Items list show you everything you can include in the Status Bar. Items that are checked are the ones currently displayed in the Status Bar.

   ➤ To add an item, find it in the list and either click on it, or highlight it and press the **Spacebar**.

   ➤ To delete a checked item, click on it again, or highlight it and press the **Spacebar**. You can also drag it off the Status Bar.

➤ To move an item, drag it along the Status Bar.

➤ To change the size of an item, drag either the left or right edge of the item's box.

3. To change the Status Bar options, select the **Options** button, make your selections in the Status Bar Options dialog box, and select **OK**.

4. When you're done, select **OK** to return to the Preferences dialog box.

The Least You Need to Know

This chapter took you through a few neat features designed to make your WordPerfect life easier. Here's a recap:

➤ To display the Preferences dialog box, pull down the Edit menu and select the Preferences command.

➤ Select the **Display** icon to customize certain aspects of the WordPerfect for Windows display.

➤ Select the **Environment** icon to change various environment settings such as your user info, and whether or not WordPerfect for Windows saves your workspace.

➤ Select the **File** icon to change the settings for things like the default document directory and the extension WordPerfect for Windows uses when you save your documents.

➤ Select the **Toolbar** icon to customize the look of the Toolbars and to edit individual Toolbars to suit your needs.

➤ Select the **Power Bar** icon to customize the appearance of the Power Bar and to add and remove Power Bar buttons.

➤ Select the **Status Bar** icon to rearrange the Status Bar info.

Chapter 29

Ten Great WordPerfect for Windows Ideas

Like most people, after forking out hard-earned cash (your own or your company's) for WordPerfect for Windows, you're probably looking to get your money's worth. Does this mean you need to fixate on each feature and memorize mundane minutiae? Not on your life! No, to get the most out of WordPerfect for Windows—or any piece of software, for that matter—you need to put it to work doing practical, useful things either around the home or at the office. To get you started, this chapter suggests a veritable bounty of handy—and sometimes even interesting—WordPerfect for Windows ideas and assorted stupid computer tricks.

1. Backing Up Your Files from WordPerfect for Windows

Computers are relatively reliable beasts, but one of these days your hard disk will crash, you'll accidentally delete your last six months' work, or a virus will trash your precious files. To help you sleep better at night, you should regularly make backup copies of your documents to a floppy disk. This way, when disaster strikes, you'll at least be able to restore your work.

Does all this mean you have to rush out and fork out big bucks for a dedicated backup program? Nah. WordPerfect for Windows' directory dialog boxes have a Copy command you can press into service as a basic backup utility. (Not sure how to wield the directory dialog boxes? Slink back to Chapter 20, "Managing Files in WordPerfect for Windows," to learn everything you need to know.) The following steps show you how it's done:

1. Place a formatted floppy disk in the appropriate disk drive.

2. In any directory dialog box, highlight the files you want to back up.

3. Select the Copy command from the File Options pop-up list. The Copy Files dialog box appears.

4. In the Copy Selected Files To text box, enter **A:** if the disk is in drive A, or **B:** if it's in drive B.

5. Select Copy. WordPerfect for Windows copies the files to the floppy disk.

6. Select **Cancel** to return to the document.

You can make backing up a little easier by changing a couple of setup options. In any directory dialog box, select the **Setup** button to display the Open/Save As Setup dialog box. Then set the following options:

➤ In the **S**how pop-up, select the Filename, **S**ize, Date, Time option.

➤ In the Sort **B**y pop-up, select the **D**ate/Time option.

➤ In the Sort **O**rder pop-up, select the **D**escending option.

Select **OK** to return to the directory dialog box. You'll notice that your files are now sorted by date and time in descending order. How does this help? Well, the documents you worked on most recently will appear at the top of the list. Since these are the ones you're most likely to back up, it's easy just to mark everything you need and crank up the Copy command.

2. Using Templates to Avoid Reinventing the Wheel

In word processing lingo, a *template* is a special document that contains predefined text, graphics, formatting, abbreviations, and styles. The template acts as a sort of skeleton from which you can create other documents.

For example, suppose you wanted to use WordPerfect for Windows to create cover sheets for faxed documents. Most of these cover sheets would probably end up with the same basic structure: a header showing your company information and maybe a logo, the word "FAX" or "FACSIMILE" in large type, headings such as "To," "Fax #," "From," and "Date," and whatever else you need to display. To save some work, you could create a fax cover sheet template that includes just those constant elements that appear in every fax. You could then fill in the variable info, such as the recipient's name and fax number, the date, the number of pages in the fax, and the cover sheet text.

The best part about templates is that WordPerfect for Windows has already gone to the trouble of creating the most common ones. In fact, the program comes with dozens of predefined templates that cover not only faxing, but also memos, purchase orders, invoices, and lots more. To show you how they work, let's go through an example. The following steps show you how to create a fax cover sheet using one of WordPerfect for Windows' templates:

1. Pull down the File menu and select New, or press **Ctrl+T**. (In version 6.0, select the File menu's Template command.) WordPerfect for Windows displays the New Document dialog box.

   You can also access the New Document dialog box by clicking on this button in the 6.1 WordPerfect Toolbar.

2. Use the **Group** list to select the category of document you want. For the example, select **fax**. A list of the available templates appears in the Select Template list.

3. If you'd like to take a gander at a template before making up your mind, highlight it and select the View button. WordPerfect for Windows displays the template in the Viewer window. When you're done, press **Alt+F4**.

4. Highlight the template you want in the Select Template list and choose **Select**.

5. If this is your first template, WordPerfect for Windows mumbles something about personalizing your templates. Select **OK**, and the Enter Your Personal Information dialog box will appear.

6. Enter your **Name**, **Title**, and so on, and select **OK** when you're done. (Don't worry, you won't have to go through this with every template; you only do it once to make WordPerfect happy.)

7. WordPerfect for Windows displays a dialog box so you can fill in the data for the template. For the fax, you need to enter the recipient's name and fax number, what the fax is about, and the number of pages (see the following figure). When you're done, select **OK**. WordPerfect for Windows displays your template in all its glory.

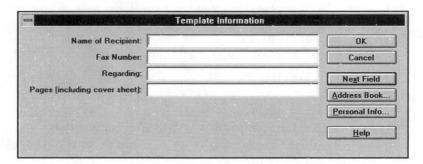

Use the Template Information dialog box to fill in your fax template data.

8. Fill in whatever other info the template needs. For the fax, you'll usually need to add a note or some comments. If you want to keep the document for posterity, don't forget to save it.

Templates are also a great way to achieve a consistent look and feel between departments. Assuming everyone uses WordPerfect for Windows, just issue the template file to each person and show him or her how to use it.

3. Creating an Address Book for Your Templates

Many of WordPerfect for Windows' templates force you to enter address data. There are the fax templates, of course, and also the templates for memos, letters, envelopes, invoices, and more. Yes, these templates save you tons of work, but pounding in all that address info every time will still seem like drudgery after a while. My approach to dull, repetitive work is "Just say NO!" In this case, you can say no to drudgery by creating a WordPerfect for Windows *address book* that contains the address particulars of your friends, family, colleagues, clients, or whomever. Here's how you add stuff to an address book:

1. The next time you create a template that requires an address, pause at the dialog box where you'd normally enter the address data. Select the Address Book button (or, for some templates, the Addresses button). WordPerfect for Windows displays the Template Address Book dialog box.

   Clicking on this button in the Utility Toolbar takes you directly to the Template Address Book dialog box.

2. Select the Add button. The Edit Address dialog box appears.

3. Use the text boxes to fill in the address data.

4. Select **OK**. WordPerfect for Windows returns you to the Template Address Book and displays the person's name in the Names list.

5. Repeat steps 2–4 to add more addresses.

6. If you're creating a template, highlight the address you want to use in the Names list and then choose Select.

4. Creating Your Own Overheads Template

WordPerfect for Windows' predefined templates cover a lot of ground, but they're not exhaustive. To bolster those that come with WordPerfect for Windows, you can create your own templates.

As an example, let's create a template for documents that can be used as overheads in a presentation. The following figure shows an example of an overhead template. You replace **[Slide Title]** with the title of the slide, and then you fill in the bullet points (**[First point]**, **[Second point]**, and so on).

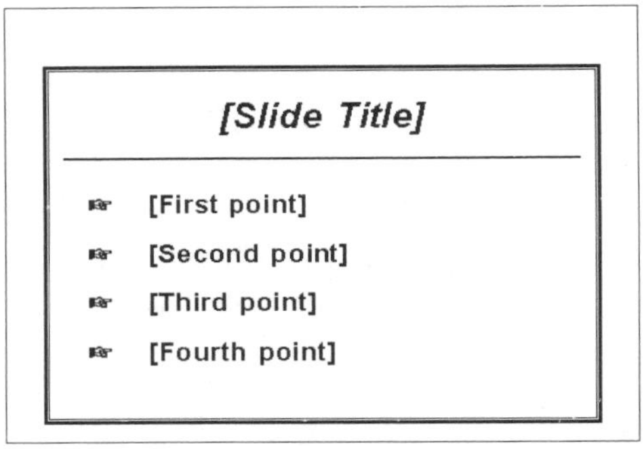

An example overhead template.

Here are the steps to follow to define and create your own template:

1. Pull down the File menu and select the New command, or press **Ctrl+T**. (Select the File menu's Template command in version 6.0.)

2. In the Options pop-up list, select New Template. WordPerfect for Windows displays a new template document.

3. Build the overhead template using the following guidelines:

   ➤ Overhead text needs to be big so people in the back of the room can see it. For my overheads, I use a 48-point bold italic font for the title and a 36-point bold font for the bullet points. Arial is a good typeface to use because the individual letters are clean and easy to read.

   ➤ I showed you how to work with bullets back in Chapter 27, "A WordPerfect for Windows Miscellany." To get the pointing hand bullets in the overhead template, select the Insert menu's Bullets & Numbers command, highlight a bullet you don't use in the Styles list, and then select Edit. In the Styles Editor, double-click on the number code in the Contents box. (For example, if you're using the Small Circle bullet, the number code will be 6,34.) In the WordPerfect Characters dialog box, highlight the new bullet (the right-pointing hand is in the Iconic Symbols character set), and then choose Insert and Close. Select **OK** to use the new bullet.

   ➤ Overheads usually look best with the page arranged in landscape orientation (where the text runs along the long side of the page). See Chapter 17, "Other Ways to Look Good," to learn how to set the orientation.

   ➤ A border around the page is often a nice touch on an overhead. To add a border, pull down the Format menu (or the Layout menu in version 6.0), select Page, and then select Border/Fill. In the Page Border dialog box, select Border Style, and then highlight the border you want from the box that appears. Select **OK** to return to the document.

   You can also display the Page Border dialog box by clicking on this button in the Page Toolbar.

➤ To maximize the readability of the slide, set the line spacing to 1.5 (see Chapter 14, "Making Your Lines and Paragraphs Look Good").

4. When you're ready to save the template, pull down the **File** menu and select **Save** (or press **Ctrl+S**). The Save Template dialog box appears.

5. Use the **Description** text box to enter a description of the template (for example, "Template for overhead presentations"); use the Template **Name** text box to enter a file name for the template (for example, "overhead"); use the Template Group list to select a group for the template (**business** is probably your best bet). When you're done, select **OK**.

6. Select Exit Template from the Template feature bar.

5. Merging for Mass Mailings

If you've ever received one of those "standard reply" letters addressed "To Whom It May Concern" or to "Occupant," you know how impersonal and cold they feel. They have about as much charm as a tax audit. But if you have to send out a mass mailing of a few dozen or even a few hundred pieces, who has time to personalize each one? The solution is to take advantage of modern technology and check out WordPerfect for Windows' Merge feature, which can automatically personalize (is that an oxymoron?) your letters, thank-you notes, or envelopes.

How does it perform such magic? It's quite simple really. Let's say you want to send out a letter to a few dozen customers, and you want each letter to begin with a friendly "Dear Frank," or "Dear Martha," or whatever. You begin by entering all the pertinent data for each person in a table in a separate file. This includes the first name, last name, address, and so on. Now you write the basic letter, and in the spot where each person's first name will appear, you place a special code that says, essentially, "insert each person's first name here." That's about it really. When you run the merge, WordPerfect for Windows goes through the table of data, and for each person, it extracts the first name, creates a copy of the letter, and inserts the name at the spot you specified. In other words, the two files are *merged* to produce a new document. (It's also pretty easy to extend the merge to include each person's last name, address, and so on.)

Step 1: Defining the Data File

The hardest part of a merge (or, at least, the most time-consuming), is creating the data file. Entering data for dozens or hundreds of people or companies is no one's idea of fun, but at least you know you'll only have to do it once.

Each person's data is contained in a file called, appropriately enough, the **data file**. The file into which WordPerfect places the data is called the **form file**.

There are a couple of ways to create a data file, but by far the easiest and most straightforward is to enter everything into a table. (If you're not familiar with WordPerfect for Windows tables, this might be a good time to review the material in Chapter 26, "Techniques for Terrific Tables.") The idea is that each row in the table represents a particular person (or company, or whatever), and each column represents a specific chunk of info, such as that person's first name, last name, address, and so on.

How do you know what information to include in the data file? Well, it depends entirely on what you want to use in the merge. In a basic letter, you'll need first name, last name, address, city, state, and ZIP code. If you're writing thank-you notes for charitable donations, you'll need to keep track of the amount of the donation so you can refer to it in the note.

Start a new document and then follow these steps to create your merge data file:

1. Pull down the Tools menu and select Merge, or simply press **Shift+F9**. WordPerfect for Windows displays the Merge dialog box.

2. Activate the **Place Records in a Table** check box and select **Data**. The Create Data File dialog box appears.

3. In the Name a Field text box, enter a name for a field in your data table, and then select Add. (Make sure the name reflects the type of data that will appear in the field, such as **First Name**.) WordPerfect for Windows adds the field name to the Field Name List box.

4. Repeat step 3 until you've entered all the fields you need. Then select **OK**. WordPerfect for Windows creates a table showing the field names in the first row with a blank row underneath.

5. If you're using version 6.1, the Quick Data Entry dialog box appears. To enter data with this dialog box, type the data for a single record into each field, and then select the New **R**ecord button. Repeat this until you've entered all the records. Then select Close. Otherwise, just enter your data directly into the table.

6. If WordPerfect for Windows asks if you want to save your changes, select **Yes** and then use the Save Data File As dialog box to enter a file name. (Don't bother adding an extension; WordPerfect for Windows adds the .DAT extension it uses for data files automatically.)

The figure below shows a data file with some data entered into the table.

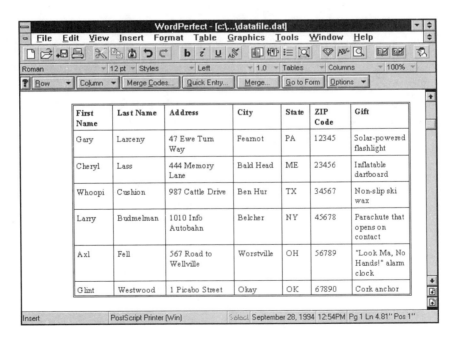

A data file with some data entered into the table.

Step 2: Defining the Form File

Your next step is to set up the form file to receive the info from the data file. This involves two things: creating the basic "skeleton" of the document you want to send out, and inserting *merge codes* that tell WordPerfect for Windows where you want it to stick the data file data. The following steps spell everything out:

1. In a new document, pull down the Tools menu and select **M**erge (or press **Shift+F9**) to display the Merge dialog box.

2. Select the Form button. WordPerfect for Windows displays the Create Merge File dialog box.

3. Make sure the **N**ew Document Window option is activated, and then select **OK**. Now the Create Form File dialog box appears.

4. In the Associate a Data File text box, enter the name of the data file you created in the last section, and then select **OK**.

5. Enter the regular document text until you reach a place where you want to insert some data file info (such as a first name).

6. Select the Insert Field button from the Merge feature bar. The Insert Field Name or Number dialog box appears.

7. In the Field Names list, highlight the field you want to use and select Insert. Repeat this for any other fields you want to add. Then select Close. If necessary, add spaces and punctuation marks (such as commas) to make the data readable.

8. Repeat steps 5–7 until the form file is complete.

9. Save the file (using the **F**ile menu's **S**ave command). When you enter a file name, don't bother adding an extension. WordPerfect for Windows automatically adds the .FRM extension it prefers to use for form files.

The following figure shows an example form file that uses codes for the columns in the data file shown earlier.

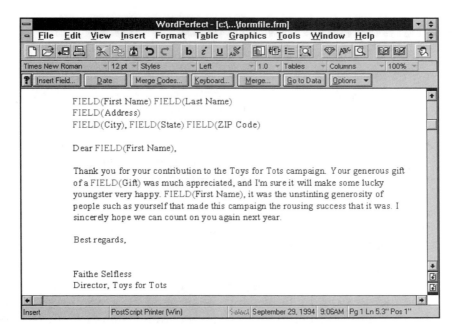

A form file with several merge codes.

Step 3: Running the Merge

Well, it's all over but for the shouting, as they say. The hard part's done, and all that remains is to perform the merge. Here's what you do:

1. Select Merge from the Tools menu or **Merge** from the Merge feature bar.

2. Select the **Merge** button. WordPerfect for Windows displays the Perform Merge dialog box.

3. Make sure the Form File text box contains either **<Current Document>** or the name of your form file, the **Data** File text box contains the name of your data file, and the Output File text box says **<New Document>**.

4. Select **OK**. WordPerfect for Windows performs the merge. In the new file that appears, each merged document is displayed on a separate page.

6. Monitoring Your Finances with a WordPerfect for Windows Checkbook

In the old days of computers (way back in the '80s!), life was simple: word processing programs were only used for writing; desktop publishing programs were only used for page layout; and spreadsheets were only used for calculating. Nowadays, however, muscular programs like WordPerfect for Windows give you the electronic equivalent of one-stop shopping. So, yes, you can write with WordPerfect for Windows, but you can also do some pretty fancy page layout stuff that used to be the domain of high-end programs. And WordPerfect for Windows' extensive table features allow you to turn the program into a veritable spreadsheet. No, it's not in the same league as Microsoft Excel or Lotus 1-2-3, but it can handle reasonably complex calculations without a complaint.

As an example, how about turning a WordPerfect for Windows document into a digital version of your checkbook register? As you can see in the following figure, you can record all the usual stuff—check numbers, the date of each transaction, the payee or description, the payment or deposit, and whether or not the transaction has cleared the bank—and you can also convince WordPerfect for Windows to track the account balance for you—automatically! No more pecking away at tiny calculator keys or fumbling with your fingers.

Checkbook Register

Bank: Last National Bank
Account Number: 1234567

Chk #	Date	Payee/Description	Payment	C	Deposit	Balance
	12/12/94	Opening balance			$100.00	$100.00
	12/14/94	Deposit			$500.00	$600.00
1	12/18/94	Christmas presents	$348.50			$251.50
	12/19/94	Withdrawal	$100.00			$151.50
	12/28/94	Salary			$500.00	$651.50
2	12/31/94	Bert's Beer Store	$221.37			$430.13

The checkbook template.

If you've read Chapter 26, "Techniques for Terrific Tables," creating the checkbook register will pose no problems. Here are a few notes about how I've set things up:

➤ The cells in the Date column have been formatted as dates. Place the insertion point in any cell in the column, and then select the Table menu's Number Type command. Select Column, select Date/Time, and then select Custom. Choose the date format you want from the Custom Date Types dialog box, and then select OK.

➤ The cells in the Payment, Deposit, and Balance columns have been formatted as Currency and aligned on the decimal point.

➤ You can make WordPerfect for Windows print the column headings at the top of each new page. Select a cell in the header row and then select the Table menu's Format command. In the Format dialog box, select Row, activate the Header Row check box, and then select OK.

The only moderately tricky concept is the formula you use to track the account balance. You begin the register by entering an opening balance transaction. Enter the current balance in your account in the first cell below the Balance header (cell G2 in my register). For subsequent transactions, WordPerfect calculates the balance by either subtracting the value of the transaction (if it's a payment) or adding the value of the transaction (if it's a deposit). Since we don't know in advance whether a given transaction is going to be a payment or deposit, we can take both into account by using the following calculation to derive the current balance:

Previous Balance – Payment + Deposit

For example, once you enter the second transaction, the previous balance is cell G2, and the transaction value is either in the Payment column (cell D3) or the Deposit column (cell F3). So the formula that calculates the new balance in cell G3 is as follows:

G2–D3+F3

Enter this formula in cell G3, and copy it each time you add a new transaction, by following these steps:

1. Place the insertion point inside the last cell that contains the formula.

2. Pull down the Table menu and select the Copy Formula command. WordPerfect for Windows displays the Copy Formula dialog box.

3. Activate the Down option and make sure the spinner value is 1.

4. Select OK. WordPerfect for Windows copies the formula to the cell below and adjusts the formula's cell references accordingly.

7. Creating Your Own Business Cards

If you're part of the growing SOHO movement (Small Office, Home Office), you can use WordPerfect for Windows to create your own snazzy business cards. The only material you need is the appropriate paper for printing the cards (the stock should be thick enough that the cards don't appear flimsy, but not so thick that your printer will choke on it). The rest just requires a modicum of imagination and creativity.

The secret to creating business cards is WordPerfect for Windows' Subdivide feature. Subdivide breaks up a single page into two or more *logical pages*. WordPerfect for Windows treats each of these logical pages as though it were a separate page on its own, so it makes it easy to format each logical page as a separate entity.

In our business card example, each logical page contains the text and graphics for a single card. Here are the steps to follow to subdivide your pages:

1. Pull down the Format menu (or the Layout menu in version 6.0), select Page, and then select the Subdivide Page command. WordPerfect for Windows displays the Subdivide Page dialog box.

   Clicking this Page Toolbar button also displays the Subdivide Page dialog box.

2. Use the Number of Columns spinner to enter the number of logical pages that will appear across the physical page. Business cards are usually 3 1/2 inches wide, so enter 2 (I'm assuming you're using 8 1/2-inch wide paper).

3. Use the Number of **R**ows spinner to enter the number of logical pages that will appear down the physical page. Most business cards are 2 inches tall, so enter **5** (I'm assuming your paper is 11 inches tall).

4. Select **OK** to return to the document. WordPerfect for Windows displays the first subdivided page.

At this point, you just enter and format the info you want to appear on the card (including any graphics you want to include, such as a logo). When you're done, move to the bottom of the "page" and press **Ctrl+Enter** to start the next logical page. In most cases, you can create each subsequent card just by copying and pasting the information from the first card. The following figure shows a subdivided page with some example business cards.

Some business cards on a subdivided page.

Subdivided pages have endless uses: name tags, phone message sheets, dinner place cards, invitations, you name it. In each case, first determine the dimensions of the object you want to create, and then use these dimensions to determine how many logical pages to create.

8. Creating a Drop Cap

A *drop cap* is the first letter of a paragraph that is much larger than the regular paragraph text, and extends down into the text. The following figure shows an example. Drop caps are often used in articles and newsletters to add a touch of class to the proceedings.

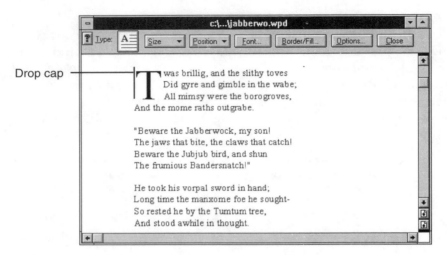

An example of a drop cap.

Here are the steps to follow to create a drop cap (note that you need WordPerfect for Windows version 6.1 to perform these steps):

1. Position the cursor at the beginning of the paragraph.

2. Pull down the Format menu and select the Drop Cap command, or press **Ctrl+Shift+C**. WordPerfect for Windows converts the first letter of the paragraph to a drop cap and displays the Drop Cap feature bar.

3. If you like, you can use the feature bar buttons to format the drop cap.

4. When you're done, select Close.

9. Keeping Track of Document Revisions

Some documents may go through a dozen amendments or more, so it becomes crucial to know which version you're dealing with. If you include the codes (not just text) for the date and time, WordPerfect for Windows updates everything each time you work on the file, so you always know when it was last modified.

The ideal place for these date and time codes is a header or footer (which I covered in Chapter 15, "Making Your Pages Look Good"). When you're in the header or footer editing screen, pull down the Insert menu, select Date, and then select the Date Code command.

If you don't want to clutter a header or footer with a date code, you can also use the Document Summary feature to keep track of revisions. Return to Chapter 27, "A WordPerfect for Windows Miscellany," to find out more.

You may also want to include the document's file name in the header or footer. To do this, pull down the Insert menu, select Other, and then select either Filename (to insert the name of the file only) or Path and Filename (to insert the file's drive and directory, as well as its name).

10. Using QuickLists to Avoid Sharing Conflicts

The QuickLists we looked at earlier in the book (see Chapter 21, "Finding Files Quickly with QuickLists and QuickFinder") are great if you have several people sharing a computer. If everyone uses different files, you can set up a QuickList for each person so she can easily work with her own files (and keep her grubby hands off yours).

The best way to do this is to create a separate subdirectory for each person. You can use the person's name to make it clear who belongs to which directory. Here's how it's done:

1. In a directory dialog box, select the Create Directory command from the File Options pop-up list. WordPerfect for Windows displays the Create Directory dialog box.

2. Use the New Directory text box to enter the full name of the new directory. For example, if you want to create a subdirectory named MARGE attached to the main WPWIN directory, you'd enter **C:\OFFICE\WPWIN\MARGE.**

3. Select Create. WordPerfect for Windows creates the directory.

When creating the QuickLists for each person, you'd use the name of her directory and the *.* file specification ("*.*" is the wild card way to designate every file in a directory). For example, if one person's directory was C:\OFFICE\WPWIN\MARGE, you'd enter the following for her QuickList:

C:\OFFICE\WPWIN\MARGE*.*

Chapter 30

It's a Setup: Installing WordPerfect for Windows

When I was a kid, I used to get nervous when I received Christmas presents that said "Some assembly required" on the box. I *knew* what this meant. First of all, it meant I couldn't play with the toy right away—a major bummer. Second, it meant that someone, usually my father or a slightly inebriated uncle, would have to do the assembling. Several hours and several missing parts later, the poor thing would have been relegated to a corner somewhere, half-assembled and sad-looking.

Installing computer software still fills me with the same apprehension. Most installation programs are written by people who assume that everybody will know what they mean when they say, "Change the BUFFERS setting in your CONFIG.SYS file to 30."

I'm happy to report that the WordPerfect for Windows installation program (it's called Setup) is at least a little friendlier than most. If you're feeling gung-ho and would like to try your hand at this installation thing, here are the steps to follow:

1. Place the disk labeled **Setup** into drive A or drive B (whichever one it fits into).

2. In either Program Manager or File Manager, pull down the File menu and select **R**un to display the Run dialog box. In the Command Line text box, type **A:SETUP** if the disk is in drive A, or

B:SETUP if the disk is in drive B, and then select **OK**. The Setup program takes a few seconds to get going, and then it displays its welcome screen.

3. Select the Install button. Setup displays the Registration Information dialog box.

4. Enter your name, company name (if you don't have a company name, feel free to enter whatever you'd like—the sillier the better), and your WordPerfect for Windows license number (which you'll find on the certificate that comes with the WordPerfect for Windows package). When you're done, select Continue. The Installation Type dialog box appears, as shown below.

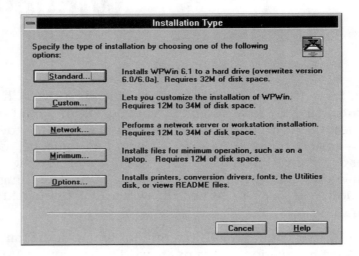

The WordPerfect for Windows 6.0 Installation Type dialog box.

5. Select the type of installation you want:

Standard   This option installs WordPerfect for Windows in all its glory (all 30 megabytes worth!). This is the easiest option, but it uses a whopping amount of disk space. If you select this button, Setup asks which drive you want to use for the installation. Select the appropriate drive and select **OK**.

Custom   This is a good option to choose if there are chunks of WordPerfect for Windows you think you'll never use (such as macros, for example). If you select this button, the Custom

Installation dialog box appears showing two check boxes:
WordPerfect and **Shared Components**. For each item, select
the corresponding **Files** button, deactivate the check boxes for
the components you don't want to install (see the following
figure), and then select **OK**. When you're done, select the **Start
Installation** button.

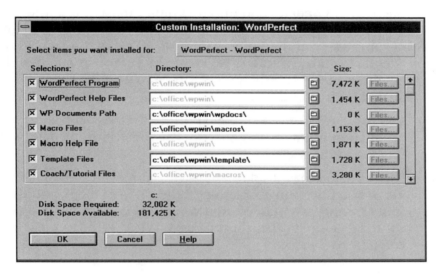

*Deactivate the check boxes for the WordPerfect for Windows components you
don't want to install.*

Minimum   If your hard disk real estate is at a premium, choose
this option, which installs a bare-bones version of WordPerfect
for Windows. If you select this button, the Minimum Installation dialog box appears to warn you that features such as the
Spell Checker and WP Draw won't be installed. Just sigh resign-
edly, and select Yes to proceed with the installation. Setup now
asks which drive you want to use for the installation. Select the
appropriate drive and select **OK**.

6. Setup starts copying files to your hard disk. You'll eventually see
   the Diskette Needed dialog box, asking you to insert another one
   of the installation disks. Remove the current disk, insert the disk
   that Setup needs, and select **OK**. You'll need to repeat this step *ad
   nauseum* until Setup has finished its file copying chores.

7. When you've trudged through all the necessary disks, you may see the Set Up Program Manager Group dialog box asking you which program group to use for your WordPerfect for Windows icons. It's probably best to let Setup create a new WPWin 6.1 group, so just select **OK** when this dialog box appears.

8. Now Setup will ask if you want to view the "README" files. These files contain updates and info that didn't make it into the manuals. Since there is the occasional tidbit in these files that might be of some use, you should probably select **Yes**. In the View README Files dialog box, select the **WPWin** button, read as much of the file as you can take, and then press **Alt+F4** to exit. Repeat for the **Shared** button, and then select Close.

9. You're almost home. Setup next displays a message telling you the installation was a rousing success. Pat yourself on the back a few times, and then select **OK**.

10. Finally, Setup may display a message telling you it has modified a file or two (including something called SYSTEM.INI), and that it's about to restart Windows. Nod your head knowingly, and select **OK** to let Setup go about its business. When Windows reappears, you'll be ready to go.

active window   The window you're currently slaving away in. You can tell a window is active if it contains the blinking *insertion point*, and if its title bar is a darker color than the other windows.

alphanumeric keypad   The keyboard area that contains the letters, numbers (the ones across the top row, not the ones on the *numeric keypad*), and other punctuation symbols.

ASCII text file   A file that uses only the American Standard Code for Information Interchange character set (which is just techno-lingo for the characters you see on your keyboard).

bit-spit   Any kind of computer-created correspondence.

block   A selection of text in a document.

boilerplate   Text that you use over and over. It's the word processing equivalent of the old maxim, "Don't reinvent the wheel."

boot   Computer geeks won't tell you to start your computer; they'll tell you to *boot* it. This doesn't mean you should punt your monitor across the room. The term *booting* comes from the phrase "pulling oneself up by one's own bootstraps" which just means that your computer can load everything it needs to operate properly without any help from the likes of you and me.

byte   Computerese for a single character of information. So for example, the phrase "This phrase is 28 bytes long" is, yes, 28 bytes long. (You count the spaces too—but not the quotation marks.)

cascade   A cool way of arranging windows so that they overlap each other, but you can still see the top of each window.

cascade menu   A menu that appears when you select certain *pull-down menu* commands.

cell   In a *table*, the intersection of a row and column. Within the table, each cell has its own address, which is a combination of the letter and number of the column and row, respectively, that form the cell.

character formatting   Changing the attributes of individual characters by adding things such as bold or italics, or by using different fonts.

character set   A collection of related characters.

check box   A square-shaped switch that toggles a *dialog box* option on or off. An "X" in the box indicates that the option is toggled on.

churn   To endlessly rewrite and revise a section of text.

click   To press and release the left mouse button.

Clipboard   An area that holds data temporarily during cut-and-paste operations.

command button   A rectangular doohickey (usually found in *dialog boxes*) that, when chosen, runs whatever command is spelled out on its label.

commands   The options you see in a *pull-down menu*. You use these commands to tell WordPerfect for Windows what you want it to do next.

delay   The amount of time it takes for a second character to appear when you press and hold down a key.

dialog boxes   Ubiquitous windows that pop up on the screen to ask you for information, or to seek confirmation of an action you requested (or sometimes just to say "Hi").

directory   A storage location on your hard disk for keeping related files together. If your hard disk is like a house, a directory is like a room inside the house. See also *subdirectory*.

disk See *floppy disk*.

double-click To quickly press and release the left mouse button twice in succession.

drag To press and hold down the left mouse button and then move the mouse.

drop-down list A *dialog box* control that normally shows only a single item, but when selected, displays a list of options.

endnote A section of text placed at the end of a document that usually contains asides or comments that embellish something in the regular document text. See also *footnote*.

extension The three-character ending to a DOS file name. The extension is separated from the main name by a period.

file An organized unit of information inside your computer. If you think of your hard disk as a house, files can be either servants (your programs) or things (data used by you or by a program).

file name The name of a file (duh). File names usually consist of a primary name (that can be a maximum of 8 characters), followed by a period (.), followed by an extension (that can be a maximum of 3 characters). Primary names and extensions can't contain spaces or any of the following characters:

> + = \ | [ ] ; : , . < > ? /

file specification A combination of drive letter, directory name, legal *filename* characters (such as letters and numbers), and *wild-card characters* (* and ?) that specifies the files you want to work with (for example, **c:\office\wpwin\wpdocs*.doc**).

floppy disk A portable storage medium that consists of a flexible disk protected by a plastic case. Floppy disks are available in a variety of sizes and capacities.

font A distinctive graphic design of letters, numbers, and other symbols.

footer A section of text that appears at the bottom margin of each page in a document. See also *header*.

footnote A section of text placed at the bottom of a page. It usually contains asides or comments that embellish something in the regular document text. See also *endnote*.

formatting   The process of setting up a disk so it can read and write information. Not to be confused with *character formatting*.

frame   A border that surrounds a *window* and enables you to *maximize*, *minimize*, move, and size the window.

fritterware   Any software that causes you to fritter away time fiddling with its various bells and whistles.

function keys   The keys located either to the left of the *numeric keypad*, or across the top of the keyboard. There are usually 10 function keys (although some keyboards have 12), and they're labeled F1, F2, and so on. In WordPerfect for Windows, you use these keys either by themselves or as part of key combinations.

hard page break   A *page break* that you insert yourself. Text always breaks at this point, regardless of the margin sizes.

header   A section of text that appears at the top margin of each page in a document. See also *footer*.

hyphenation   The process in which WordPerfect for Windows splits larger words in two at the end of a line and inserts a hyphen. This can help improve the spacing in your paragraphs.

Insert mode   A WordPerfect for Windows mode in which the characters you type are inserted between the existing characters in a document. Press the Insert key to toggle between this mode and *Typeover mode*.

insertion point   The vertical bar you see inside WordPerfect for Windows' typing area; it tells you where the next character you type will appear.

insertion point control keys   The keys (which you'll find on a separate keypad or mixed in with the *numeric keypad*) that you use to navigate a document.

kilobyte   1,024 *bytes*. Usually abbreviated as just *K*.

landscape orientation   When the lines on a page run parallel to the long side of the page. See also *portrait orientation*.

margins   The empty spaces that surround your text on the page. WordPerfect for Windows' standard margins are one inch high on the top and bottom edges of the page, and one inch wide on the left and right edges.

maximize   To increase the size of a window to its largest extent. See also *minimize.*

megabyte   1,024 *kilobytes* or 1,048,576 *bytes.* The cognoscenti write this as *M* or *MB* and pronounce it *meg.*

menu bar   The horizontal bar just below the title bar in the WordPerfect for Windows screen. The menu bar contains the *pull-down menus.*

minimize   To reduce the size of a window to its smallest extent. See also *maximize.*

mouse potato   The computer equivalent of a couch potato. Someone who spends lots of time in front of his screen.

numeric keypad   A separate keypad for entering numbers on most keyboards. It actually serves two functions: when the Num Lock key is on, you can use it to enter numbers; if Num Lock is off, the keypad insertion point movement keys are enabled, and you can use them to navigate a document. Some keyboards (called extended keyboards) have a separate insertion point keypad so you can keep Num Lock on all the time.

ohnosecond   The brief fraction of time in which you realize you've just made a HUGE blunder.

option buttons   *Dialog box* options that appear as small circles in groups of two or more. You can choose only one option from a group at any time.

orphan   A first line in a paragraph that appears by itself at the end of a page. See also *widow.*

page break   A line that appears across the screen, telling you where one page ends and the next one begins.

point   To move the mouse pointer so it rests on a specific screen location.

port   The connection you use to plug in the cable from a device such as a mouse or printer.

portrait orientation   When the lines run parallel to the short side of a page. This is the standard way most pages are oriented. See also *landscape orientation.*

pull-down menus   Hidden menus that you open from WordPerfect for Windows' *menu bar* to access the program's commands and features.

quadruple-click   To quickly press and release the left mouse button four times in succession. Quadruple-clicking a paragraph selects the entire paragraph.

RAM   Stands for Random Access Memory. The memory in your computer that DOS uses to run your programs.

repeat rate   After the initial *delay*, the rate at which characters appear when you press and hold down a key.

right-click   Press and release the right mouse button.

right ragged   Left-justified text. The right side of each line doesn't line up, so it looks ragged.

scroll   To move up or down through a document.

scroll bar   A bar that appears at the bottom or on the right of a window whenever the window is too small to display all of its contents.

soft page break   A *page break* inserted automatically by WordPerfect for Windows. The position of the break depends on the margin sizes.

spamming   To write (or speak) ramblingly and aimlessly on a hodgepodge of subjects. ("I got his memo, but you could tell he was just spammin' me; the guy doesn't know what the heck he's talking about.")

style   A predefined collection of formatting and layout options that you can apply to text all at once.

subdirectory   A *directory* within a directory.

table   A rectangular grid of rows and columns that can hold text, numbers, graphics, and the results of formulas.

text box   A screen area in which you type text information such as a description or a file name.

triple-click   To quickly press and release the left mouse button three times in succession. In WordPerfect, triple-clicking a sentence selects the entire sentence.

type size   A measure of the height of a font. Type size is measured in *points*; there are 72 points in an inch.

Typeover mode   A WordPerfect for Windows mode in which text you type replaces characters instead of being inserted between them. Use the Insert key to toggle between this mode and normal typing (*Insert mode*).

watermark   A translucent image or section of text that prints "underneath" existing text on a page.

wild-card characters   Characters used to designate multiple *files* in a *file specification*. The question mark (?) substitutes for a single character, and the asterisk (*) substitutes for multiple characters.

widow   The last line in a paragraph that appears by itself at the top of a page. See also *orphan*.

window   A screen area where WordPerfect for Windows displays your documents.

word processing   Using a computer to write, edit, format, and print documents. A high-end word processor, such as WordPerfect for Windows, also enables you to add complicated features such as *footnotes* and indexes, and even has desktop publishing options that let you do true page layout stuff.

word wrap   A WordPerfect for Windows feature that starts a new line automatically as your typing reaches the end of the current line.

WYSIWYG   What-You-See-Is-What-You-Get. The feature that makes it possible for you to see on your computer screen what you end up getting from your printer. It's pronounced *wizzy wig*.

Index

More Fun Learning from Alpha Books!

If you enjoyed this *Complete Idiot's Guide* then check out these other books!

The Complete Idiot's Guide to PCs
ISBN: 1-56761-168-0
Softbound, $14.95 USA

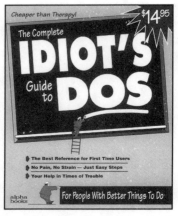

The Complete Idiot's Guide to DOS
ISBN: 1-56761-169-9
Softbound, $14.95 USA

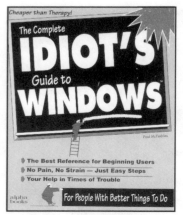

The Complete Idiot's Guide to Windows
ISBN: 1-56761-175-3
Softbound, $14.95 USA

Also Available!

**The Complete Idiot's Guide
to 1-2-3, New Edition**
ISBN: 1-56761-404-3
Softbound, $14.95 USA

**The Complete Idiot's Guide to
1-2-3 for Windows**
ISBN: 1-56761-400-0
Softbound, $14.95 USA

**The Complete Idiot's Guide
to Ami Pro**
ISBN: 1-56761-453-1
Softbound, $14.95 USA

**The Complete Idiot's Guide to
Buying & Upgrading PCs**
ISBN: 1-56761-274-1
Softbound, $14.95 USA

**The Complete Idiot's Guide to
Computer Terms**
ISBN: 1-56761-266-0
Softbound, $9.95 USA

**The Complete Idiot's Guide
to Excel**
ISBN: 1-56761-318-7
Softbound, $14.95 USA

**The Complete Idiot's Guide
to Internet**
ISBN: 1-56761-414-0
Softbound, $19.95 USA

**The Complete Idiot's Guide
to The Mac**
ISBN: 1-56761-395-0
Softbound, $14.95 USA

**The Complete Idiot's Guide
to VCRs**
ISBN: 1-56761-294-6
Softbound, $9.95 USA

**The Complete Idiot's Guide
to WordPerfect**
ISBN: 1-56761-187-7
Softbound, $14.95 USA

**The Complete Idiot's Guide to
WordPerfect for Windows**
ISBN: 1-56761-282-2
Softbound, $14.95 USA

**The Complete Idiot's Guide
to Word for Windows**
ISBN: 1-56761-355-1
Softbound, $14.95 USA

**The Complete Idiot's Guide
to Works for Windows**
ISBN: 1-56761-451-5
Softbound, $14.95 USA

Who cares what you think? WE DO!

We take our customers' opinions very personally. After all, you're the reason we publish these books. If you're not happy, we're doing something wrong.

We'd appreciate it if you would take the time to drop us a note or fax us a fax. A real person—not a computer—reads every letter we get, and makes sure that your comments get relayed to the appropriate people.

Not sure what to say? Here are some details we'd like to know:

- ☛ Who you are (age, occupation, hobbies, etc.)
- ☛ Where you bought the book
- ☛ Why you picked this book instead of a different one
- ☛ What you liked best about the book
- ☛ What could have been done better
- ☛ Your overall opinion of the book
- ☛ What other topics you would purchase a book on

Mail, e-mail, or fax it to:

Faithe Wempen
Product Development Manager
Alpha Books
201 West 103rd Street
Indianapolis, IN 46290

FAX: (317) 581-4669
CIS: 75430,174

Special Offer!

Alpha Books needs people like you to give opinions about new and existing books. Product testers receive free books in exchange for providing their opinions about them. If you would like to be a product tester, please mention it in your letter, and make sure you include your full name, address, and daytime phone.